SECOND DEATH

EDINBURGH CRITICAL STUDIES IN SHAKESPEARE AND PHILOSOPHY

Series Editor: Kevin Curran

Edinburgh Critical Studies in Shakespeare and Philosophy takes seriously the speculative and world-making properties of Shakespeare's art. Maintaining a broad view of 'philosophy' that accommodates first-order questions of metaphysics, ethics, politics and aesthetics, the series also expands our understanding of philosophy to include the unique kinds of theoretical work carried out by performance and poetry itself. These scholarly monographs will reinvigorate Shakespeare studies by opening new interdisciplinary conversations among scholars, artists and students.

Published Titles

Rethinking Shakespeare's Political Philosophy: From Lear to Leviathan
Alex Schulman

Shakespeare in Hindsight: Counterfactual Thinking and Shakespearean Tragedy
Amir Khan

Second Death: Theatricalities of the Soul in Shakespeare's Drama
Donovan Sherman

Shakespeare's Fugitive Politics
Thomas P. Anderson

Forthcoming Titles

Making Publics in Shakespeare's Playhouse
Paul Yachnin

Derrida Reads Shakespeare
Chiara Alfano

The Play and the Thing: A Phenomenology of Shakespearean Theatre
Matthew Wagner

Shakespearean Melancholy: Philosophy, Form, and the Transformation of Comedy
J. F. Bernard

SECOND DEATH

Theatricalities of the Soul in Shakespeare's Drama

♦ ♦ ♦

DONOVAN SHERMAN

EDINBURGH
University Press

Edinburgh University Press is one of the leading university presses in the UK. We publish academic books and journals in our selected subject areas across the humanities and social sciences, combining cutting-edge scholarship with high editorial and production values to produce academic works of lasting importance. For more information visit our website: www.edinburghuniversitypress.com

Edinburgh University Press Ltd
The Tun – Holyrood Road,
12(2f) Jackson's Entry,
Edinburgh EH8 8PJ

First published in hardback by Edinburgh University Press 2016

Typeset in 11/14 Adobe Sabon by
IDSUK (DataConnection) Ltd, and
printed and bound in Great Britain by
CPI Group (UK) Ltd, Croydon CR0 4YY

A CIP record for this book is available from the British Library

ISBN 978 1 4744 1145 5 (hardback)
ISBN 978 1 4744 2609 1 (paperback)
ISBN 978 1 4744 1146 2 (webready PDF)
ISBN 978 1 4744 1147 9 (epub)

CONTENTS

ACKNOWLEDGEMENTS

Second Death has had many lives, and as the book has leapt from incarnation to incarnation, innumerable people have helped it along the way. I want to thank first my roster of fantastic mentors at the University of California, Irvine who oversaw this work in its early stages. Anthony Kubiak and Ian Munro supplied warmth, wit and wisdom; Bryan Reynolds offered a sounding board for my initial frazzled brainstorms and continues to lend his uncanny mixture of patience, intelligence and mischief. Julia Reinhard Lupton has exhibited staggering generosity in reading and responding to many drafts of this book; she remains a trusted and inspirational mentor. Many academic conferences have supplied testing grounds for this work, and in these strange, vital and ephemeral settings I have found communities of receptive readers and listeners to various early versions of the book's chapters: Michelle Liu Carriger, Glenn Kessler, Elise Morrison, Lloyd Kermode, Julia Obert, Jonathan Gil Harris, Andrew Hartley, Eileen Joy, Amy Cook, Daniel Keegan and Joy Palacios all took time, over the years, to respond deeply. The Shakespearean Performance Research Group, an offshoot of the American Society for Theater Research, is worth singling out as a particularly invigorating staging-ground for many of the ideas herein.

Seton Hall University has, over the past few years, provided a model community for fostering scholarly dialogue and goodwill; I am lucky to be among such supportive colleagues. Karen Gevirtz, Angela Weisl and Jonathan Farina lent their formidable powers of scrutiny to reviewing early drafts of the book. Mary Balkun has helped me steer through many professional eddies and currents; Marianne Lloyd and the rest of the Untenured Faculty Organization have kept me on track. The staff at Walsh Library has indefatigably culled crucial resources from far and wide. I am also grateful to the university for giving me a University Research Council grant over the summer of 2014, and to the Department of English for a course release in the fall of 2015. I was fortunate to attend the National Humanities Center Summer Institute for Literary Study in 2013, at which I was doubly fortunate to study *The Winter's Tale* under the peerless guidance of Sarah Beckwith. Kevin Curran and the staff at Edinburgh have been immensely inventive and kind – this book is fortunate, and I am humbled, to have such an esteemed home.

There is neither space nor readerly patience enough to express my debts to the other sympathetic and thoughtful people who have had a hand (or in some cases, a paw) in bringing this book to fruition. An emphatic thanks, though, is in order to my family for their love and good cheer: hugs to Rachel, Kirby, Max, Mary, Spencer, Christine, Toph, Amy, Olive, and of course Kasey. Since I began work on this book, Natalie Sherman has done me the good favour of arriving in the world, and her gumption and liveliness offer happiness in a hitherto unknown register. Finally, and most powerfully, I thank my wife, Kasia, to whom this book is dedicated. My real gratitude cannot ever be fully expressed; suffice it to say that her love, understanding, humour and patience have surely provided this project with a soul of its own.

Earlier drafts of two chapters have previously appeared in publication, and I thank the journals where they appeared for granting permission to these later versions. One such edition of Chapter 2 was published as 'Governing the Wolf: Soul and Space in The Merchant of Venice' in *Journal of Medieval and Early Modern Studies* 43:1, pp. 99–120, copyright 2013, Duke University Press, republished by permission of the rightsholder: www.dukeupress.edu. And parts of Chapter 4 were originally published in *Shakespeare Bulletin*, 27, Issue 2, Summer 2009, pp. 197–221, copyright 2009, Johns Hopkins University Press.

SERIES EDITOR'S PREFACE

Picture Macbeth alone on stage, staring intently into empty space. 'Is this a dagger which I see before me?' he asks, grasping decisively at the air. On one hand, this is a quintessentially theatrical question. At once an object and a vector, the dagger describes the possibility of knowledge ('Is this a dagger') in specifically visual and spatial terms ('which I see before me'). At the same time, Macbeth is posing a quintessentially philosophical question, one that assumes knowledge to be both conditional and experiential, and that probes the relationship between certainty and perception as well as intention and action. It is from this shared ground of art and inquiry, of theatre and theory, that this series advances its basic premise: Shakespeare is philosophical.

It seems like a simple enough claim. But what does it mean exactly, beyond the parameters of this specific moment in Macbeth? Does it mean that Shakespeare had something we could think of as his own philosophy? Does it mean that he was influenced by particular philosophical schools, texts and thinkers? Does it mean, conversely, that modern philosophers have been influenced by him – that Shakespeare's plays and poems have been, and continue to be, resources for philosophical thought and speculation?

The answer is yes all around. These are all useful ways of conceiving a philosophical Shakespeare and all point to lines of inquiry that this series welcomes. But Shakespeare is philosophical in a much more fundamental way as well. Shakespeare is philosophical because the plays and poems actively create new worlds of knowledge and new scenes of ethical encounter. They ask big questions, make bold arguments, and develop new vocabularies in order to think what might otherwise be unthinkable. Through both their scenarios and their imagery, the plays and poems engage the qualities of consciousness, the consequences of human action, the phenomenology of motive and attention, the conditions of personhood, and the relationship among different orders of reality and experience. This is writing and dramaturgy, moreover, that consistently experiments with a broad range of conceptual crossings, between love and subjectivity, nature and politics, and temporality and form.

Edinburgh Critical Studies in Shakespeare and Philosophy takes seriously these speculative and world-making dimensions of Shakespeare's work. The series proceeds from a core conviction that art's capacity to think – to formulate, not just reflect, ideas – is what makes it urgent and valuable. Art matters because unlike other human activities it establishes its own frame of reference, reminding us that all acts of creation – biological, political, intellectual and amorous – are grounded in imagination. This is a far cry from business-as-usual in Shakespeare studies. Because historicism remains the methodological gold standard of the field, far more energy has been invested in exploring what Shakespeare once meant than in thinking rigorously about what Shakespeare continues to make possible. In response, Edinburgh Critical Studies in Shakespeare and Philosophy pushes back against the critical orthodoxies of historicism and cultural studies to clear a space for scholarship that confronts aspects of literature that can neither be reduced to nor adequately explained by particular historical contexts.

Shakespeare's creations are not just inheritances of a past culture, frozen artifacts whose original settings must be expertly reconstructed in order to be understood. The plays and poems are also living art, vital thought-worlds that struggle, across time, with foundational questions of metaphysics, ethics, politics and aesthetics. With this orientation in mind, Edinburgh Critical Studies in Shakespeare and Philosophy offers a series of scholarly monographs that will reinvigorate Shakespeare studies by opening new interdisciplinary conversations among scholars, artists and students.

Kevin Curran

INTRODUCTION

CONSPIRING ELEMENTS

What is a soul?

The question seems both radical and obvious. In fact, it is radical *because* of its obviousness: a soul must, by necessity, act as a self-evident entity. It resists explanation because it remains when explanation ends. Whether spiritual or merely rhetorical, we talk about souls as connotations of quintessence; a description seems too flimsy a costume for it to wear. Its common usage gives us, however, a hint at the paradoxical qualities that lurk under this overfamiliarity. 'Soul' may be used as a metonym of identity – 'he's a kind soul' – or as something that can be possessed – 'she has a good soul'. Both of these benign-sounding possibilities lead to thorny conclusions if allowed to live side by side: on the one hand, simply being a soul implies a fusion with the non-corporeal; on the other, having one suggests a fragmented character whose speaking-self lays claim to a presumably silent, though still crucial, component.

In a general sense, this book stages its questions in this space between being and having, where identity fluctuates in its interplay with the soul's sameness and otherness. Specifically, in the pages that follow, I explore these questions as they resonate in early modern England, a site perfectly suited for such an inquiry, given its entanglement in competing belief-systems and poetic imaginations. The long wake of the Reformation dispersed Protestant ethos throughout residual facets of Catholicism, while the rise of humanism introduced translations of classical polytheistic texts into circulation. This network of religious and scholarly ideologies, which Stephen Greenblatt calls a 'whole, weird, tangled cultural inheritance', made conceptualisation of the soul a multifaceted and unsteady process.[1] Broadly speaking, Anglican theology sought to eliminate its representational capacity, Catholic recusants retained belief in its conscious caretaking, and Neoplatonist and Aristotelian pedagogy conceived of its metaphysical vitality. These characterisations, of course, are highly reductive. Endless conceptual shading exists within this basic structure, with individual artists, politicians, ministers, and other figures borrowing, amending, and creating more nuanced properties. As a result of these disparate understandings, the soul seemed to be both hyper-legible *and* removed from perception – something that was beyond any earthly means of apprehending the world, yet also something that needed to be thought through, reckoned with, and compartmentalised.

Recent scholarship has examined the spiritual richness of early modern England by turning to religion as both historical and theoretical apparatus.[2] Efforts to radicalise and reinterpret the writings of Saint Paul, or follow Jacques Derrida's seminal reading of *Hamlet* as a 'hauntological' text of ideological spectres, or recover chthonic powers by illuminating uncanny textual resonances with sacred rituals – to name only a few salient examples – have marked the 'return to religion' as a palpable shift in the wake of the more language- and meaning-obsessed conversations of post-structuralism. And yet, strangely, within this return the soul has been ignored. Conversations around the soul tend to focus more on 'spirits' or – as with Derrida – 'ghosts'. Although the ghost of Hamlet's father does make a cameo in this book's conclusion, I do not, in the main thrust of this exploration, seek to add to that already rich discourse.[3] While the connections between souls and ghosts, and the temptations to transfer spectral tropes into myriad critical contexts, are clearly many, I am more interested in the relations of the soul to the living. As my title implies, this book will certainly examine the soul in terms of dying and death, but my focus is always on how the dynamic of the soul as it cleaves itself from the body in death reflects a complex condition of the soul when still lodged within the living. I aim to relate the soul to the kinetic and fleshy world of experience, rather than an ethereal understanding of a world beyond. In fact, the very distinctions of tangible and intangible, human and non-human, and life and death are what become complicated; one of the most puzzling aspects of the soul in early modernity is precisely that it muddles the borders between these dualities, slipping into the spaces between registers. Likewise, this book does not focus on demons and devils – the monstrous manifestations that populate the lore and literature of the sixteenth and seventeenth centuries. While oftentimes such beings are linked to the soul, a consideration of their voluble mythos is outside the scope of this study. My desire is to look at the soul, squarely and head-on, as a very real aspect of what Gail Kern Paster, borrowing from Pierre Bourdieu, calls the 'internal habitus' of the subject.[4] Paster's deployment of this term focuses on humoral and physiognomic systems; I am interested instead on what might be called *spiritual* habitus. How did people relate to their souls? This question returns us to this chapter's opening stab at obviousness, the potentially unanswerable 'What *is* a soul, anyway?'

In his 1599 work 'Of Soule of Man, and the Immortalitie thereof' – the final and dominant section of his long poem *Nosce Teipsum* – Sir John Davies attempts to figure out this riddle, and in doing so he gives us an especially lyrical plumb line into the cultural depths of the era. By questioning the soul's status, he dips into politics, justice, aesthetics, natural philosophy, and of course, spirituality, all while trying to skirt the contradictions that lurk in the very premise of his inquiry. The poem hopes to show how the soul can be both spiritual and essential, self and other – both *is* and *have*. This introduction takes up a reading of his poem as a useful road map of the multivalent networks explored in the chapters that follow. Davies demonstrates how those networks always teeter on the edge of shattering the coherence of the singular, undisturbed subject. A study of the soul becomes, in a sense, a study of the fragility of self-understanding and existential reification. First, Davies gives voice to those who suggest the soul resides in the physical realm:

> One thinks the *Soule* is *Aire*, another *Fire*,
> Another, *bloud* defus'd about the hart;
> Another saith, the *Elements* conspire,
> And to her *Essence* each doth give a part.[5]

The possible components of the soul that Davies debates, with light exasperation, mingle the elemental and humoral with the theological. The 'aire' recalls the breath into the figure of clay in Genesis – the literal inspiration for the Hebrew word for soul, *nephesh*; the fire implies a Purgatorial instrument of divine purification, displaced and recentreed within the human corpus; the 'bloud' describes its actual physiognomy; and the synthesis of elements that 'conspire' together denote a mystical, metaphysical balance. Davies continues to survey the soul's competing theorists, gesturing to Lucretius ('Epicures make them swarmes of Atomies, Which do by change into our Bodies flee') and variations of Neoplatonism before letting his irritation finally give way. Blood, air, fire, atoms, and others that possibly supply the fabric of the soul are, Davies tells us, only decoys, feints in a larger divine battle: 'God only wise, to punish pride of Wit, / Among mens wits hath this confusion wrought, / As the proud Towre whose points the clouds did hit, / By Tongues confusion was to ruine brought.'[6] The whole, weird, tangled culture that we peer at in hindsight was evident at the time to Davies, who attributes the mess to God's plan to prevent a unified, Babel-like edifice of singular belief.

So what is a soul, then, according to Davies, if not biological, elemental, or atomic? After all, as he later recounts, the soul cannot be thought of as possessing any kind of physical attributes at all, since 'If th'Elements which have no life, nor sense, / Can breed in us so great a power as this, / Why give they not themselves like excellence, / Or other things wherein their mixture is?'[7] How could something without a soul, like a stone or patch of earth, itself provide our soulfulness? If they were so powerful, wouldn't they have souls themselves? The comic tenor of this digression arises from the notion of a soul occupying the same corporeal space as we do. The poet's solution to the quandary of spiritual concretisation concerns itself equally with the soul's positive and negative attributes. Following his dismissal of the soul's tangibility, he admits that 'though this substance is the root of sense, / Sense knows her not, which doth but bodies know'.[8] The Neoplatonists and Lucretians, misguided though they may be, at least provide for the possibility of human contact with the soul. By dismissing them, Davies embraces a vision of the soul that cannot be sensed, but must control the sensory apparatus by translating sensation into the 'phantasie' of the imagination, a non-corporeal presence that nonetheless irrefutably alters the corporeal form of its host. Davies carefully maps out the progression of the soul from its initial breath of God into the womb, charting its ability to act as 'handmaide to the mind' without ever actually touching the 'Ledger Booke' that 'lyes in the braine behind, / Like *Janus* eye, which in his *poll* was set'.[9] The soul, Hamlet-like, can clear the tables of the mind, codifying thought into memory, experience into archive. Besides fantasy, the soul guises itself as wit and will, sibling forms that similarly drive the body into movement through invisible, untouchable means.

Davies's tripartite model of a soul is not, by design, original. By claiming the soul as fantastical, wilful, and witty, he borrows Aristotle's famous proposal that souls exist in vegetative, sensitive, and rational forms, contextualising the ancient philosopher's division within a courtly and humanistic argot. His reclamation of this formula, furthermore, serves decidedly Christian aims by allowing him to link the tripartite to the Trinity, thus giving us a perfect syncretic moment of neoclassical and Anglican overlay that borrows liberally from Greek forbears to assert a broader divine plan, all while admitting to the explanatory power – albeit in ironised form – of the dizzying crowd of other options for spiritual dissection. The poem indexes competing claims to understanding the soul. This is not an inventive proposal; in fact, it is exactly the opposite, an illumination of how the cultural and social forces of his day, already gathering around him, produced a necessarily disjointed subject. His tour of the soul's passage through the body and his careful mapping of the intangible mingling with the physical serve what the poem asserts is a deeper logic, but in order to access this logic he must limn a field of incoherence. Davies gives us a human figure that by definition and design must be fundamentally split; identity here becomes a frontier between begrudgingly collaborative, though essentially distant, fields.

His poem explicitly states that the Renaissance human – the famous measure of all things – was already, in its contemporary apprehension, a fundamentally hybrid knot of disparate forces. In his rhetorical structuring, Davies even casually suggests that humanity itself is at stake in making the soul legible; the poem frequently and favourably mentions that the soul acts as a 'bee' that shuttles sensory information from the world into the body: 'From flowers abroad, and bring into the braine, / She doth within both waxe and honey make, / This worke is hers, this is her proper paine.'[10] Furthermore, the poem continually hails the soul as female – never 'it', always 'she' – to assert both its virginity and its domesticity: Davies compares the body to a gracious host and the soul to a polite and thoughtful guest whose '*quickening* power in every living part, / Doth as a Nurse, or a Mother serve, / And doth employ her *oeconomicke* Art, / And busie care, her household to prefer'.[11] Here '*oeconomicke*' hearkens back to its ancient definition, lately revitalised in political theology, as the care of the family. The soul performs as a dutiful wife who keeps its physical trappings in order. Finally, Davies returns to that hoariest of poetic comparisons, the sun, to describe the soul's sway over the body. Like the sun, the soul changes its effects on the body as its rays reflect in different directions and alter the 'seasons' of mood and affect. The image twists a theory of Ptolmey, who in his *Tetrabiblos* draws the connections between the soul and the planets: '[T]he aspects to the sun and the angles shown by the planets that are related to the class of qualities under consideration' surely affect the 'character' of the soul, along with 'that particular natural quality of each one of the planets which relates to the movements of the soul'.[12] Such language is analogical, but the need for Davies to turn to the animal, feminine and astral when conceiving of the soul reminds us of the fact – again, one both obvious and radical – that the early modern soul, itself the signature stamp of humanity, could not be conceived as strictly human. Asking after the soul leads the poet down a rabbit hole of metaphorical exhaustion, choosing images united only in their mutual lack of resemblance to the civilised subject.

This book builds on Davies's inquiry by expanding beyond the poem's purely textual scope and instead thinks of the soul theatrically. This imperative informs my focus on, primarily, works of drama – texts that only reach their realisation when enacted. Furthermore, even when texts do not explicitly engage with theatre, the book examines them as meditations *on* theatre by analysing seemingly non-dramatic works, such as John Foxe's *Actes and Monuments* or Heinrich Bullinger's sermons, as discussions on lived praxis. In another sense, though, the theatre presents a broader pattern of behaviour. A citizen in London in the late sixteenth and early seventeenth centuries was not simply unknowingly bearing citations of the divisions in her surrounding ideological climate. The soul manifested itself in the theatrical rituals, both quotidian and heightened, by which the human subject rendered him- or herself cohesive and coherent. Hence, while 'The Soule of Man' provides an instructive guide through the paradoxes of the soul, it is overly neat, untainted by the possibility of bodily action. There is a quality of smoothness to poetry like Davies's that lends a lustre of sensibility to what is more properly a porous, anxious, and lively assemblage, one that freely performs a mixture of human and inhuman, self and other. It is one thing to determine the soul as a transcendental, intangible force; it is another thing entirely to puzzle out how that force makes itself perceived. Theatre thus gives us an apposite site in which we can explore the more earthy repercussions of the tensions that Davies highlights.

Looked at from a different angle, though, the theatre seems like the last place in which to examine the soul. Indeed, by proposing this course of study, I am suggesting an impossible task – to locate the transcendental within the determinedly ephemeral. The theatre comprises itself of the very elements that Davies, and the powerful ideologies to which he gives voice, place in direct opposition to the soul: bodies, time, space, matter. It is, however, this exact impossibility, and the energies it manifests, that comprises this book's focus. In its literary and performative manifestations, the theatre mediates itself in relation to something *beyond* its capacities – an implied world, character, or quality that the audience fabricates through the perception of arranged concrete cues. As Katherine Eisaman Maus observes, the early modern stage is 'radically synecdochic, endlessly referring the spectators to events, objects, situations, landscapes, that cannot be shown them'.[13] With its noises within and without, alarums and battle cries, floods of messengers and reports of offstage developments, the theatre sculpts itself out of vivid absences – it always demands, in Coriolanus's phrase, a 'world elsewhere' (III, iii, 134). This dynamic resonates with the means by which the soul maintained its own necessary distance from complete definition. Like the theatre, the internal disposition of the early modern subject contains the potential attainment of the sublime while always engaging in the immediate world of sensation and display. Poetry such as Davies's helps us neatly compartmentalise the soul as a concept, and numerous poems, treatises, and sermons pontificate as to the soul's exit from the body. But what about the soul as *lived* practice? How does the soul reveal itself within the theatre, then? How can something that necessarily keeps at bay its description resolve itself within a forum that demands clear definition?

The first chapter of the study, 'This Tough World', proposes an answer to these problems by suggesting that the soul can still be resolutely theatrical while refusing to be mimetic. Drawing from the work of Ludwig Wittgenstein, Stanley Cavell, and others, Chapter 1 proposes that the mode of being that emerges in the interstices of this proposal is expression rather than representation. The chapter then draws out a genealogy of the major discourses surrounding the soul, beginning with its emergence in classical metaphysical doctrine, following through its appropriation in Catholic discourse, and finally ending in its reconfiguration in the Reformation. My aim in presenting this progression of thought is to illuminate its traces within the societal and theatrical spaces explored in the book's chapters – not for their mere replication, or citation, but for the complications that the theatre makes evident in its aesthetic crucible.

The subsequent three chapters build on the philosophical ideas of the first to examine their implementation as theatrical strategies utilised by Shakespearean characters who become souls, of sorts, within their respective dramas: Shylock, Coriolanus and Leontes. The contours of this inquiry become most palpable in analysing the work of Shakespeare; his dramaturgy perpetually evokes the possibility of transcendence – manifested variously as the sublime, the unknown, or the forthrightly godlike – through the rough arrangements of the everyday, and, hence, his work comprises the book's primary concentration. Shakespeare by no means commands the absolute centre stage of *Second Death*, however. While each chapter features an extended reading of a Shakespearean play, each also utilises that reading as a structure that allows for connections among a wider literary and cultural web of associations. Furthermore, in keeping with my intention to always keep an eye on embodied performance, each chapter pairs its Shakespeare text with a specific phenomenon culled from the cultural landscape. These phenomena negotiate the soul in death; Shakespeare's plays, I contend, help us see the more problematic way the soul's presence exists in the living.

Chapter 2, 'Governing the Wolf', examines *The Merchant of Venice* alongside the phenomenon of metempsychosis (the transmigration of the soul) and branches out into Christopher Marlowe's *Dr Faustus,* Montaigne's 'An Apologie for Raymond Sebond', John Donne's 'Holy Sonnet VIII', and a collection of Neoplatonist and humanist pedagogical texts. Chapter 3, 'Wounding the Wound', presents an extended consideration of *Coriolanus* along with Thomas Middleton's *Second Maiden's Tragedy*, John Foxe's *Actes and Monuments*, *The Survey of London* of John Stow, and *Ancient Funerall Monuments*, by John Weever. For Chapter 4, 'Mourning the Present', I examine *The Winter's Tale* in conversation with a wide collection of poetic remembrances of Prince Henry and other pastoral elegies, Milton's 'Lycidas', and the sermons of the arch-Reformist Heinrich Bullinger. The conclusion, 'The Semi-Theatrical Prejudice', offers a playful and speculative exploration of the case studies that precede it. With *Hamlet* as a guide, I explore how theatrical performance in Shakespeare lives precariously at the contact point of here and there, body and beyond, to reframe the successive 'problems' of performance posed by Shylock, Coriolanus and Leontes in the previous chapters as instead invitations to embrace a wider grammar of immediate experience, rather than a more rigid grammar of specific meaning. I end with a consideration of how the soul's mode of performance uncannily echoes our contemporary sense of 'virtuality'.

By examining the central figures of this study – Shylock, Coriolanus and Leontes – alongside the soul, we can see in their antagonisms an uncanny echo of the soul's relationship to humanity, a drama that played itself out every day in the human characters that lived in the England outside of Shakespeare's fictional universes. In fact, these three figures, as manifestations of the soul, oppose themselves not only to their apparent foils *within* the play. They also aim their disruptive wills against the very representational logic that constituted the theatrical world *without* – that is, the early modern stage that establishes and tries to contain their fictions. They begin to doubt the signifying processes of their lives, but they also doubt the process of the theatrical event into which they are cast. Such sceptical behaviour is characteristic of a wider ambivalence. People in the sixteenth and seventeenth centuries were constantly being told how to deal with their souls: they should doubt representation, but they had to exist in a world dependent on representation; they should resent the bodily and temporal, but they lived in bodies and in time. The soul, one could reasonably imply, is an unearthly, impossibly wonderful thing, in distinction to our fallen and ravaged selves. On stage, though, the soul does not appear as ideal. In the theatre's quest to purge it from its representational fabric – to exile, dismember, or eulogise it as lost – the soul starts to look like just the opposite: a villain, a pariah, or a madman.

As Davies realises quickly in his 'Immortalitie', any neat notion of human life itself comes under fire once we question the status of the soul. This ambiguity explains in part the meaning of this book's title, which is in part borrowed from the Book of Revelation's description of the soul's 'second death' on judgement day:

> And I saw the dead, small and great, stand before God; and the books were opened: and another book was opened, which is the book of life: and the dead were judged out of those things which were written in the books, according to their works. And the sea gave up the dead which were in it; and death and hell delivered up the dead which were in them: and they were judged every man according to their works. And death and hell were cast into the lake of fire. This is the second death. (20: 12–15)[14]

The second death is the death of the soul, an eternity of pain and suffering. To a contemporary ear, however, it also evokes the term 'second life', which refers to an online world where users control their 'avatars' – on-screen figures that operate as extension of selfhood, both connected to identity and necessarily separate from it. On the one hand, the soul, like the avatar, emblematises a second life, an internalised capacity for vitality that can be thought of as our inner forces, *anima*, or the housed breath of God. On the other, the soul is a second death that stands in opposition to our consciousness, unattainable and unfathomable.

One of the theoretical tactics of this study results from the complex spiritual dance that results from the simultaneous life and death of the soul. Even though this book studies the negotiation of the living, the cultural figures surveyed alongside the primary texts – for Chapter 2, metempsychosis; for Chapter 3, the memorial; for Chapter 4, the elegy – all revolve around death. In death, the soul's separation and fundamental difference becomes explicit and clear, but this same separation exists in life, even if it is less remarked on. Each chapter, then, folds its study of the soul's properties in its more visible deathly negotiations *back* into a consideration of its role in the living – or, more accurately, its role in the braided strands of life and death that constitute an early modern human. The theatre, a place of life and death both, lays bare these paradoxical forces and exposes, despite itself, the rituals that maintain the soul's distance and clamour for its ecstatic proximity. Like the soul, what we consider life can seem the same as us, but also other. It can be – and be had.

CHAPTER 1

THIS TOUGH WORLD

In the final scene of *King Lear,* shortly after Lear dies, Edgar instructs Kent to 'Look up, my lord', to which Kent sombrely replies: 'Vex not his ghost; O, let him pass. He hates him / That would upon the rack of this tough world / Stretch him out longer' (V, ii, 311–12).[1] What is passing by these men? Lear's ghost, it would seem, departs from the stage. His spirit tarries briefly in the tough world. While addressed as a ghost, however, the play does not indicate that Lear is an embodied ghost, as with Hamlet's father, Richard III's victims, or other phantasmagoric entities that physically traverse the scene and have living actors cast in their roles. The kind of ghost on display – or more precisely not on display – is presumably the fresh soul departing from Lear's body. This soul exits quickly: Edgar finishes out the line of Kent's request with 'O he is gone indeed.' No sooner is decorum asked for to authorise Lear's spiritual exit than that exit is completed. It is done invisibly, though somehow felt by the characters who eulogise his departure. Lear has finally become the 'nothing' that notoriously repeats throughout the play – or, perhaps more accurately, he has now actualised the title conferred by the Fool of 'Lear's shadow' (I, iv, 221).

This brief moment exists on the threshold of materiality and immateriality. Tension emerges between the invisible and insubstantial ghost of Lear and the 'tough' world that Edgar and Kent live in. This world is 'tough' not only in the sense of 'unfair' but also physically textured, tangible, durable.[2] The passage of Lear's spirit offers a more melancholic version of King John's wry observation, in the spasms of death, that his soul now has 'elbow room' (V, vii, 28). That king's line is tinged with irony, as the departing soul should not worry about 'room' in the more earthy sense of physical allowance. There is, here, something darkly comic in the attempt to describe the ineffable soul in the quantifying terms we reserve for our bodily sensorium, as if the soul occupied a set amount of space.

The implied staging of the scene in *Lear* keeps his soul from our sight, denying its appearance not only in the world depicted but also from the similarly physically constituted theatrical world that depicts it. In one sense, there is a clear historical reason why this might be. The early modern theatre, as popularly understood, was not a place to reveal the soul. Jonas Barish elaborates this idea in his reading of a sermon by William Perkins: 'God has provided us with not only a soul but a body, and not only a body but the prescribed covering for the body, and not only the covering but the precise degree and kind of adornment allowable for that covering . . . Players are evil because they try to substitute a self of their own contriving for the one given them by God. Plays are evil for analogous reasons.'[3] Antitheatricalist sentiment in Shakespeare's England rebelled against many forms of medieval piety and tended to focus on the preservation of the sacredness of images; to supply a moving image – a stage picture – of a soul, previously an articulable notion in Catholic modes of dramatic presentation, would be profanation. Huston Diehl explains that

> [t]he intensity of the rage vented against images by rioting iconoclasts has the same source as the intensity of the horror felt by disapproving bystanders who witnessed the iconoclastic acts: a deeply held belief, however threatened, in the power of images. Whether that belief is tested by willing participation in iconoclastic events or challenged by unwilling observation of them, the implicit relation between visible images and God is suddenly disrupted and forever changed. The intimate bond late medieval culture had established between the visible and the divine is irrevocably severed.[4]

Such antitheatricalism would find its return – albeit with vastly different motivation – in the Romantic era, a period whose critics and artists were often bent on venerating, rather than chastising, early modern playmakers. In his review of *A Midsummer Night's Dream* starring Edmund Kean as Bottom, William Hazlitt notes that the play, 'when acted, is converted form a delightful fiction into a dull pantomime. All that is finest in the play is lost in the representation. The spectacle was grand: but the spirit was evaporated, the genius was fled . . . The *ideal* can have no place upon the stage, which is a picture without perspective; everything there is in the fore-ground.'[5] The problematic condition of the production is that it *was* a production; the sublime has to meet, awkwardly, the pragmatic logic of putting on a show at all. It thus seems natural that Lear's departing essence of human life – his soul – would not be visible within the realm of the actual – the stage.[6]

Lear deals with many variations of the strained relationship of theatrical space to spiritual presence. (Of course, the pre-Christian setting of *Lear* does not articulate a completely clear reflection of early modern theology, but it certainly accommodates it, as several powerful readings have shown.[7]) The resigned observance of Lear's departing invisible soul follows right on the heels of his tortured attempts to determine Cordelia's liveliness. 'I know when one is dead and when one lives; / She's dead as earth', Lear proclaims as he lays her body to the ground – only to immediately demand that someone 'Lend me a looking-glass; / If that her breath will mist or stain the stone, / Why then she lives' (V, iii, 258–61). The heartbreaking stage business that follows involves him holding a feather to her mouth and rationalising his desperate belief that she might be alive – Did the feather move? Perhaps she is trying to speak, but has a soft voice? Look, her lips are moving! – even as Kent, Albany and Edgar soberly attempt to dissuade him. From a theatrical standpoint, Cordelia's death comprises a notoriously cruel turn of fate because the traces of her life, the fluttering breath or mist, are most likely impossible for the audience to detect. For Thomas Betteridge, this visual impossibility creates narrative failure: 'The promise, and temptation, that Shakespeare hold out to his audience at this moment is that they can make sense of Cordelia's murder – they can create a narrative, deploy a historical myth, tell a sad tale, anything, just to fill in the expanse of nothing that opens at the end of the play.'[8] Ellen MacKay, further peeling back the layers of this troubling scene, also notes the haze that results from the impossible evidentiary demands placed on the spectators. The failure is not only narrative, however, for MacKay – the invisible breath indicates a vexing quality at the heart of performance itself: 'The *summa* of Lear's tragedy is thus its subsumption of the audience in the theatre's quintessential dilemma: the undecidable nature of the performed "fact".' But beyond this problem of staging something so miniature that it eludes the scopic grasp of the stage, a deeper difficulty lurks in the fact that the actor *is* breathing, and as such 'production does the play wrong' – and so we see 'the actor's inevitable failure to live up to the demands of the part'.[9] The theatre demands the death of the actor while Lear demands the life of the character, and we are stuck between trusting Lear's flawed reportage or believing that the play has actually killed someone. Shakespeare perversely uses the tough world of the stage to obscure signs of life, just as he will shortly have us believe we have witnessed Lear's soul because it has not appeared at all.

The deaths of Cordelia and Lear thus concern the search for a difficult-to-detect *and* difficult-to-dismiss component of human life: the departing ghost, on the one hand, and the rise and fall of breath, on the other. But to further complicate things, the play repeatedly testifies that simply being alive – breathing, blood pulsing, maintaining sentience – is not necessarily the same as having a soul. To have a soul is in fact precisely the difference between being animated and being distinctly and incalculably human. It is simple enough to determine if these characters are alive: they move about, have consciousness, possess vital organs, and so forth. This kind of life, mere animation, is what Lear desperately searches for as he waits for the feather to move. He is simply checking to see if she is alive. As a result, he issues a plaintive cry against the abundance of life in seemingly lower creatures: 'Why should a dog, a horse, a rat have life / And thou no breath at all?' (V, iii, 305–6). He is not, on the surface, looking for a spiritual aspect of her being – he would settle for the animal life that fills dogs, horses and rats.

The search for the difference between the bare constitution of life and the construction of a fully-formed person, so vividly demonstrated in the contrast of these two deaths, comprises a major thematic throughline in *Lear* as a whole. As Lear asks, surveying Edgar's feigned madness, 'Is man no more than this? Consider him well. Thou ow'st the worm no silk, the beast no hide, the sheep no wool, the cat no perfume. Ha? Here's three on's us are sophisticated; thou art the thing itself. Unaccommodated man is no more but such a poor, bare, forked animal as thou art' (III, iv, 101). In a meticulous reading of this speech, Laurie Shannon notes that the play 'not only anatomizes man, philosophically, and finds him wanting; it taxonomizes man, literally, and finds him naked'.[10] The thing that separates us from the animals is invisible, without the obvious distinction that making silk, leather, wool, or perfume lends us. The compulsion to account for evidence of the unaccountable soul propels the dominant trajectory of Lear's character, from domineering patriarch who demands precise quantification of love to the wandering figure who surrenders to the unknowable whims of the universe. The shadowy nothing that Lear has become in death, then, is precisely the supplementary quality that allows him to be more than merely life and breath – more than merely accountable. But how do we locate this in the living? How do we know we have a soul, and are not simply life-machines that breathe and move?

This chapter builds a theoretical and historical framework for wrestling with these questions. The problem of how our spiritual selves can be known in a representative medium is one that characterises Shakespeare's dramaturgy as well as major pillars of Western thought, from the Greeks to early Christianity to the post-Reformation world of the early modern era. But this problem also appears in a much more contemporary work of philosophy, Ludwig Wittgenstein's *Philosophical Investigations*. Wittgenstein's work, anachronistic though it may seem to the present concerns, actually helps illuminate many ideas already uncannily at play in the philosophies of the soul that are more historically appropriate for an analysis of early modern literature. Wittgenstein gives us a way to think through how the soul might make itself known in the fallen, mimetic world of the theatre by suggesting that the soul is, in fact, *ever*-present – but in order to see it, we have to shift our definition of 'presence' so as to escape limiting categories of representation, reference, presence, and absence altogether. This is not a question only of the difference between the mere life of Cordelia's breath and the sublime spirit of Lear's departing spirit, but also of how the latter can appear – must appear – in the former. Wittgenstein helps introduce a peculiar property of the soul that will provide a central claim of this book by claiming that it is expressive – or, put differently, that it is theatrical without being representational. The passage from *Philosophical Investigations* begins as follows:

> Suppose I say of a friend: 'He isn't an automaton.' – What information is conveyed by this, and to whom would it be information? To a *human being* who meets him in ordinary circumstances? What information *could* it give him? (At the very most that this man always behaves like a human being, and not occasionally like a machine.)
>
> 'I believe that he is not an automaton', just like that, so far makes no sense.
>
> My attitude towards him is an attitude towards the soul. I am not of the *opinion* that he has a soul.[11]

Wittgenstein goes on to make the iconic pronouncement that 'the human body is the best picture of the human soul' before concluding with a consideration of a specific idiomatic gesture: 'And how about such an expression as: 'In my heart I understood when you said that', pointing to one's heart? Does one, perhaps, not *mean* this gesture? Of course one means it. Or is one conscious of using a *mere* figure? Indeed not. – It is not a figure that we choose, not a simile, yet it is a figurative expression.'[12] The passage takes the form of a debate in which different efforts at surmising the existence of a soul are evaluated not in terms of their accuracy in knowledge – not as to whether they correspond to a 'reality' of the soul – but rather as to the decorum and effects of their use. The statement that the body is the best picture of the soul has the ring of a resolution to an argument, as if slightly resigned to settle on the most effective, rather than the perfect, solution to the problem of the soul's visualisation. Finding its absolute embodiment seems a lost cause: Wittgenstein steers the conversation on the soul away from notions of meaning, information, knowledge, or even ontological composition, and toward a consideration of what the soul *does:* it expresses a picture and comprises a gesture, but it does not prompt an exploration for proof of its existence.

To tease this out further, the difference that Wittgenstein illuminates here can also be thought of as one between representation – this *means* something – and expression – this *does* something. Stanley Cavell elaborates on this distinction in his meditation on Wittgenstein's aphorism:

> The human body is the best picture of the human soul – not, I feel like adding, primarily because it represents the soul but because it expresses it. The body is the field of expression of the soul. The body is *of* the soul; it is the soul's; a human soul *has* a human body . . . It does not seem more comprehensible (though of course no less figurative) to say that this 'having' is done by me: it is I who have both a body *and* a soul, or mind. An ancient picture takes the soul to be the possession of the body, its prisoner, condemned for life.[13]

One of Cavell's strategies, here and throughout much of his reflection on Wittgenstein, is to replace a vocabulary of knowledge and meaning with one of acknowledgment and expression. Rather than think of a conjuration of reference at the mention of a specific word or phrase, he encourages us to see the word or phrase as its own singular gesture. These gestures in turn constitute our habits and movements – the sum of our intentional and inadvertent bodily manipulations. We cannot divorce ourselves from these manipulations; as such, we are, in Cavell's phrase, 'condemned' to be expressive. And the soul is the condition of this condemnation. So the soul is not separated from the body: it is in fact the fated totality of what is expressed by the body.

While the body may produce expression, however, it does not necessarily produce meaning. In fact, the belief in the production of meaning, while tempting, ultimately acts as a deceptive distraction from the omnipresence of expressiveness. In the passage in which Wittgenstein determines the body as the best picture of the soul, the interlocutors elaborate on this idea when they debate the phrase 'In my heart I understood when you said that' when accompanied by a gesture of pointing at one's heart. The gesture, one speaker asserts, *is meant*: 'Of course one means it.' But to be meant is not the same as having a specific meaning, much less to always have that meaning. Marie McGinn explains that '[T]here is no gap between the concept of intention, say, and the movements of a cat stalking a bird; the intention is not merely 'associated' with this intent look, these cautious movements, this readiness to spring, etc., *but is the meaning of all these things*.'[14] If we follow this line of thinking, the soul becomes less a mythical nothingness that is inaccessible to our perception. Instead, it chafes against the ruse of thinking of language and bodily movement as representational at all. It is there under our noses, in our movements, all the time.

The tension between expression and representation colours the dialogues in *Philosophical Investigations*, which frequently feature the device of a conversant who demands a hidden and fixed definition to reveal itself – who insists that every figure is actually a symbol, every gesture a sign. In one emblematic instance, one such voice demands to know whether a drawing of a kettle of boiling water has water in it: 'Of course, if water boils in a pot, steam comes out of the pot and also pictured steam comes out of the pictured pot. But what if one insisted on saying that there must also be something boiling in the pictured pot?'[15] According to Cavell, the significance of this question lies not in the possibility of an answer, but in the curious insistence of the interlocutor in asking: 'everything is free and self-confessed, nothing up the sleeve, there is not even a sleeve; and *yet*, and notwithstanding all that, this man doubts – or maybe not so much doubts as pangs – something is on his mind, he has some reservation, he is not free and clear . . . (If he has both, they will come forth with insistence.)

This is the philosopher's cue; he enters by providing the words.'[16] The 'philosopher' figure, here, is the comforter who reassures the desperate questioner that something must be lurking under the surface, some secret that must out itself. This assurance acts as an epistemological salve: rather than condemn us to expression, the philosopher seems to liberate us into a realm of meaning-making, where our gestures are not singular and non-representational but instead translatable and accountable as signification, like currency in an exchange.

The theatre gives us, broadly speaking, an apt medium for the seductive, though ultimately empty, message of this philosopher-figure. One dominant narrative of the theatre's ontological status – especially Shakespeare's theatre – is that it operates in a representational, rather than expressive, mode. It insists on standing in for meanings elsewhere. The very term 'theatrical' can often be synonymous for 'imitative'; the stage is a place where something stands in for something else, a secondary reality that allegorises the primary one within an aesthetic structure. This conception, born from Plato and Aristotle, haunts the centuries of theatrical theory that follow, whether in the obsessive attempts of Neo-classicism to pay homage to the Greek founders or the self-conscious, outright rejection of imitative principles by Brechtian epic theatre. In the theatre, someone can lift up a broom and say 'behold my sword' or sit on an empty floor and say 'I guess Iceland is pretty warm this time of year!' – and an audience will not, for the most part, be confused: meaning is produced through grammars of space and bodily manipulation, as well as, of course, language. In early modern England, the potential for theatre to create meaning through imitation gave it a doubled edge. The stage could create splendour, but also idolatry. It could educate and seduce. In a prefatory verse to the folio of the works of Beaumont and Fletcher, Francis Palmer mobilises the potential danger of the stage as a form of hagiographic praise: 'How didst thou sway the Theatre! make us feele / The Players wounds were true, and their swords, steele! / Nay, stranger yet, how often did I know / When the Spectators ran to save the blow? / Frozen with griefe we could not stir away / Untill the Epilogue told us "twas a Play" '.[17] While the virtuosic imitation of martial and tragic actions can provide grounds for praise, the application of such skill towards the replication of holiness would clearly comprise a form of blasphemy. Seen through this lens, it is easy to understand the fervour of anti-theatricalism remarked upon by Barish, Diehl, and others: the soul is fundamentally inimitable and thus has no place in a medium of counterfeiting.

Shakespeare's works, in particular, precariously and gloriously balance the potentially dangerous and transcendental aspects of mimesis. His plays would not precisely fit the praise levelled at Beaumont and Fletcher: rather than aim for seamless replications of reality, they gleefully stuff themselves with disguises, deceptions, false narratives, hidden plots, plays-within-plays, and other reflections of and fissures within their own medium; they establish networks of imitative practices and test – and at times break – their capacity to evoke reality. Witness, for example, the scene of recognition between Posthumus and Iachimo in *Cymbeline*, as the latter convinces the former that he has seduced his beloved, Imogen; Posthumus's challenge is that 'If you can make't apparent / That you have tasted her in bed, my hand / And ring is yours' (II, iv, 56–8).[18] What ensues is a deft use of theatrical vocabulary. First, Iachimo describes her bedchamber in absurdly specific detail – including the ominous image of a bathing Diana that adorns the chimney-piece – but finds Posthumus unmoved. The crucial manoeuvre is the revelation of Imogen's bracelet, a wedding token from Posthumus but now, according to the story, given to Iachimo in a fit of desire. This briefly does the trick; after weakly suggesting that she might have 'pluck'd it off / To send it me' (ll. 104–5), he relents – 'O, no, no, no, 'tis true' (l. 106) – only to steel himself once again with incredulity while demanding 'some corporal sign about her / More evident than this' (ll. 119–20). Iachimo then delivers the final blow, a report of a mole on her breast. Of course, Imogen has remained faithful; Iachimo has simply found a crafty way of manipulating objects and descriptions so as to conjure a specific meaning. He moves through categories of effective mimetic deception: relating in detail the scenery, then proffering an object, and finally invoking her body. He acts the part of Cavell's seductive philosopher, there to answer whether a picture of a kettle can contain boiling water. The terms he uses are, significantly, theatrical elements, from setting to prop to actor. The scene relates a poetics of stage illusion by elaborating on the power of properly imbuing physical components with the ability to represent something else beyond themselves, and as such Iachimo exemplifies what we might call a mimetic economy: the valuation and trafficking in modes of meaning-making that both constitute the evoked 'reality' of the plays and comment on the theatrical methods used to constitute this reality for the audience.

That Shakespearean drama playfully twists and reflects upon its own ability to represent reality is not, of course, a new observation to make of his work, nor of early modern drama more generally. Ben Jonson, for instance, frequently pushed the mimetic power of his plays to the point of self-negation.[19] My aim, however, is to find how such playfulness gives us a powerful forum in which we can explore the conundrum exemplified in *Lear* – how the soul is both essential to existence but seemingly impossible to locate. Shakespeare might seem like precisely the wrong place to stage this exploration; after all, a world that endlessly engages in representation would be diametrically opposed to a figure that insists on expression. But it is actually *because* of this glut of representational insistence that the contours of the soul's presence can more sharply be distinguished: the soul's expressivity does not act independent of representation but in direct opposition to it. In fact, the soul expresses itself precisely through a *rejection* of representation. This notion is one crucial to many foundational works on the soul: it could mark its appearance as a failure of grammar, not its perfection. As Margaret Ferguson explains in her reading of St Augustine's *Confessions*:

> The inability to free even an allegorical notion of distance from conceptualization in spatial terms is Augustine's acknowledgment that his own language traps him in the very unlikeness he is trying to define precisely because there is something in the nature of language which necessitates a spatial understanding of a difference – an unlikeness – that is not spatial (quantitative) at all.[20]

The soul must resist allegory and spatialisation. To succumb to the belief of its elegant evocation through language, textual or bodily, is to deny its otherworldliness. Tautologically, if the soul can 'mean' anything, then it cannot be a soul. We may, then, be able to indicate the soul's appearance by performing its absence, as Edgar and Kent do when they avert their gaze from Lear's departing spirit. But while Lear's soul may be invisible when it leaves the body, when it is lodged *within* the body it can still find strategies of marking itself that exist in the nebulous area between the seen and unseen, artificial and authentic, aestheticised and real. The soul finds itself not sublimely locked away, but instead within the irreducible presentness of life. In this way, while it is not mimetic, it is still capable of theatricality.

And yet: how can something be theatrical without being representational? And how can the rejection of mimesis, so often taken as synonymous with the theatre, itself be something that is staged? The distinctions here are crucial. Theatricality is the act of rendering oneself a spectacle – not in a pejorative sense of artifice, but literally something that *is seen*; the word 'theatre', after all, derives from the ancient Greek *theatron*, or 'seeing-place'. Samuel Weber elaborates that theatricality is 'a distance that ostensibly permits one to view the object in its entirety while remaining at a safe remove from it'.[21] For Weber that 'ostensibly' marks the subtle distinction of theatricality from the theatre's mere separation of audience and stage. Theatricality troubles its own constitutive divisions by playing within the implied 'hollowness' of the specular interval and working to mark 'separation as a kind of inner space rather than an interval in-between'; it furthermore 'takes place *in the hollow of this separation*, which it deploys and to which it responds'.[22] Theatricality, as such, exists not by creating a hollow but within the hollow itself: it is an action, or in Weber's term a 'medium', rather than a static thing. It is not necessarily a space but within a spac*ing*, an active and anxious ongoing process of deploying space, of distancing oneself while inviting scrutiny; it bypasses representability or imitativeness and insists on the implication (and thus creation) of a spectator. Toril Moi, for instance, employs this valence of the word in her reading of Ibsen's *A Doll's House*, when she notes that the persistent 'theatricalization' of Nora and Helmer – the married couple at the centre of the drama – 'might give rise to the idea that the two of them are, as it were, pure performers. But their fantasies reveal them as much as they conceal them.'[23] Deploying and responding to distances, these characters are not necessarily separated, nor are they taking on different roles or attenuating their own identities. Instead, they reveal, perhaps even fabricate, themselves through their theatricalisation, through a series of gestures that cannot easily be resolved into a grammar of meaning but instead insist on their performances as the things themselves.

Moi's topic is resolutely modernist – perhaps the modernist dramatic text par excellence – and not, on the surface, related to the realm of Shakespeare's plays. So I would like now to trace these strategies in the foundational – though fluid – philosophical and theological discourses on the soul that characterised the early modern era, and with which Shakespeare's work engaged in a profound and often contentious dialogue. These are many of the texts surveyed with a sigh by John Davies in this book's introduction, the tangle of classical and Christian influences that create such a deeply imbricated series of beliefs. One line of inquiry to advance is to resist thinking of the soul in idolatrous (which is to say, mimetic, or as an inevitable victim of corruption by mimesis) or Romantic frameworks, and instead find how its picture roosts itself in the manipulations of the body – not symbolically but expressively; not representationally but in direct antagonism with representation itself, in a host of gestures that defer, conceal, smother, or seek to obliterate the possibility of hidden absolute meaning – and yet also a bodily grammar that indicates, without correlating symbolically to, something *more* than the sum total of its means. The paradox that emerges from this dynamic is this: through the resistance of the theatre's capacity to insist on meaning, the soul finds its own theatrical embodiment.

The Body Outside Itself

This overview of the soul's theorisation begins with Plato, who similarly stands as the foundational figure in many genealogies of the theatre. Along with Aristotle, Plato gives us a potent way to think through the relationship of these two fields, and as a result, these two thinkers demand particular attention, focused as they are on how the soul relates to the central elements of performance – action, movement, and representation. Careful attention to such classical formations of the soul is furthermore warranted due to their towering influence over the philosophical and theological traditions in their wake, particularly in early modern England, where early Greek thought filtered itself through humanist education and the remnants of early Christian beliefs that remained lodged in the shifting sediments of religious practice.

In Platonic metaphysics, the soul crafts a connection by which the human may ascend to attain capital-T Truth or fall into hollow sensuality. One of the most famous models of this principle occurs in *Phaedrus* (as is typical with Plato, despite his disavowal of imitation he relies on symbolic imagery) where the soul becomes framed as tripartite: two aspects are horses, one white and pure, with a 'determination to succeed' and propelled by 'self-control and respect for others'; the other black and 'crooked, over-large, a haphazard jumble of limbs' who, far from being lofty and pure, is 'an ally of excess and affectation'.[24] The third component, the charioteer, tries to pilot these repelling forces. The charioteer, caught in the middle, struggles to steer the two beasts, and must harshly discipline the downward-pointing animal; he 'wrenches the unruly horse's bit back out of its teeth, splashing its curse-laden tongue and jaws with blood, pinning its legs and haunches to the ground, and causing it pain'.[25] The black horse demonstrates dangerously excessive corporeality in its own construction as a numberless 'jumble of limbs' and its desire for bodily pleasures. But the means of the black horse's punishment are located within its own body. The pilot must inflict pain and cause secretions of blood, sound and sweat. The goal is to attain a lack of reaction when faced with beauty, in the form of a learned fear that now prevents desire to take hold and stills the body in apprehension of tactility. As Robert Watson explains, 'The art of virtue is the art of driving this chariot, the art of repressing the base animal impulses of the lesser horse and tempering the occasional excesses of the finer one.'[26] Virtue is an 'art', a *techne*, a technique of repression that demands a carefully scripted process of disciplining excess. To not give in to desire is not the same as doing nothing: it is instead an active, bodily depiction of the resistance to the lure of desire.

Plato's *Republic* reframes *Phaedrus's* imagery in describing its own three-part structure: the appetitive division, the 'irrational' aspect that is 'friend to certain ways of being filled and certain pleasures'; the rational division, which operates in resistance to the emotional and pleasurable impulses of the appetitive; and finally the 'spirited' division, which is 'the natural auxiliary of the rationally calculating element, if it has not been corrupted'.[27] The spirited aspect, formerly figured as the charioteer in *Phaedrus*, serves as the synthetic result of the proper mastery of the appetites. The telos for both individual and city is justice: Socrates concludes that 'to produce justice is to establish the elements in the soul in a natural relation of mastering and being mastered by one another'.[28] Woven through the prescriptive progression offered in *Phaedrus* and *Republic* is a meditation on the role of the body within the soul's proper governance. The body is not simply disparaged in this process, however. It is trained to perform a specific role in relation to the soul, while the soul responds to the determinedly non-material coaxing of music and reason to become more pure. The *Republic* presents this dynamic in a concise Homeric allusion: 'He struck his chest and spoke to his heart', Socrates recites favourably.[29] Plato does not merely present a duality in which the body, as the soul's opposite, is cast away; it is instead enlisted in its own distancing. The form of gesture here, of striking one's chest, is a theatrical display, one similar to Wittgenstein's example of pointing to one's heart. Of course, scenes of hair-pulling, clothes-rending and chest-pounding attend many classical scenes of excessive affect, but the Odysseus scene is notable for its employment of this gesture for precisely the opposite effect, to contain his body's more impulsive and less rational impulses. The movement, furthermore, does not correlate to a *meaning* of the soul – it is not mimetic – but it still figures something in its own self-defined grammar: it gestures at how it cannot act as a clear referent at all.

The elusive relationship of the soul to mimesis is a signal theme in Plato's work, which does not, contrary to some interpretations, simply antagonise all forms of performance. As Paul Kottman notes, the *Republic* 'expels a broad horizon of dramatic representation from the domain of politics while at the same time relying upon precise figurations culled from this same horizon in order to perform that expulsion'.[30] Kottman tracks, here, the subtle changes undergone by the notion of mimesis in Plato's dialogues to uncover a careful rhetorical move that strategically expropriates certain imitative aspects while retaining a sense of vitality in what Kottman calls 'the scene': the immediate interaction of audience and actor that evades Plato's famous disgust at mere imitation. Rather than *just* being imitation, the theatre that survives in the ideal state – upon which its politics is founded – is capable of retaining the soul's bodily powers of enactment without the dangers of representation. What emerges is a form of expression distinct from the traditionally mimetic that 'cannot be fully grasped in terms of the fictional or artistic character to political life, or in terms of its referential relation to outside reality'.[31] Kottman's thesis approaches a Platonic understanding of non-representational performance that avoids dismissing his philosophy as merely antitheatrical – such a performance skirts 'fictional or artistic character' by not resolving into form, but still constitutes a singular action. Here we see one way the nothingness of Lear's soul can be evoked even while lodged in a body, still firmly in the tough world: through expressions of mimetic futility.

While drastically differing from Plato in many regards, Aristotle echoes his mentor in defining the calculative part of the soul as seemingly divorced from the corporeal. Yet he also, like Plato, cryptically links the two. He leaves open the possibility of expressing the soul by disavowing its link to clear meaning. In explaining why animals cannot possess rationality, he observes that they are capable of movement, and that 'it is not the calculative part and what is called the intellect that produces this movement'.[32] The human soul must have a part that is not linked to physical movement. Whereas young Phaedrus risks corruption by giving in to his bodily desires, or a similarly impetuous young man in the *Republic* risks misunderstanding justice by following his appetites, in Aristotelian terms this surrender hazards a more classificatory confusion: submitting to lesser forms of the soul blurs the distinction that prevents these figures from self-definition as merely moving, overly sensitive bodies – which is to say, as Lear imagines, merely a dog, horse, or rat, or, more generally, in Aristotle's similar litany, a 'horse, dog, man, or God'.[33] A double-bind ensues: humans possess aspects of the soul that animals do not, but they cannot directly show this process because, if rationality enacted itself as performance, it would simply resemble another form of animality. Here, both Lear's spirit and Cordelia's breath threaten to blur into one, as if to suggest that man *is* no more than this – he is simply a body that inhales and exhales.

If the distinction of humanity could actually be an action, it would not make us human, because reliance on action is the signature quality of the animal. What Aristotle proposes as a way out of this conundrum is a radically internal form of performance, divorced from action, staged in the non-corporeal theatre of consciousness. But this unmarked process of ascertaining potential still depends on the active, speaking, temporal world to structure its possibility. As Michael Frede explains, thinking presupposes a body but cannot be reduced to it; it is linked, but not explicitly dependent:

> the exercise of the intellect, Aristotle wants to say . . . unlike the exercise of the other so-called mental faculties, does not involve the use of a bodily organ. For otherwise our cognitive abilities would be hampered by the restrictions the organ puts on them, the way the sense-organs limit what we can perceive. But this does not mean that the exercise of the intellect does not presuppose a body.[34]

Once again we are confronted with a kind of expressive, rather than representational, manipulation demanded by the soul that resists the simple either-or of imitative or non-imitative. David Charles identifies this movement as 'inextricably psycho-physical' and proposes that, for Aristotle, movement results not simply from the body or the soul but the 'person (or composite)', that 'moves the hand, grieves, etc'.[35] Aristotle elaborates on this notion of soulful action further in *Nicomachean Ethics*, where he sets out his agenda in exploring the results of 'an activity of soul and actions accompanied by reason, the work of a serious man being to do these things well and nobly, and each thing is brought to completion well in accord with the virtue proper to it'; if these characteristics are met, 'then the human good becomes an activity of soul in accord with virtue, and if there are several virtues, then in accord with the best and most complete one'.[36] An activity of soul aligned with virtue results in proper human action – where intention, virtue, deliberation, and effects constellate into a unified subject. The body, again, becomes instrumentalised by the soul, capable of reflecting it through rigorous self-examination.[37]

In his provocative and playful essay 'On the Soul' – the title is a clear homage to Aristotle, who also comprises the piece's focus – Jean-Luc Nancy elaborates on *De Anima*'s simultaneous divorce and commingling of body and soul. Nancy aims to escape 'an understanding of the ineffable interiority behind this word, a sublime or vaporous identity escaping from the prison of the body'; instead, he proposes that the soul 'doesn't represent *anything other* than the body, but rather the body outside itself, or this other that the body is, structurally, for itself and in itself'. In short, the soul 'is the body's difference from itself, the relation to the outside that the body is for itself'.[38] With characteristically sinewy prose, Nancy gives us a way out of the binary of soul *or* body, presence *or* absence; instead, he banishes a model of the soul as sublime and unknowable to suggest that the soul is the body's awareness of itself, a contact point between the body and something else – and this contact point both is the body and bounds the body. The body possesses a doubleness, not as a shadowy spectre but as an extension of its perceptions that creates and incorporates the gap between the body and the outside world – a kind of theatricality, in Weber's sense, that does not simply separate audience from performer but continually reinscribes and re-creates distancing. This distancing is both not the body and the body – it is, in short, the soul as a form of theatricality without symbolism or the promise of a secret, 'true' meaning.

This sense of continual, replicating doubleness threatens to postulate itself *ad infinitum* – the soul is the body and not the body but by marking the not-body it is an extension of the body, and so on – and parallels, as a result, the soul's slippery relation to selfhood in early Christian doctrine, which repurposed and retrofitted classical formulations of the soul in its exegetical commentaries. In his *Confessions*, Augustine incorporates Platonic and Aristotelian ideas in his hermeneutical practice to examine the nature of his faith:

> Then I turned towards myself, and said to myself: 'Who are you?' I replied: 'A man.' I see in myself a body and a soul, one external, the other internal. Which of these should I have questioned about my God, for whom I had already searched through the physical order of things from earth to heaven, as far as I could send the rays of my eyes as messengers? What is inward is superior . . . In that respect, my soul, I tell you that you are already superior. For you animate the mass of your body and provide it with life, since no body is capable of doing that for another body.[39]

The Augustinian model of the soul merges the divine capacities of Platonic dialectic with the animating force of Aristotelian classification. The soul is resolutely interior, and hence not located in the 'physical order of things' that Augustine has futilely investigated. This interiority recalls Plato's metaphysical investment in resisting the lure of exterior appetitive pleasures and constructing justice through inward restraint. Augustine addresses his soul as his 'self' ('I tell you . . .') though he cannot truly be the totality of his self without his soul. As such, the 'I' in the passage is not exactly Augustine but rather his sensory aspect, the part that can perceive, the performer as spectator-narrator: we see dramatised here the Aristotelian paradox by which the animal aspect of humans provides the only hope in outlining the rational quality that lends them their distinct human-ness.

With apparent contradiction, then, the Augustinian soul is internal *and* insubstantial, separate from the body *and* within it. The body is filled with the soul: it expresses it constantly, is animated by it – but the soul cannot emerge or simply be chosen as a medium of communication. What becomes articulated in his knowingly futile address to his soul is a choreography of gesturing *elsewhere*, somewhere internal beyond his understanding – a highly aestheticised acknowledgment of the soul's presence that also admits to its apparent absence – but via a non-semantic, theatrical strategy that signals the soul without consigning it to either complete absence or facile simulacrum.

The architects of the Protestant Reformation would both build upon and subvert Augustine's ideas to bring new and complex ways of negotiating the body's role in expressing the soul. To take 'The Reformation' as a cohesive and singular movement is, of course, a fallacy; as Peter Lake and Michael Questier explain, 'the process of Protestantism' is in fact 'the result – as, if you like, the sum total of – a series of acts of synthesis, assimilation, appropriation and *bricolage*. The resulting cultural and religious transactions and exchanges were always contested and partial, subject to the input and influence of a large range of individuals and groups.'[40] In response to an admission of the diverse assortment of beliefs that Lake and Questier describe, literary scholarship of the period has found nuanced readings of Reformation texts that avoid any simplistic narratives. One reductive account of the era was that of an overall de-spatialisation of spirituality – the erasure of Purgatory, the emphasis on faith rather than works – and with this, more of a plunge inward of the soul, further and further removed from the possibility of realisation in temporal form. But as Nandra Perry observes, in her study of the devotional practice of *imitatio Christi* in the early modern era, the works of humans still had the capacity to evoke divinity, and the word still possessed the ability to reflect the Word: 'Practiced skillfully' – a crucial caveat – 'early modern *imitatio* is a technique for constructing original, but broadly meaningful, systems of signification from the remnants of an authoritative, but irrevocable, past. It is a delicate art, balanced perilously between the extremes of slavish traditionalism and radically destabilizing innovation.'[41] Philip Sidney's *Defence of Poesy*, which records the first English use of 'mimesis' in terms of artistic practice,[42] provides for Parry a paradigmatic example of the skillful and delicate art *and* a cautionary tale of how devotional imitation can quickly turn into fallen idolatry. Specifically, it is the *Defence's* compulsive focus on bodies that provides the most volatile such mixture: '[I]f the bodies scattered throughout the *Defence* offer a key to Sidney's thinking about poetry's methods and aims, they can also be used to map his anxieties about its potential abuses.'[43] The body is, for Sidney, the battleground for divinity's connection. Even in an era filled with communities who often professed an allergy to divine representation, strategies persisted to suture a connection between God and physical praxis.

The signal gesture of the interiorisation of the soul is well known to the point of possible cliché, but still worth rehearsing. Martin Luther's famous concept of *sola fide*, 'justification by faith alone', promoted the utter isolation of the spirit from the sensory, temporal world. Focusing on St Paul's invocation that 'he who through faith is righteous shall live' (Rom 1: 17), Luther shifts the terms of divine practice, making faith not the object of worship but its medium. In his origin story, Luther relates how upon reading Paul's words he 'began to understand that the righteousness of God is revealed by the gospel, namely, the *passive* righteousness with which merciful God justifies us by faith'.[44] By situating grace outside of the logic of cause and effect, Luther suggests a kind of spiritual health that proceeds of its own accord, passively, without being affected by perceptible actions. Grace cannot exist temporally, in 'portions or pieces, separately, like so many gifts; rather, it takes us up completely into its embrace for the sake of Christ our mediator and intercessor, and in order that the gifts may take root in us'.[45] These 'gifts' are divorced from the attribution of time or space: it is not an act by which grace is received, but instead the totality of an inward existence. Indeed, the process is wholly inward, no longer internalised from external manifestations. In *Secular Authority* Luther applies his doctrine specifically to the soul:

> For over the soul God can and will let no one rule but Himself. Therefore, where temporal power presumes to prescribe laws for the soul, it encroaches upon God's government and only misleads and destroys the souls. [. . .] When man-made law is imposed upon the soul, in order to make it believe this or that, as that man prescribes, there is certainly no word of God for it.[46]

Faith is, for Luther, non-human. It is by definition pure and solely the property of God. The hubristic assumption that human action can have any effect on the flourishing of grace within the soul is absurd and, furthermore, a threat to spiritual health. The best way to tend to the soul is not to clear the depths of memory through careful ritual, nor to restrain desire and privilege rationality, but to keep the body out of the equation entirely. The theology that Luther founds, though it would be endlessly complicated by Anglican praxis, intensified by Puritanism, and outright rejected by still-vibrant subcultures of Catholicism, clearly suggests with bracing provocation that the soul and God have their own communication and the human can at best simply witness it, as mute and ineffectual as the farm animals who witnessed Christ's birth – or as Kent and Edgar, who make room for an unseen and intangible being to whisk by them.

As Parry's reading of Sidney suggests, however, this witnessing is itself an *act* negotiated through a proliferation of ritual. And rather than focus on the imitative processes of signification that Parry analyses, it is possible to illuminate the more expressive, even quotidian, means by which the human body could assemble its own self-contained meaning. These are the less bombastic, more subtle strategies that thread through Shakespearean drama alongside more florid demonstrations of representative manipulation: the gestures that actively resist conscription into a mimetic economy and instead demonstrate themselves as singular and unassimilable. Such gestures are still on display, still visible; the distance instantiated between the soul and body is, again, a theatrical one that produced a series of staged behaviours that insist on their own singularity and lack of referentiality. The body is, in divine terms, utterly inconsequential, but this inconsequentiality possesses its own capacity to move, inflect and gesture. The resulting ambivalence over the indexicality of imagery does not result in the eradication of visual media, but rather charges the scene of art's emergence with self-inquiry; as Michael O'Connell notes in concluding his readings of Shakespeare's works, what is remarkable is

> their willingness to enlist the image in the endeavor of definition. I have argued that the metadrama of his plays represents a

> response to iconoclasm, and it is significant that the defenses of theatricality implicit in those metatheatrical moments at the same time encompass various forms of skepticism about representation. There is never an uncomplicated devotion to the word or to the image in isolation.[47]

Such complication need not only emerge in forthrightly artistic works such as Shakespeare's. It can also symptomatically be created in even the most seemingly dogmatic tracts. As Thomas Betteridge suggests, a newly aggregated Reformist sense of aesthetics grew in concert with the flourishing of newly solidified and separate churches – a process known in more contemporary historical theory as 'Confessionalisation' – that reflected the divide between the nonsensical manipulations of earthly registers and the unified and singular being of God. Betteridge argues that, despite the specific institutional orientation of different church identities, Confessionalisation 'embodied a specific model of selfhood based upon the struggle to achieve confessional purity and its poetics consistently valorised the plain simple truth of the Word of God against the dangers of textual play and linguistic ambiguity'.[48] As a result, rather paradoxically, authors as diametrically opposed as Thomas More and William Tyndale shared a reliance on, rather than an outright rejection of, tropes of playful textual manipulation as a means to seduce and lure – and ultimately spurn – the reader. The promise of a complex system of meanings and secrets to uncover proves to be a house of cards that the pure Word of God (regardless of the religion that believes *in* that specific manifestation), in its forthright and holistic presence, can topple.

In other words, the performing body could be seen not simply as opposed to pure faith, but instead the field onto which the struggles of iconoclasm and holiness become inscribed and within which they occur. The possibility of performance ensuring faith was questioned, but the potential connection to God through revelation and engagement with the body remained the telos for most religious life. Retaining both of these principles demanded a carefully remapped spiritual and physical terrain. Calvin, in the *Institutes*, labours to accomplish this double gesture. On the one hand, following the Lutheran demand to banish temporality and further interiorise divine connection, he denounces representational practices. On the other, like Plato, he retains a lexicon of representation in charting the nature of inward belief: 'Christ is the most perfect image of God, into which we are so renewed as to bear the image of God in knowledge, purity, righteousness, and true holiness.' The replication of images extends from God to Christ to humans within their souls; however, due to the singular devastation of the Fall, the soul is 'vitiated and almost destroyed', and 'nothing remaining but a ruin, confused, mutilated, and tainted with impurity'. Furthermore, the nature of these 'images' is beyond simple external resemblance, as 'the likeness must be within, in himself. It must be something which is not external to him but is properly the internal goodness of the soul'.[49] Outlining a 'likeness' that is somehow entirely subsumed, Calvin is reticent to abandon entirely the language of imitation. Instead he reclaims it within a semantic realm that barely skirts contradiction – a resemblance that is not seen at all, a representation in search of a referent. Calvin nimbly navigates the representative complexities faced by Protestant theologians who sought to craft a theory of the soul. The early modern debate on 'soul sleep' helps exemplify the stakes of this philosophical quandary. To believe in soul sleep is to believe that wandering souls, freed upon death, go on to possess bodies. (It echoes, in this regard, debates over metempsychosis, discussed in the next chapter.) Protestants became split in their affirmation of this idea between, as Diarmaid MacCulloch puts it, 'popular beliefs about ghosts and indeterminacy after death'.[50] Believing that the soul could possess a body would lend the soul corporeal form, and thus an aesthetic quality, and would in turn graft itself onto existing popular folklore about wandering corpses. But affirmation of soul sleep loses the mysticism of the soul's unknowability. Luther was in favour of the belief and Tyndale agreed, but not so Calvin, who, true to his interiorising impulse, insisted that reports of wandering corpses were occasions of demonic possession.[51]

Official modes of English Protestantism adapted this set of circumstances into a theo-political doctrine that retains both the capacity for ritual and the ineffectiveness of mere action. The Homily of Faith, from 1547, professes that

> nothing commendeth good men unto God so much as this assured faith and trust in him. Of this faith, three things are specially to be noted. First, that this faith doth not lie dead in the heart, but is lively and fruitful in bringing forth good works. Second, that without it, can no good works be done, that shall be acceptable and pleasant to God. Third, what manner of good works they be, that this faith doth bring forth.[52]

The homily reassures its followers that, while faith is divested from the temporal world, it is not 'dead in the heart'. Once more we are faced with concern over spirituality's necessary unknowability appearing, for all purposes, to be at the edge of non-existence. Indeed, the homily continues, we need to reverse the causality of faith: good works do not lead to good faith; faith must be the firm foundation from which good works emerge. This foundation must remain unknown, but its unknowability must be expressed.

The stakes of allowing the non-physical foundation of faith to flourish properly are high – quite literally life and death. Strands of English puritanism in the Renaissance adapted the Reformist philosophy of the homily to such a degree that humans *qua* humans seem almost overdetermined as nearly dead. As Henry Greenwood explains in his sermon 'A Treatise on the Great and Generall Daye of Judgement Necessarie for Every Christian', because 'the soule is the life of the body, so God is the life of the soule; take away the soule, the body dieth; take away God, the soule is dead'. So far so good: this is a rather traditional view of the soul's connection to God. But Greenwood interprets the Fall as the primal scene of this separation: 'So that Adam that day died in soule, being separated from the Lord; yea that day Adam was made subject to death in this life, and in the life to come; that day he had the beginnings of death seasing upon him, for hee was presently cast out of Paradise into the ragged world.'[53] The ragged world, like the tough world that cannot hold Lear's soul, absorbs Adam as the residual cast-off of God's broken contract – and contact – with humanity. What Adam needs is to reinstatiate that connection, but what is available to him are only the fragments and ruins of the tangible, de-souled environment. Faith can only be rekindled from within by mending the interiorised act of Edenic expulsion that constitutes the preordained condition of the soul within the body.

The divorce of the soul from the body that sin leads to, coupled with the soul's habituation, even when correctly placed beyond the realm of the body's registers, can potentially lead to the body's figuration as fallen – tough, ragged – or even abject. The melodramatic excesses of Jacobean tragedy meditated with especial attention on this excremental vision of corporeality. As Bosola, in John Webster's *Duchess of Malfi*, describes:

> Thou art a box of worm-seed, at best but a salvatory of green mummy. What's this flesh? A little crudded milk, fantastic puff paste. Our bodies are weaker than those paper prisons boys use to keep flies in, more contemptible, since ours is to preserve earthworms. Didst thou ever see a lark in a cage? Such is the soul in the body; this world is like her little turf of grass, and the heaven o'er our heads, like her looking glass, only gives us a miserable knowledge of the small compass of our prison.[54]

This model of spiritual life is more accurately one of death: the body is a putrefying wisp of material through which the soul passes. Bosola's description serves as his response to the Duchess's question 'Who am I?' with the 'I' here a nightmarish version of Augustine's pronoun, the body who is aware of, but not coextensive to, the soul. 'I' am simply the body, the turf, the 'paste'. For Bosola, humans can at best be stewards to the soul as it briefly floats through the world.

In short, the theology that took root in the Reformation – as endlessly pluralised, mediated, and ideologically varied as it was – opens up spaces for complex forms of soulful performance untethered to a purely mimetic mode of operation. There is no clear road map as to what such a practice would look like. Certainly internalised faith could be evoked textually, but less clear is how a bodily grammar could be marshalled to show that the soul was vibrant and aligned with a divine purpose. Embodying the soul, then, could be less a clear praxis of meaning-making and more an active and visible denial of meaning, a way to show the body's inconsequence and irrelevance as mere witness. To be faithful was to be on the cusp of not doing anything particular at all.

Justice for the Unseen

The genealogy outlined here can be translated into an arsenal of strategies to evoke the soul theatrically without allowing it to become represented – a set of bodily practices such as concealment, deferral, withholding, silence, whispering, stillness, and other highly visible, though obstinately non-mimetic, behaviours. These strategies differ wildly across such different eras, cultures and works, but one binding theme to these highly disparate and idiosyncratic discourses is *justice*. Plato demanded that the telos of the polis be justice, and this idea, in various incarnations, doggedly sticks to the soul throughout its centuries of rigorous and varied investigation. 'Justice' could mean, as it does for Plato, the ruling of absolute right. But the more abstract understanding of 'doing' justice similarly helps us understand the soul's persistent characteristics. Whether interpreted by Hellenistic philosophers, patristic commentators, medieval theologians, or Protestant reformers, the soul indexes the desire that there be *something more* than the apparent sum of the human's parts. This is the same desire plaintively cried for by Lear. It is the stuff of human distinction and, when overly scrutinised, of human tragedy.

Writing on Aristotle's notion of the soul as form, Michael Frede articulates this potentially destructive desire by comparing the body's digestive system to a hypothetically identical one created synthetically: 'Presumably the same process, as described in material terms, could be reproduced artificially. But if it were, it would not be a case of digestion. And this is not because it lacked some details or some mysterious quality the natural process has, but because it, as a whole and its details, *would have to be explained differently*.'[55] The soul demands a different mode of explanation by asserting an essential quality: the soul of a dog is its quiddity, its essential dog-ness, which nothing else can have, not even a perfectly replicated dog. This nearly tautological definition points to 'justice' of the more quotidian sort: we have to 'do' justice to what something really is by explaining it in terms of an absolute essence. In a way, these twin ideas of justice weave through all the disparate definitions of the soul. It must remain, to a degree, unseen, but it must be understandable as a way to measure the extent to which the seen can be defined. 'Doing' justice is not the conjuration of absolutely meaning but the proper delineation of the insubstantial.

The scene from *Lear* that opened this chapter references one notion of justice – the punitive, punishing kind – in Kent's description of the 'rack of this tough world'. The 'rack' of the world effects a retributive action for a supposed transgression. In Lear's case, his apparent crime is according to Kent that 'He but usurped his life' (V, iii, 316). Lear has lived past his allotted life on earth and stolen extra time, and for this crime the world has stretched him out to cause pain and suffering. But the alternate spelling of the word as 'wracke', found in the quarto and folio editions, helps illuminate a deeper sense of justice. The world has been ruined by civil strife; in Albany's colourful turn of phrase, the kingdom has become 'the gored state' (IV, iii, 319). The world is also inherently a 'wracke', though, because of its status as just the world and not a realm that can accommodate souls and spirits: the doubled sense of 'tough', as both durable and unfair, reflects itself in the doubled sense of '(w)rack'. The tough world of bodies and things pressurises us to be just, but the world itself has already redundantly been punished and ruined. When released, the soul cannot reveal itself directly – it only slips by. But neither could it reveal itself in the puffs and shells of bodies in the first place. Humans are condemned to be part of the same world that denies their spiritual presence.

Understanding the soul as a site of justice reframes it as a site of theatre, though not a traditionally understood one where someone or something stands in for something else. The soul needs to be made understandable enough without imprisoning itself in semiosis, without pretending to be invested in the tough world that expels it. This delicate balancing act in turn requires a specific set of organised actions: the physical world has to conscript itself into behaviour that denies its direct connection to the soul while structuring a space in which the unknowable can become symptomised. The body becomes the best picture of the soul. This kind of picture-making consists of deferrals, concealments, whispers, breaths, silences, elisions and other ripples through fields of representation. Furthermore, such a bodily grammar would find an overlap among the many thinkers discussed in this chapter, despite their ideological differences: the self's interior spiritual components rely, indirectly, on a theatrical grammar located in the body, even as the soul defines itself as necessarily distinct from these components. The close attention to specific figurations of the soul's dynamic with the physical world, furthermore, has helped to establish a detailed historical vocabulary for the following chapters. Indeed, many of the specific ideas mentioned above will reappear as central components to my readings, so understanding their placement in discourses of the era will help texture their usage. What are the specific ways resistance to meaning could make itself theatrical – that is, how can one strategise a way to show a lack of meaning? We have the philosophical structure of an answer, but not a corporeal or characterological one. The theatre of Shakespeare and his contemporaries demonstrates such an answer acutely, and the remainder of this book explores this proposition in depth.

CHAPTER 2

GOVERNING THE WOLF: SOUL AND SPACE IN *THE MERCHANT OF VENICE*

The Merchant of Venice pits relentlessly economising forces against figures who insist on unknowable interiority. The play, in its compulsive acts of accounting, repeatedly measures, weighs, and translates value into tangible replacements, stand-ins, and prostheses. As Simon Critchley and Tom McCarthy observe, one can simply flip 'through the text to almost any passage' to discover 'variants on owing, exchanging, bequeathing, expending, accounting, and converting applied as the default vocabulary for all manner of subjects and phenomena one would not normally consider to be "economic"'.[1] Antonio and Shylock, seeming antagonists, both stubbornly and even perversely oppose this radical broadening of economic processes, and as a result, they share an uncanny bond beyond their actual bond of monetary promise. Both have a deep disdain of explaining their motives, and their expressions of denial lend symmetry to the dramatic action: the play opens with Antonio dismissing attempts to identify the cause of his sadness, and the trial climaxes with Shylock dismissing attempts to identify the cause of his hate. Throughout, both of them resist, with varying repertoires of techniques, any attempt to place their inner selves on a grid of valuation.

Looked at differently, the conflict of the play could easily be described in terms precisely opposite to what I have sketched out here. Shylock could represent the more economic side with

Antonio, along with his fellow Venetians, embodying a belief in grander and more abstract principles, such as mercy, friendship and love. As a Jewish usurer, Shylock accommodates – and as a canny performer, he manipulates – a host of associations that characterise him as obsessively valuing, counting, assessing and correlating worth. And the Christian citizens of Venice habitually deny the seduction of surface value; they celebrate instead the moral lesson impressed onto Bassanio at Belmont: 'The world is still deceived with ornament' (III, ii, 74).

This chapter will try to have it both ways. Shylock is indeed an economising figure, but in a radically different manner than the Christian Venetians. When read as an elaboration of the soul's placement in the 'tough world' of space and tangibility surveyed in the previous chapter, *Merchant* reveals a deeper negotiation of how the unknowable can be reflected – though not determined – through the ornament of physical means. What Shylock, and to an extent Antonio and Jessica, offer us is not simply a reflection of the soul's unknowability but instead a meditation on how that unknowability can be expressed without resolving itself into a strict assignment of meaning – or, put more broadly, without resigning itself to an understanding of 'meaning' as fixed at all. Throughout the play, Shylock deliberately engages with the resolutely trivial minutiae that the soul defined itself *against*, but does so in a way that highlights the irrelevance of ornamentation, rather than deifies it as capable of transmitting spiritual presence. Other characters, meanwhile, constantly talk of soulful valences in casual declarations of commitment. The soul, as a result, is economised through language and mimetic ritual, even as it is purported to be outside of language. Maintaining proper social and even existential cohesion, for the Venetians, depends upon the carefully scripted and performed deferral of acknowledging how ruthlessly economic one must be to function as a subject.

Two understandings of the soul, then, will emerge in this reading. One is Shylock's embodiment and expression of the soul, which uses language gesturally, almost playfully, to floridly show its own rootedness in an immediate and particular context that cannot host the soul's atemporal nature. The second is the more socially normalised behaviour of his tormentors, which compartmentalises the soul as if it were an aesthetic commodity – or, more accurately, as if language could compress and stretch the fabric of everyday life into something spiritually potent. Late in the play, a lengthy digression, self-consciously marked as trivial, acts as an uneasy contact point between these two conceptions. In the trial scene, the witty and bawdy Gratiano, furious with Shylock, levels an extended threat that revels in its imagery even as it forecloses on its own possibility. His admonishment mentions the belief, attributed to the Greek thinker Pythagoras, that souls could migrate from a dying body into a new host. As such, Gratiano's speech allows for a consideration of how the physical world interacts with the spiritual, and how the human body becomes inscribed with the irreconcilability of the two:

> Thou almost make me waver in my faith,
> To hold opinion with Pythagoras,
> That souls of animals infuse themselves
> Into the trunks of men: thy currish spirit
> Govern'd a wolf, who hang'd for human slaughter –
> Even from the gallows did his fell soul flee,
> And whilst thou layest in thy unhallowed dam,
> Infus'd itself in thee: for thy desires
> Are wolvish, bloody, starv'd, and ravenous. (IV, i, 128–38)[2]

In framing his tale of a wolvish soul and fetal Shylock as impossible, yet mapping that impossibility with syllogistic precision, Gratiano fulfils his reputation for speaking 'an infinite deal of nothing' (I, i, 114). His claims comprise a collection of 'nothings' because they base themselves on the admittedly fictional idea of soul transmigration. But Gratiano also speaks 'nothing' in a more literal sense: he identifies an empty space, a nothingness, through which the guilty wolf-soul would fly. This space is the normal sort, the one that typically houses things, actions, and people, rather than souls – the space through which we move. Gratiano's disavowal of metempsychosis suggests that the soul is kept at bay from this world.

By elaborating on this space in the context of souls, however, Gratiano also tacitly brings up a different kind of nothing: the space between the soul and the body. The distinction between these types of spaces is made succinctly by Plotinus, the Neoplatonist celebrated by humanists in the early modern era, in book four of his *Enneads*. He stresses to the reader that the soul should be maintained separate from the self 'not in a spatial way' but rather in its 'alienation in relation to the body'.[3] Plotinus, in carefully parsing these definitions, worries that his advice to keep the soul separate could be misinterpreted as an order to move it into space itself. He means instead to be mindful of the internal spacing that keeps the soul separate from the registers of sensory being, lest it be forced into Platonic corruption like the downward-plunging, lustful horse of the *Phaedrus*. Soul transmigration threatens to blur Plotinus's distinction by allowing the space of alienation from the body to become the space of distance. As a result, souls would become realisable and detectable things – hence, Gratiano's assurance that no actual souls would be moved in the deliverance of his vitriol. The proposition of souls passing through knowable space threatens to disrupt the maintenance of internal coherence. These two notions of space, in turn, line up with the two understandings of the soul that thread through the play. A strict barrier must be kept up between the inner space of the soul, the ethereal space outside of our perceptions – but still part of who we are – and the outer space of our physical reality. If this barricade fails, we compromise and cheapen the unknowable qualities of the soul and threaten to reveal how our inner selves depend on something non-human. The soul must remain imprisoned, unseen, unmoving.

And yet souls are always on the move in *Merchant of Venice*. They move idiomatically, in speeches that reduce the soul to a fungible trope or helpful linguistic tool to signify lyrical devotion or, more broadly, to gesture towards a kind of courtly extravagance. And they move prosthetically, in material surrogates to be exchanged and manipulated as demonstrations of spiritual proficiency. Invoking the soul in this casual and metaphoric manner is surely a Renaissance commonplace, but *Merchant* keeps challenging the casualness of the soul's figurativeness by congealing its rhetorical uses into material realisation. The most glaring examples of this over-literalisation are orchestrated by Portia and in service to amatory connection. The casket-game allows prospective husbands to rehearse physically the abstract act of looking beyond Portia's beauty and into her innermost self. And the ring-game substitutes inanimate tokens for unfaithful partners, playing out a test run of the soul-bond of marital dedication with objects. As David Schalkwyk has shown, the embodiment on stage of poetic convention renders visible how Renaissance poetry is essentially a social and performative medium, one whose communally received nature becomes elided when read in private. The addressee of a sonnet, for instance, is absent in the text but implicated when read to someone in a play. In the theatre, Schalkwyk relates, 'the corporeality of speaker and audience, or the real circumstances either of receipt or miscarriage, are difficult to ignore, and performative uses of language are set in fully developed contexts of interactive dialogue'.[4] The result is a visible process of 'embodied reciprocity'.[5] Portia, too, stages lyrical tropes in her games, but she cheats at Schalkwyk's formula by using inanimate actors, as if culling the potential of theatricalising poetic turns of phrase without the risk of reciprocity that attends the literalising of convention within the bodies of actual people.

It is telling, then, that the one moment Portia expresses embarrassment at her fluid manipulation of spiritual abstraction occurs when actual people are implicated, rather than rings or caskets. In elaborating Bassanio's love of Antonio to Lorenzo, she shifts her vocabulary from mimetic resemblance to one of actual transformation, but stops short of imagining it taking place, just as Gratiano stops short of imagining metempsychosis. She notes that for companions

> That do converse and waste the time together,
> Whose souls do bear an equal yoke of love,
> There must be needs a like proportion
> Of lineaments, of manners and of spirit.
> Which makes me think that this Antonio
> Being the bosom lover of my lord,
> Must needs be like my lord. If it be so,

How little is the cost I have bestowed
In purchasing the semblance of my soul
From out the state of hellish cruelty. (III, iv, 12–21)

Portia allows, here, the entwinement of their selves as a result of their copious time together, an inadvertent theatricality by which they mimic each other externally – by approaching 'like proportion / Of lineament' and 'manners', but also by the internality of their 'spirit', a deeper link than behavioural or physical traits that allows a spiritually transitive link to Antonio. It follows, Portia reasons, that if she and Bassanio love each other, and Bassanio loves Antonio, they must all bear semblance inside and out. The soul of Bassanio finds its 'image' in Antonio, and Portia realises she can purchase this semblance – of Bassanio and herself – as an act of salvation. The chain of Antonio to Bassanio to herself relies on an understanding of 'soul' that is adaptable and textually pliant, a sanitised model scrubbed of its resistance to the world and packaged as a synecdoche of romantic connection.

Portia cuts herself off when, in following this progression further, she intensifies the rhetoric of semblance into one of alteration, realising with a start that 'This comes too near the praising of myself, / Therefore no more of it' (III, iv, 22–3). In following her claim that love creates physically and spiritually accurate representations of lovers, Portia allows, briefly, that it approaches their actual re-creation. Rather than fashion souls as twinned through a love cultivated through idleness and contemplation – thus far, a thoroughly Platonic model – she allows soul to become self and connection to become sameness. Harry Berger Jr, in his study of embarrassment in *The Merchant of Venice*, sees Portia's discomfiture as self-conscious humility that disguises a deeper embarrassment caused 'by the husband with whom she has contracted to share life after Happy Ending, and by the professional scapegoat [i.e., Antonio] he is attached to'.[6] Portia's language scaffolds itself with the language of selflessness, but what that language *performs* is an admission of her vulnerability in the face of a competitor to Bassanio's love. She startles herself with vulnerability and, to countervail this openness, she stages a reciprocal humiliation of Antonio in the courtroom, where she draws out his suffering at length.

In describing a semantic fallacy that resembles Portia's rhetoric, Wittgenstein also links embarrassment to the soul's usage in language. As elaborated in the previous chapter, the soul, for Wittgenstein, is no more than the particularised and immediate sum of the body's grammar. But the word 'soul' and its ilk are so often used to disguise the fact of the soul's asignifying material presence. In *Philosophical Investigations*, Wittgenstein notes that when 'we cannot specify any *one* bodily action which we call pointing to the shape (as opposed, for example, to the colour), we say that a *spiritual* activity corresponds to these words'.[7] The context here is an extended meditation on what it means to point at something: are we pointing at its shape? Its colour? Its material composition? What is the 'shape' that we would point at – is it an isolated thing we can analyse? Wittgenstein critiques an atomist position that would have the object in question be the sum of its properties, each expressible as a proposition. But when faced with the possibility that we cannot identify what it even means to point 'at' a quality of the object, and thereby that we begin to lose the thread of how the object is composed – and what it even is – we tend to cover up this gap with the label 'spiritual'. This point is made more directly in *The Blue Book*, a collection of the early drafts and notes on *Philosophical Investigations*: 'we already know the idea of "aethereal objects" as a subterfuge, when we are embarrassed about the grammar of certain words, and when all we know is that they are not used as names for material objects'.[8] A phantom 'object' is created when the atomist confronts the impossibility of the act of naming actually conjuring up fixed meaning.

Linking Wittgenstein's use of embarrassment to Berger's, we can identify Portia's embodiment of the idiomatic soul as a demonstration of her avoidance of wrestling with the actual soul's irreducibility, its lack of connection to the values and properties that she so relentlessly assigns to words and objects. An appeal to the spiritual covers over embarrassment at her words' lack of referentiality; Portia's version of 'soul' is, ultimately, a commodity to be traded in order to uphold the fiction of an ethereal, quasi-substantial spirituality.

Her embarrassment results from confronting the fiction of her model of the soul when she realises that it cannot so easily point to and correlate with herself, Antonio, and Bassanio – that it cannot be legible if made present in human bodies. This realisation, furthermore, seems to drive her need for vengeance on Antonio: the love that he has inspired in Bassanio has irrupted, momentarily, the play of commodified souls in which Portia specialises.

Portia's brief moment of confronting the fabrication of her idea of the soul echoes Gratiano's invocation of metempsychosis in the trial, which, even if hypothetically raised, similarly marks a point at which the two understandings of the soul I have been drawing out – as unknowable but expressible, for one, and as economisable as a means of avoiding facing unknowability, as another – collide, and as a result the unsteady foundations of the characters' spiritual structure become threatened. The act of parsing out soul from self calls attention to an inherent incoherence at play in relating these two terms at all. In Gratiano's example, the introduction of the soul into the elements that comprise Shylock, even rhetorically, prompts discomforting questions of who, exactly, Shylock is: a body that hosts the soul, or the soul itself? And if he is acting inhumanly – like a wolf – is this due to his corporeal or spiritual self? And even if they do not fly about, do animals even *have* souls? Shylock's behaviour in the play stubbornly resists the smooth play of signification that allows for a shortcut around these questions; Gratiano's frustration, like Portia's embarrassment, signals a desperate desire to remain wilfully blind to the seams left over in the construction of a 'naturally' spiritual being.

Metempsychosis, then, by demonstrating the fundamental incoherence at the heart of the soul's conception, allows for the curtain of the spiritual economy, disguised as perfect translatability, to be lifted. In what follows, I will explore this claim more in depth, but before returning to *Merchant*, I want to first develop this idea further by turning to other early modern texts that engage with the prospect of spiritual migration and, as a result, show the uneasy tension between both the soul's economisable and unrealisable versions. Mentioning metempsychosis leads to moments of embarrassment, frustration, and other reactions that somehow force the speaker to look away, to avoid dealing with the soul head-on and retreat instead to an understanding of the soul that can be accounted, valued, traded, correlated. Wrestling with transmigration risks the danger of conflating Plotinus's two spaces, which would reveal the soul's – and, by extension, all of our – alienated essence, along with our own vulnerable and trapped state on the other side of the barrier, in mere space.

Much of the chapter will centre on Shylock, who freely participates in the financial economy as he prevents exchanges in the mimetic economy, and lingers, as a result, in Venice as an embarrassing reminder of the soul's impossibility. His insistence on expression, rather than mimesis, colours his bodily and rhetorical grammar with the impossibility of the clear signification of the soul. He theatrically asserts only the sum totality of his actions and words and stymies philosophical desires for a wider representative schema. *The Merchant of Venice* stages the failure of Shylock's expressive grammar within its engine of economisation, and closes with a rapid, floridly artificial recovery from this failure. In doing so, the play replicates the internal spacing by which early modern life fabricates itself in relation to its alienated centre. Alongside Shylock's demise, Jessica's and Antonio's more subtle, though still somewhat tragic, narratives suggest another fate of the hopelessly expressive within the mimetic world: the melancholic and solitary exile *within* the community. These two are subsumed within, and at times fetishised by, society as emblematic of precisely what they avoided losing – the inhumanity of foreign identity, for Jessica, and a collection of flesh, for Antonio. Both are fashioned as somehow both a body without a soul and a soul unable to incorporate itself, adrift in physical space.

Pythagorean Delirium

In the early modern imagination, metempsychosis existed as a far-fetched idea that also prompted serious philosophical consideration. It invited meditations on the implications of its possibility and, at the same time, brusque dismissals of it ever happening. Speculations of how metempsychosis would occur bracket themselves with sober declarations of its absurdity, but acknowledging its illusory nature only seems to enhance the utility of bringing it up in the first place. The structure of Gratiano's speech echoes many such considerations: 'I know souls cannot migrate, but *if they could* . . .' While metempsychosis might have been impossible to conceive in the post-Reformation landscape of Shakespeare's England, the dramatic energy of reciting Pythagoras's belief, and the narrative structure it lent, seemed too potent to resist.

This dynamic already exists at the source, Arthur Golding's 1567 translation of Ovid's *Metamorphoses*, whose prefatory epistle to his patron articulates a desire to philosophise on metempsychosis while qualifying it by selectively appropriating its Aristotelian influence. Pythagoras offers, for Golding, a way to connect early modern religious spirituality to classical mythos, and thus acts as a guide for the translator's endeavour to strike a careful syncretic balance of publicising Ovid to a Christian audience without descending into blasphemy. Golding first observes that one of Ovid's central lessons is that 'eche substance takes / Another shape than that it had', a moral that he 'makes / The proof by shewing through his woorke the wonderfull exchaunge / Of Goddes, men, beasts and elements, to sundry shapes right straunge.'[9] The phantasmagoric transformations of Ovid become tamed into a less occult process in the Christian present; Golding downplays the physical transformation in favour of the subtler exchanges of souls. Ovid, Golding notes, 'bringeth in Pythagoras disswading men from feare / Of death, and preaching abstinence from flesh of living things.'[10] But this migration of Roman ethos to English religion needs careful elaboration:

> But as for that opinion which Pythagoras there brings
> Of soules removing out of beasts to men, and out of men
> To birdes and beasts both wyld and tame, both to and fro again:
> It is not to be understand of that same soule whereby
> Wee are endewd with reason and discretion from on hie:
> But of that soule or lyfe the which brute beasts as well as wee
> Enjoy.[11]

After glossing Aristotle's three kinds of soul, Golding suggests that the third, which 'gives understanding, wit, and reason' is 'it alonly which with us of soule dooth beare the name'.[12] Pythagoras, for Golding, nervously officiates the wedding of classical tripartite division to post-Reformist radical interiority: the rational soul, Golding asserts, is what an early modern reader would just call the soul, which stays put during transmigration. Golding furthermore assures the reader that the soul that migrates from human to animal, or vice versa, may be vegetative or sensitive, but it surely cannot be rational – the distinctly human soul cannot leap into the body of, say, a horse.

When Pythagoras actually appears in Golding's *Metamorphoses*, however, in book 15, his own formulation suggests a subtler and more anxious process than the preface would have us believe. Ovid's Pythagoras offers Numa, the second king of Rome, an extended lesson in political ethics that draws on the preceding tales. He acts as a translator, of sorts, within the poem – it is no wonder Golding foregrounded the Greek thinker when explaining his own efforts to transpose one hermeneutic system to another. Soul migration comes up after another quick rehearsal of Ovid's theme – 'All things doo change' – as an elaboration of how the soul fits this grand precept:

> This same spright
> Doth fleete, and fisking here and there dooth swiftly take his flight
> From one place to another place, and entreth every wyght,
> Removing out of man to beast, and out of beast to man.
> But yit it never perrisheth nor never perrish can.[13]

The grounds for Golding's previous Christianising amendment are clear: Pythagoras makes no mention about what kind of soul can fly from body to body. He only notes that the soul is eternal and mobile, and that bodies are both disposable and porous, always potentially open to reception. Pythagoras goes on to explain the permanence of the soul by drawing on a ubiquitous metaphor:

> And even as supple wax with ease receyveth fygures straunge,
> And keeps not ay one shape, ne bydes assured ay from change,
> And yit continueth always wax in substaunce: so I say
> The soule is ay the selfsame thing it was and yit astray
> It fleeteth into sundry shapes.[14]

This process of migration is characterised not by a proper dialectical incorporation of soul and body but instead the precise failure of any kind of mingling of colliding forces whatsoever. Instead, the soul registers the spectral presence of the body without altering its constitution. The eternal quality of the soul meets, headlong, the temporal qualities of the body, and while the soul, like wax, can change its form, its essence remains the same. But what is this essence? Is it separate from the essence of the creature that it leaves? And what remains in the bodily host? Golding is hasty to shore up this discussion and gloss over the problems posed to coherent identity, but it is just on those matters that Pythagoras lingers.

The model of the soul articulated by Golding and Ovid deftly threads together many contradictions: it is divorced from identity, but essential to life; it splices out its more humble and earthy animal and vegetative components while retaining a connection to something holy and sublime – but somehow its loss is still a threat to subjectivity; it always remains the same, but it bears traces of its hosts. A road map of sceptical critique presents itself as soon as one considers, even briefly, the mechanics of transmigration, and the exemplary case of just such a dismantlement is laid out carefully and humanely by Montaigne, in 'An Apology for Raymond Sebond'. Montaigne, like Ovid, is careful to praise the figure of Pythagoras himself as someone who practiced kindness toward animals by refusing to eat meat – a very real side effect of what Montaigne ultimately sees as a phantom belief. Even if metempsychosis is simply a mystical folly, the consideration of its possibility still has utility by introducing the question of animal souls and thus animal rights, which in turn allows Montaigne to question the fragility of what he calls the 'imaginary sovereigntie' that separates human from subjugated beast.[15]

Montaigne is, in fact, attracted to an exegesis of metempsychosis *because* of its impossibility. He notes, echoing Plato, that in the 'fantasie' of eternal souls is embedded 'some consideration of divine justice'.[16] But what of those souls themselves? What happens when we must ponder the logistics of their travel and inhabitance, when they become points on a grid rather than fragments of an unseen absolute power? In considering the actual process and labour of souls – in pushing past their 'aethereal' quality and attempting to resolve their identity within an atomist framework – Montaigne first brings up the Epicurean objection to metempsychosis by wondering if 'the soules removed from their abode would throng and strive together, who should get the best seat in this new case: And demaund besides, what they would passe their time about', and furthermore, 'contrary-wise, if more creatures were borne, then should die; they say, bodies should be in an ill taking, expecting the infusion of their soule, & it would come to passe, that some of them should die, before they had ever bin living'.[17] The prospect of transmigration is countered, here, with the rational calculus that must emerge from its practice. Montaigne's sticking-point centres on space – the tough kind in which we live, and into which the souls would have to fly – and priority: while the 'divine justice' of metempsychosis finds purchase in his religious beliefs, the simple question of where the souls would go, and how they would assign themselves, upends the equation. If there weren't enough bodies, the souls would have to pass idly about, in purgatorial condemnation. Conversely, and more chillingly, if there were more bodies than souls in waiting, then the bodies may die without ever having a proper spiritual inhabitant and thus never truly having been living – surely a divinely unjust consequence. A soulless death would be an end that never began.

For Montaigne, the ludicrousness of soul migration arises in the application of rational and physical properties – the observable laws of spatial behaviour – to something that must elude registers of the performative. As Portia shows, in her nimble navigation of its rhetorical potential, the soul could be endlessly discussed and packaged as a lyrical trope if it remained permanently unembodied. But as Portia's speech and Gratiano's screed also demonstrate, an awkwardness results from the realisation of these tropes in a more earthly realm. The soul revels in its inscrutability and as a result can supply a poetic engine for theological inquiry, as John Donne explores in his 'Holy Sonnet VIII': 'if our mindes to these soules be descry'd / By circumstances, and by signes that be / Apparent in us, not immediately, / How shall my mindes white truth by them be try'd?'[18] Donne, here, sees the soul as the battleground between sentience and holiness. The soul and mind – the cosmically placed and the subjectively intentional – must be related, he insists, even as his questioning voice belies the dread of facing the gap between the inscrutable language of the former and the familiar faculties of the latter. As befits the traditional arc of his sonnets, this panic refashions itself as a salve of faith to treat the wounds of his fear. The unknowability ultimately strengthens his dependency on God: 'Then turne / O pensive soule, to God, for he knowes best / Thy true griefe, for he put it in my breast.'[19] Donne creates a deepened faith that arises from his anxiety, one that necessarily is in crisis because it demands a lack of signification in order to operate. He is capable of using the terror of facing the incomprehensible split of his self as the essence of its spiritual balm. His sonnet marks the passage from not-knowing to the limning of non-knowledge as a manifestation of the divine.

But the prospect of wrenching the soul outward invites consideration of its embodiment by revealing the discontinuities, gaps, and contrary forces lurking under the smooth surface of the soul's textual conception. The citation of metempsychosis marks the limit of the spiritual even as it dissolves that limit by inviting speculation on how the soul would gain physical coherence. Like *The Merchant of Venice* itself, metempsychosis acts as a testing-ground for the powers of accountability to apprehend and digest the spiritually apophatic; both are thresholds of forces that demand both divine absence and hungrily consumed, material presence.

The theatre, then, stands as the forbidden zone for the fantasy of the soul's clean emergence. The uneasily erotic banter between Lorenzo and Jessica in the final scene of *The Merchant of Venice* particularises the discomfort of the soul on stage as a mode of romantic failure, and as a result troubles the play's recurring theorisation of the body as capable of seamless spiritual transmission. After increasingly unsettling allusions to tragic circumstances befalling young lovers – each citation opening with the phrase 'In such a night' – the young lovers decide to linger outside, despite the return of Portia and Nerissa. Lorenzo's justification for doing so borrows from the Neoplatonist understanding of the soul's link to heaven, with imagery that hints at the more immediate concern over the role of the body's fallibility in the face of cosmic forces:

Sit, Jessica. Look how the floor of heaven
Is thick inlaid with patens of bright gold.
There's not the smallest orb which thou behold'st
But in his motion like an angel sings,
Still choiring to the young-eyed cherubins.
Such harmony is in immortal souls,
But, whilst this muddy vesture of decay
Doth grossly close it in, we cannot hear it. (V, i, 58–65)

What begins as an appeal to celestial wonder ends with a resigned acceptance of the body's overdetermined state as a closed and muffled chamber that prevents the soul from reconnecting with its divine origins. This model of the body as sealed-off container of the soul is precisely what Portia's casket-game, in its inanimate theatre, presents as a more flexible situation, one in which the soul can readily be accessed through the humble vesture of lead. The 'grossly' figured body returns at the close of the scene, and play, with Portia's charge that the seemingly cuckolded men 'speak not so grossly' (V, i, 266). But Gratiano's bawdy language in response to the women's ring-trick, while jovial, also counters Portia's advice by insisting on the body as the primary site of erotic negotiation; his closing vow to 'fear no other thing / So sore as keeping safe Nerissa's ring' cements this commitment to speaking so grossly (V, i, 306–7). His scatology, read against Lorenzo's Platonic musings, punctuates the pastoral resolution with anxiety over the possibility of an irreducible body, a 'muddy vesture' that makes no claims to spiritual connection and onto which fidelity and identity become legibly mapped. Lorenzo's comparison of the floor of heaven to 'patens' of gold, ornate trays that would hold the host in Eucharistic ceremony, tacitly attempts, Golding-like, to Christianise his classical allusions. But the transubstantiation of flesh is exactly what he ultimately doubts. The flesh instead lingers, despite Portia's complaint, as failed remnant of, rather than as conduit to, cosmic connection.

Internal Migrations

If part of the anxiety and allure of metempsychosis results from the revelation of the soul's lack of tangible resolution in the world – its failure of translating inner space into outer – then the contrary proposition also reveals itself as problematically compelling: that even when housed within the human subject, the soul lacks coherence. A heightened demonstration of this dynamic occurs in Christopher Marlowe's *Dr Faustus*. As portrayed in his harrowing final speech, on the night of Faustus's planned demise, the only thing that can save him is Jesus's blood, which must remain offstage, overdetermined as outside signification and narrative. The audience cannot see this salvation; like the similarly grisly pound of flesh that hovers over Antonio's hearing, it is imagined but never staged. Facing a vision that eludes form but offers grace, Faustus desperately calls for Lucifer and the vision disappears. This final deliverance lost, he turns from Christianity altogether to wish ruefully that 'Pythagoras' *metempsychosis*, were that true', would allow his soul to 'fly from me and I be changed / Unto some brutish beast. / All beasts are happy, for, when they die, / Their souls are soon dissolved in elements; / But mine must live still to be plagued in hell.'[20] The exact details of his wish are stranger than they may first appear: crucially, he is not exactly wishing that he die, but rather that he pass into oblivion by transferring his soul to a beast's body. His language suggests that becoming a beast would be complete through the relocation of his soul alone – his human body remains a matter of circumstance. This version of Pythagorean passage seems to solve Montaigne's problem of zeroing out the ledger of immortal souls and bodies – rather than living eternally, Faustus's soul would dissipate into the materiality of the world upon its animal death.

But Faustus cannot have his wish. Even if a potential scandal of improper allotment would be avoided, he balks at conjuring forth his soul from his body. The problem of translating souls does not stem simply from Montaigne's numbers game (are there enough bodies for souls, enough souls for bodies), but instead a deeper irreconcilability. The bird evokes Golding's transmigration compromise, which holds that the rational soul remains in the body and the vegetative and sensitive parts fly into an animal. But if that were the case, Satan would still have a soul to enslave for all eternity in Hell – it just wouldn't be the *entire* soul. Faustus, though, seems to imply that if 'Pythagoras' *metempsychosis* were true' he would have an escape, as if he could identify his animal self as more than a fragment of his complete self – as, instead, coextensive with his fully realised being. Much as a metempsychotic Shylock would not be exactly animal or human, but rather an entombment of one within the other, Faustus would not be exactly dead or alive, but trapped within a beastly effigy. As a result, the suggestion of an animal soul moving into a human body, or a human soul moving into an animal body, implies a deeper threat to subjectivity by calling into question the pre-existing relationship of the human soul to the *human* body, a paradox easily glossed over, as Golding demonstrates, unless forced into the bodily behaviour of the theatre. Once Pythagoras appears on stage, the tenuous relation of soul to body to animal undermines the seamless construction of the self: if his soul could fly forth into a bird, there would no longer be any Faustus – to say nothing of the consideration of the bird itself already having a soul occupying its body. If Faustus, as a soul, can occupy a bird's body – and if Shylock is not Shylock but a lupine soul occupying his body – then an extended theatrical demonstration of these differences would make explicit the slippery task of identifying who these soul-possessing humans were. They are, it seems, already untranslatable, at odds, and migratory as a fundamental condition.

The classical notion of transmigration, wished for over and over in early modern culture, has a tacitly and anxiously related scene of bestial soul migration in Christian lore, one that occurs twice in the New Testament and is mentioned by Shylock himself when defending his dietary restrictions. The story has Jesus encounter a possessed man 'with an unclean spirit, who had his dwelling among the tombs' (Mark 5: 2–3). The 'spirit' turns out to be many demonic inhabitants, not one, and Jesus's solution is to engage successfully in the type of Pythagorean exorcism only dreamt of by Faustus:

> Now there was there nigh unto the mountains a great herd of swine feeding. And all the devils besought him, saying, Send us into the swine, that we may enter into them. And forthwith Jesus gave them leave. And the unclean spirits went out, and entered into the swine: and the herd ran violently down a steep place into the sea, (they were about two thousand;) and were choked in the sea. (5: 11–13)

Despite the sudden end, questions linger: How do the spirits speak? How can they exercise agency to make their own demands for migration? Who was this man, whose home among the tombs troubles his own status as living or dead, once they left? Perhaps most pressing, though, is the fleeting circumstance that follows their escape from a human host – the moments in which the unclean spirits occupy the pigs. What is the ontological status of these pigs-possessed-by-spirits? Once again, the animal provides the catalyzing body between death and life by effecting the soul's entrapment. By catching the escaped souls and plunging them into oblivion – by moving them out of the space – the pigs unburden the narrative from considering who the subject is that encounters Jesus in relation to his divide between soul and self, or the fact that there is division at all, capable of reassignment by messianic will.

Shylock curiously invokes the scene of the pigs in refusing Bassanio's invitation to dine with him: 'Yes, to smell pork, to eat of the habitation which your prophet the Nazarite conjured the devil into. I will buy with you, sell with you, talk with you, walk with you and so following. But I will not eat with you, drink with you nor pray with you' (I, iii, 30–4). A traditional Jewish purification regulation for consumption would stem from interpretations of Leviticus, where the pig is listed among those that are hooved but do not chew their cud (11: 7–8). Shylock's alternative citation – which, like many of his references, makes Antonio deeply uneasy – acts as a stinging critique of this foundational Christian scene as complicit with the practice of 'conjuring', a word with occult associations. *Doctor Faustus,* after all, repeatedly labels Faustus's illicit and distinctly un-Christian actions as a form of conjuring, both in terms of illusion and mimesis, as Andrew Sofer notes: 'conjuring models a performative speech act that threatens to blur the distinction between theatre and magic'.[21] And yet Shylock applies the term to a messianic figure, not a demon. Shylock also insists that the souls stubbornly remain within the pork, transferred, presumably, from the living pigs – a kind of failed metempsychosis. By reminding Bassanio of the possibility of souls surviving, Shylock brings to the fore the uneasiness of soul migration that Montaigne locates – but rather than dismiss metempsychosis as impossible, Shylock finds its possibility sponsored by the religion that repeatedly dismisses it.

Thinking of the pigs-as-occupied-by-spirits, as Shylock uncomfortably asks us to, lets us stay in the strained, multi-hyphenated language of subjects that are not quite subjects, and of justice questioning its assumptions about the totality of its recipients – the pigs not as pigs but as hybrid beings; Shylock himself, as inadvertently hinted at by Gratiano, not a holistic character but rather a dynamic relationship of soul to body. These liminal subjects are not exceptions, but rather explicit examples of what is already going on inside the early modern subject: an immanent metempsychosis that divides the inner space. In other words, the difficulty of imagining how a soul appears within the space outside the body should not prevent us from realising that it is equally challenging to apprehend while inside.

This is not to deny the possibility of a soul in performance but to propose how the body can express the soul – a mode of expression that represents a threat to the dire political and even ontological logic of Venice in *Merchant.* Gratiano seems assured that Shylock's wolf-like nature – his mercilessness – means he must have the soul of a wolf. But his soul could not lend itself as evidence any more than Faustus could conjure forth his own spiritual essence from his body and plunge into a bird. If humanity depends on having a soul, it depends on something incapable of cleanly symptomising its proof: other techniques of showing soulfulness need arise in place of the mimetic or figural. A popular humanist retelling of a story from Plutarch's *Morals* – which is itself a version of the Circe's island episode of the *Odyssey* – attempts to outline how the soul's distance still gains a theatrical dimension, despite – or because – of its total entrapment within the body's prison. In his *Circe*, Giovanni Gelli tries to find a way to demonstrate the soul's existence without making recourse to the affectations of the body. In the original myth, Circe has transformed Ulysses's companions into pigs. However, rather than drowning themselves, these pigs remain in the story to discuss the benefits of their newfound piggishness with their former compatriot. Gelli, following Plutarch, relays the scene as a Socratic engagement between Ulysses and the animals on the island, with Ulysses attempting to convince the animals to abandon the sensual comforts of their new bodies. Since, in each case, the animals can talk, speech cannot be used as a simple way to show the human's advantage.[22] The hapless Ulysses thus has a difficult task: How can he prove that humans are superior to animals? What difference can there be, once language is excluded, between beast and man?

The answer is, following Aristotle, the rational soul – the part that, Golding comforts us, still stays within its original corporeal home. But this solution provokes an even direr situation. Ulysses must prove that the soul exists and is somehow of a different quality in his body than it is in the animals' physical states. The only medium at his disposal to prove this point, however, is his own body. A lion wittily uses this very contradiction against him, stating that since 'our bodye beynge none other thinge, then a wagan that carieth our *soule*, yf he be feable and weake: the soule canne not doo perfectlye her operations, or els with very gret difficultie'.[23] Defending corporeal strength as a corollary to the soul, the lion posits that a strong soul needs a strong body. The lion's strength, it follows, indexes the strength of his soul, even if the body is merely its wagon: rather than the decaying and muddy vestures that Lorenzo returns to in his attempts at divine sublation, the body properly reflects the health of its cargo.

Ulysses's solution in countering this accusation is simple: he stops moving altogether.[24] We gather this general demeanour from Circe herself, who enters the colloquy to mock his stoic nature:

'thou standest all the day musinge, nowe under the shadowe of some tree, on a stone, now by the waves of the Sea, with thy mind so farre drowned in imaginations, that thou semest unto me almost a *bodye without a soule*'.[25] Circe holds Ulysses accountable for the precise crime he accuses the animals of – being non-human. The irony is that Ulysses, in trying to prove he has a soul, becomes one, rendering himself a stony monument to the silence and stillness of a rational entity removing itself from the trappings of the body. This conclusion surfaces in another early modern citation of the Circe myth, the naturalist Edward Topsell's massive compendium *A Historie of Foure-Footed Beastes*. The entry for 'Pig' allegorises the episode as an interior drama within the contested soul-body territory. The story, Topsell counsels, should be 'interpreted in this manner, *Circe* to signifie unreasonable pleasure, *Ulisses* to signifie the soule, and his companions the inferior affections thereof, and so were the companions of *Ulisses* turned into swine by *Circe*'.[26] Ulysses evokes the soul without quite representing it. The comedy of the scene arises from the similarity of a non-performing human to an animal, a comparison that gets confusing, as noted by a pig in Philemon Holland's translation of the Plutarch source material. A pig, in Holland's version, asserts that if men praise wisdom and temperance, they 'doe but goe in the companie of beasts'.[27] The alienation from the body, a distance from the senses needed to keep the soul properly preserved, pushes the human soul into something quite beastly when exposed. The entrapment of the absolute, when executed with perfect facility, efficiently – and too effectively – creates the disguise of the monstrous.

In his sermon 'Mercy to a Beast', the Puritan minister John Rawlinson draws on the soul's monstrousness as a surprisingly touching call for empathy, rather than frustration, wondering if because 'a righteous man regard the life of his beast, because it is his; ought he not then much more to regard the life of his soule; which is so his owne, Have pity on thine own soule, pleasing God. Please him better thou canst not, than if thou have pity upon thine own soule.'[28] The elusive meaning of the sign 'soul' – its insistence on a *lack* of referent, its spacing from the senses and the world – is here a call to exert a faithful charity. The mercy that Rawlinson implores his congregation to demonstrate stems from an embrace of the limits of the articulable, a deliberately incontinent economy of forgiveness. However, the opposite conclusion could also be reached, as with the Catholic minister Thomas Watson, who issues the dire warning that if man is 'not regardinge hys dignitie, contempning the commaundement of God his maker, and folowing his owne sensual appetite', he becomes comparable to 'unreasonable beasts' because he has 'changed the similitude of God, wyth the similitude of beastes, and the honour of hys first image beyng taken away, by carnal desyres and beastly lyving, was made like a beast'.[29] The animal trope provides innocent and docile dependence for Rawlinson, a perfect stand-in for the soul, but for Watson the same imagery emphasises carnal sensuality. While the soul is clearly not reducible to a coextensive part of the human, it refuses a clear, static set of associations when rhetorically fashioned.

While opposed, Rawlinson's kindness and Watson's repugnance do not pretend to universalise the soul and instead recognise its necessary distance within the body, yet at the same time its need to remain outside of human perception. The condition of the early modern soul, then, suggests an always-restive process of failed metempsychosis even within the very constitution of humanity. Given its insistent circling around questions of spiritual health and justice, and its demands to test the bounds of civic society, *The Merchant of Venice* is poised to be read as a commentary on this thwarted process. The theatrical world of Shakespeare's Venice, it follows, does not confront in Shylock something alien that needs conversion. It faces instead the internal and essential non-humanity of its own soul, and in expurgating Shylock it attempts to exonerate its civil society from having a core that, if viewed headlong, it would despise.

An Infinite Deal of Nothing

What edges to the fore in an overview of metempsychosis literature is an issue central to *The Merchant of Venice*: the search for a proper way to signal unified self-construction. Or, more accurately:

a proper way to disguise as unified a fundamentally *in*coherent self-construction. In a characteristically metacritical take on *Merchant*, Jacques Derrida suggests that its central, fraught topic is translation, the same that greets him when his work is transmitted in English and hovers over the works of Shakespeare when it seeks currency in other languages. (Translation, too, preoccupies Golding doubly, both as a literal translation of language and a theological translation out of classicism.) The endless economising in the play, Derrida maintains, can be thought of as acts of translation that culminate in the conversion of Shylock to Christianity, a fantasy of absolute transformation of one term to another, word to word, value to value, Jew to Christian. Derrida links Shylock's religious conversion to the monetary values of the pound of flesh: 'This relation of the letter to the spirit, of the body of literalness to the ideal interiority of sense is also the site of the passage of translation, of this conversion that is called translation.'[30] Translation, for Derrida, is a 'sublime and impossible task' whose unfeasibility operates in *Merchant* as 'an incalculable equivalence, an impossible but incessantly alleged correspondence'.[31] Derrida's reading posits that the constant play of dissembling signs creates the illusion of an impossible truth – the absolute and unreachable meaning behind translation, most saliently manifested in the totalising mercy that Portia seems to offer Shylock. The play constantly gestures to the absolute as accessible and gently received as rainfall, hiding the grinding subjugations of its economy behind a 'theatre of absolute forgiveness'.[32]

Thinking of forgiveness as a kind of theatre, a creation of truth that disguises its own fakery, links the ability Derrida detects in Portia – her mastery at synthesising the tangible elements at her disposal into a simulacrum of spiritual cohesion – to the ability to participate successfully in the mimetic economy (and, to remove one more frame, in the staging of a Shakespeare play), a system of representation that in turn undergirds the more visible economies of finance, ethics and politics. This careful dance of theatrical meaning-making is hyperbolically announced in the first scene, in which, after Antonio declaims that he knows not why he is so sad, his acquaintances get to work helping him – futilely, it turns out – to discover the mysterious cause. Salarino, the first to speak, suggests that Antonio's mind is at sea because his merchant ships are as well:

> Your mind is tossing on the ocean,
> There where your argosies with portly sail
> Like signiors and rich burghers on the flood,
> Or, as it were, the pageants of the sea,
> Do overpeer the petty traffickers
> That cur'sy to them, do them reverence
> As they fly by them with their woven wings. (I, i, 7–13)

The basic thrust of the sentiment is simple: you are needlessly worried about your business ventures. But the terms of Salarino's comfort hint at a subtle and telling distinction. Antonio's ships, with their full sails, are first compared to 'signiors and rich burghers on the flood' – aristocratic gentlemen. This analogy almost immediately feels insufficient, as marked by Salarino's amendment of 'Or as it were', a pivoting phrase that allows him to embroider the comparison further by describing these signiors as the 'pageants of the sea'. This image sticks, at least temporarily, and gains descriptive power as Salarino develops it. Antonio's ships are a nautical spectacle, a medieval procession of glorious sights that causes lesser traders to bend in supplication. Salarino's suggestions, like those of the others on stage, will be swatted away by Antonio before this collection of peers, like the ships in Salarino's speech, exit in curtsying reverence to the greater pageant of Gratiano and Bassanio.

While dismissed by Antonio, though, Salarino's comparison of mercantile activity to pageantry illuminates *Merchant*'s constant aestheticisation of capital, from Portia's game to the masque that conceals Jessica and her father's ducats to the expensive feast that distracts Shylock from his daughter's departure. At the close of the opening scene, Antonio will shorthand this conflation of livelihood with actual life by noting to Bassanio that his 'purse, my person, my extremest means / Lie all unlocked to your occasions' (I, i, 138–9). Salarino's prescription for Antonio's melancholy anticipates the translation of purse to person – of emotional health to successful economic transactions – and exaggerates that assumption by suggesting that economic transactions can take on the glorious appearance of a proper subject, a fat nobleman who basks in the shows of deference showered upon him from suppliants or a perfect spectacle that attracts an awestruck audience.

Portia, as Derrida detects, stands at the calm centre of this network of illusory equivalences and translations; she is continually marked by her ability to manipulate signification. Ronald Sharp argues that 'Portia respects forms and conventions but uses them for higher purposes, and in this regard I would suggest that she treats symbols, such as the ring, in precisely the same way that she treats law and religion.'[33] But what are these 'higher' purposes? To treat conceptual terrains such as law and religion as if they were symbols is to undermine the very possibility of a hierarchy of devotions. She does not, it follows, respect the will of an unseen purpose, but rather constructs this very purpose through the configuration of its phantom symptoms. She demonstrates an ability to fashion the fantasy of a coherent self, a perfect realisation of the golem fantasised by Salarino; she maintains the myth that she is neatly linked to the divine and proves strategically capable of eliding the possible incoherence of the soul – the internal space that a meditation on metempsychosis would flag. The fullest demonstration of this ability occurs in her celebrated speech on mercy:

> The quality of mercy is not strained:
> It droppeth as the gentle rain from heaven
> Upon the place beneath. It is twice blest:
> It blesseth him that gives and him that takes.
> 'Tis mightiest in the mightiest; it becomes
> The throned monarch better than his crown.
> His scepter shows the force of temporal power,
> The attribute to awe and majesty,
> Wherein doth sit the dread and fear of kings.
> But mercy is above this sceptered sway;
> It is enthroned in the hearts of kings,
> It is an attribute to God himself,
> And earthly power doth then show likest God's
> When mercy seasons justice.

Mercy, like the soul, extends heavenly energy to the earthly realm but refuses earthly embodiment. It is, like Portia's portrait, enthroned within materiality but not possessed by it. In a turn of phrase obsessed over by Derrida, Portia holds that mercy 'seasons' justice – that it does not comprise or outright affect justice so much as alter its essence, like the malleable wax with which Ovid's Pythagoras symbolises the soul. Portia's mercilessness is clear in her treatment of Shylock and Antonio, but her disquisition on mercy does more than ironise her use of virtuous language. She shows how the fiction of divinity must be effected through distinctly non-divine means – and the necessity of publically and communally cathecting to the spiritual terrain of politics, regardless of how brutally that terrain is constructed. Portia's contract with the people of Venice stipulates that mercy will remain divine if they allow her to construct mercy in any way possible. She is, in effect, a merchant, but a merchant of identities, one whose economy is mimetic rather than material.

What Shylock insists on, by contrast, is that fundamental aspects of the self, such as spirit, blood and flesh, cannot simply be rhetorically transferred. Instead, they are fundamentally banned from realisation. But Shylock himself is decidedly not banned – at least, until he is. He continually insists on his presence and celebrates his power to interrupt and linger, and he manifests this inability as a set of theatrical actions – as an *excess*, not as an attempt at minimisation. The residual tensions over the status of the soul, surveyed in the first chapter, become realised through Shylock's performing body. His oppression surely signals panic at the prospect of juridical dissolution, as the Duke maintains, but it also threatens to present the soul as both divorced from understanding and essential to life – the alternately divine and monstrous slipperiness of internal self-spacing. What Shylock demonstrates is something similar to Ulysses's unresponsiveness, a fulfilment of metempsychosis not as aesthetic capital but as an admission of the inherent fiction *of* economic self-definition. In short, Shylock fulfils two seemingly paradoxical purposes: he reveals the soul's impossibility by expressing himself *as* a soul.

Shylock begins to articulate this double bind after setting the terms of the loan with Antonio: 'A pound of man's flesh taken from a man, / Is not so estimable, profitable neither / As flesh of muttons, beefs, or goats' (I, iii, 161–3). Shylock defines the pound of flesh by what it is not: it is not a commodity to be purchased or to give the buyer profit. But it is also not 'estimable', in two senses of the word. It is not as rarified, but also it cannot be estimated or valued at all: it is both not worth as much and incapable of worth altogether. Both definitions circulated in Shakespeare's time and the word seems to play on both meanings, or to find a subterranean connection between a lack of translation and its near opposite, a highly valued correspondence.[34] The pound of flesh somehow denies and encourages valuation. This logic of inestimability is repeated in the trial itself, when Shylock is pressed as to the possible justification for his demand:

> I'll not answer that!
> But say it is my humour. Is it answered?
> What if my house be troubled with a rat,
> And I be pleased to give ten thousand ducats
> To have it baned? What, are you answered yet?
> Some men there are love not a gaping pig!
> Some that are mad if they behold a cat!
> And others when the bagpipe sings i'th'nose,
> Cannot contain their urine: for affection
> Maistrice of passion, sways it to the mood
> Of what it likes or loathes. Now, for your answer (IV, i, 43–53)

Disingenuous reasons overlap each other in attempts to deflect the question. The refrains of conditional words – 'is it answer'd?', 'What if . . .', 'are you answered yet?' – fail to answer any inquiries but instead defer any translation, as Shylock hopes each attempt satisfies the insistent offer of locating monetary equivalence. The passage ends, comically, with the suggestion of an answer, although what follows only summarises his previous list of rationales and proffers the admission that he can 'give no reason, nor I will not, / More than a lodged hate and a certain loathing / I bear Antonio' (IV, i, 60–2). The careful rhetorical construction of his argument does gesturally what it cannot show textually. Shylock places his reasoning beyond possibility ('I can not') and election ('I will not') and associates himself with the forces of nature that press upon subjective experience, rather than something firmly within experience.

His desire cannot be explained by objects, cannot find its model in a casket-game. He aligns himself instead with 'affection', a force that will take on horrifically enlarged sense of importance later in this book, with Leontes in *The Winter's Tale.*

Time and again, Shylock short-circuits attempts to use language as anything more than a utility to negotiate material and monetary means, as when he tells Bassanio that Antonio is a 'good' man, a claim that prompts Bassanio to ask if he 'had any imputation to the contrary' (I, iii, 13). But Shylock's description reports on Antonio's financial, rather than moral, standing, and the usurer's elaboration corrects Bassanio's assumption: 'My meaning in saying he is a good man is to have you understand me that he is sufficient, yet his means are in supposition' (I, iii, 14–16). Shylock continues with a detailed list of Antonio's holdings before repeating that the merchant is 'good'. Antonio may or may not be a good man, but he is a sufficient one, capable of repaying his debts. This swift credit-check focuses only on the quotidian and immediate: Shylock summarises a collection of goods dispersed at sea. But he is careful to separate Antonio's sufficiency from any claims to his worth as a person; these goods do not coalesce into a wealthy burgher or spectacular pageant. Speech, for Shylock, can work its way through an economic exchange and talk through details of financing, but it stops short of correlating itself to virtue, much as it does in the trial scene's long deferral.

The rules for Shylock's speech are counter-intuitive, given its obvious content. He relentlessly talks about money, so to characterise him as unconcerned with money is surely absurd. More accurately, though, we can observe that his words drive a wedge between themselves and metaphysical worth. He is as concerned with valuation as he is with sketching the limits of his language's ability to figure value at all. His carefully phrased rejoinder notes that his 'meaning in saying he is a good man is to have you understand me that he is sufficient', a needlessly prolix phrase if viewed as the comic logorrhea of an anti-Semitic stereotype but a subtle one if viewed as simply a careful declaration of what Shylock is acknowledging. Meaning functions as an *action* – his meaning is to have Bassanio understand him, and what he wants Bassanio to understand is that Antonio is in good standing, but just barely. Value that correlates to anything outside of the immediate concerns of the conversation doesn't come up as a topic. The casket-game models a kind of language-game that Shylock wants no part of: no linguistic surrogacies of selves, no embarrassment at calling an empty space ethereal and spiritual, no linking people to ideas willy-nilly, no attempt to penetrate the vestures of clay. And as Wittgenstein and Berger remind us, the result of this kind of particularising behaviour is embarrassment, and from embarrassment arise anger, vengeance and justice.

The arsenal of language Shylock has at his disposal, with its gratuities, repetitions, and denials of its own capacities, places a roadblock in the trading routes of the play's mimetic economy. Shylock's behaviour marks a performative grammar in the Wittgensteinian sense: a collection of usages, of examples without the pretence to definition, a form of life rather than a series of stand-ins for meaning. But he is surrounded by those who traffic in definitions and conceptual assignations with the same robust propulsion as Antonio's scattered argosies. Shylock's behaviour is prefigured as a burlesque of Antonio's melancholy by Gratiano, who, after beginning with the warning that he will knowingly act like a fool, advises his friend to avoid self-styled seriousness:

> There are a sort of men whose visages
> Do cream and mantle like a standing pond,
> And do a wilful stillness entertain
> With purpose to be dressed in an opinion
> Of wisdom, gravity, profound conceit,
> As who should say, 'I am Sir Oracle,
> And when I ope my lips, let no dog bark'. (I, i, 88–94)

Gratiano correlates sadness with a withdrawal from sensual life and mocks the reticence and pomposity of those who believe their every word will be golden. Such 'wilful stillness' goes against nature – though Lorenzo will quickly mock his friend for talking so much he forces others into the role of 'these same dumb wise men' (I, i, 106). This comic stillness will return as embodied irritant in Shylock's resistance to the festivities of carnival and his inability to be 'moved' in both senses at the trial, where he declaims that 'There is no power in the tongue of man / To alter me' (IV, i, 237–8).

The bond between Shylock and Antonio stretches beyond the agreement they make during the play; that bond, for ducats and possibly flesh, ratifies a deeper connection the two seem to always already possess, one figured in the still waters of the melancholic. While Antonio teasingly invites attempts to decode his knotted and unknowable interiority, Shylock theatrically deflects and shores up the limits of his expressiveness. But both remove themselves from the exchanges of knowledge that mark the play: self-knowledge, knowledge of the law, knowledge of love, knowledge of idiom. It seems appropriate, then, that their potential exchange would be a violent demonstration of incomprehensibility, a bleak parody of the mimetic currencies that propel the rest of the characters. Antonio's unknowability can only be possessed, not deciphered, and can furthermore only be possessed in the horrific and nearly comical fashion on the 'inestimable' pound of flesh, a concentration into materiality of his lack of legibility. As Drew Daniel suggests, the removal of the flesh renders graphic not only Antonio's unknowability but his contrapuntal invitation to be analysed: 'It is this ambition to be known through a violation of interiority that the melancholic solicits, and that the extraction of the pound of flesh threatens to realize so gruesomely.'[35] The answer to the question of Antonio's sadness can only appear in the play as a violent rearticulation of the process of questioning: a manifestation of the desire to know through the literal penetration of the surface to recover meaning. The action of carving out the flesh, like Shylock's repetitive and recursive speeches, is gratuitous, luridly excessive in its macabre realisation. It also plays on Shylock's earlier, knowingly perverted citation of the spirits fleeing into the suicidal pigs. If the souls of the exorcised demons live on in the dead flesh of the pigs, then surely Antonio's soul must be soaked into his own dead tissue. And it would thus be Shylock's to own – a too-real totem of the soul's absence.[36]

Appropriately, Jessica is caught in the penumbra of the representational practices of Shylock and the Venetians: she calls herself 'a daughter to [Shylock's] blood' but 'not to his manners' (II, iii, 18–19). She finds herself only partially capable of the full transference practiced by Portia, who easily connects manners to lineaments to spirit; the blood, for Jessica as with her father, is not subject to translation. Her belief in blood's immutability is challenged by Salarino, who tells Shylock that there 'is more difference between thy flesh and hers, than between jet and ivory, more between your bloods than there is between red wine and Rhenish' (III, i, 34–6).[37] Jessica's and Salerio's alternate comprehensions of blood ties provide a gentle echo of the tensions in the trial scene, where the Christians, who, like Saint Paul, cannot be reduced to their bodies (Rom. 7: 15–20), are afforded the luxury of manipulating the formation of the body to their liking. For Shylock, though, faith in meaning beyond the components of signification propels him to reject any perceived misuse of the body and word.[38]

From what we see of Jessica and Shylock's actual relationship in their brief exchange in Act II, Scene V, Salerio's insult seems fitting. Their dialogue transposes Shylock's belief in the body's total encasement of blood onto his anxiety over his house's possible infection; their speech is marked with the repeated imagery of cutting off connections to the outside and preventing penetrations of space. Responding sincerely and fearfully to Launcelot's tongue-in-cheek warning of a Christian celebration proceeding outside his house, Shylock leaves Jessica with instructions to stay inside: 'Clamber not you up to the casements then, / Nor thrust your head into the public street / To gaze on Christian fools with varnished faces; / But stop my house's ears – I mean my casements – / Let not the sound of shallow foppery enter / My sober house' (II, v, 30–5). The slip of 'ears, I mean my casements' connects the faith Shylock has in the proper maintenance of his body to that of his environment. The significance of his house is as fixed and removed from comprehension as his conception of the body; both are incapable of making their borders porous. He insists on enclosure in his own private signifying system and is terrified of polluting his and Jessica's house-body with traces of Christian imagery, especially when they assume the form of sensual revelry – a glorious pageant like the one imagined by

Salarino as the magical synthesis of Antonio's ships. Shylock tethers the spirit within an impenetrable space. Like Ulysses, he demands recusancy from the temptations of the body, unconnected as they are from his codified faith.

Shylock's final instructions to Jessica, 'shut doors after you' (l. 51), breaks their connection rather than preserves her inclusion. Lorenzo will soon abscond with her and Shylock's riches. When he learns of her departure, Shylock invokes her as 'My own flesh and blood' (III, i, 31), thus maintaining the filial connection of the body in the face of commodification – the zealously economic lines attributed to him, 'O, my ducats! O, my daughter!' (II, viii, 15) are, it must be emphasised, in fact not his but the hiss of rumour, a mimicry of his injury repeated or fabricated by Salanio. The loss of Jessica, in fact, refuses any equivalence in value. In Kenneth Gross's observation, neither 'gold nor child is quite confused with the other; neither is tradable for the other; there is not easy logic of exchange here'.[39] The ducats-daughters equivalence wielded by Salanio mirrors the Christians' own seamless rhetorical conflation of value, but pins a grotesque re-enactment of this fluid exchange onto the character incapable of imagining it. Similarly, the ring that Jessica trades for a monkey devastates Shylock because he cannot shift its reference; it remains connected to Leah, his deceased wife – another presence that cannot be seen. When Tubal relays the news to him, Shylock breaks from the logic of economic loss and places the ring, like the pound of flesh, outside of expressible meaning: 'I would not have given it for a wilderness of monkeys' (III, i, 110–11). Julia Reinhard Lupton traces this trajectory of failed exchange in terms of the typological transformation of Jew to Christian that so fascinates Derrida, a process that leaves traces of its conversion even as it aspires to universality. According to Lupton, by passing over 'the double threshold drawn by Jewish and Venetian laws', Jessica can exchange the ring for a monkey 'because the complex set of affiliations it has bound together (marital/familial, religious/coventental, legal/communal) have been broken apart and refigured'. But the Pauline migration of one identity to another still 'keeps track of the travel expense when Jessica no longer can or will, gathering the receipts of historical transformation and handing them over to Shylock as their nominal possessor'.[40] Shylock absorbs the shocks of Jessica's flight through a declaration – and reminder – of her incommensurability. This declaration starkly contrasts with the other rings in the play, the gifts from Portia and Nerissa to their partners. Bassanio stakes his entire life on his ring's care, stating that when it 'Parts from this finger, then parts life from hence, – / O then be bold to say that Bassanio is dead!' (III, ii, 184–5). Of course, he does not die when he gives the disguised Portia the ring; his words are simply words, banal aphoristic ingredients, shifting tokens in a constant game. Shylock, however, by removing himself from the mimetic economy altogether, ultimately loses out to a world where identities can be exchanged, troped, hidden, and slipped from casket to casket and body to body – the constant transmigration effected by the theatre itself.

The demand of the pound of flesh, then, represents the frontier between Portia's semiotic mastery and Shylock's resistance to meaning – he is unable to imagine the literal seepage of one substance, blood, from another, flesh. He tries to keep the unsaid and untransferable meanings of the pound of flesh, like those of his house, rings and daughter, untouched by the material reality of its existence. Portia, however, casually alters its meaning-making ability along with its physical composition with the fluency of her transference of self from casket to suitor. The result of this imagistic and spiritual continence is Shylock's demonisation. As with Ulysses's unwilling resemblance to an animal, Shylock's attempt to extricate himself from the sensual, corporeal and representational marketplace of meaning leaves him looking less like a human and more like a beast – like a wolf. However, the apostate Jew could also, like Ulysses, embody the ideal of the Christian ethos he resists, as the perfect stillness of interior holiness, the manifestation of the soul kept properly at bay from the sensual world of theatricality. But this selfsame stillness also threatens to call out the illusion by which the world construes it, not as an unseen belief but as a configuration of signs, an infinite deal of nothing. Derrida's tragedy of translation is not merely that of mercy exercised by Portia, then;

it is the tragedy of Shylock exposing to Venice the essential lack of compatibility that their own theological culture has crafted within their selves. Shylock mirrors their own souls back to them as animal and terrifying.

As a result of Shylock's inscrutability, he loses his own self-definition. His penultimate words before exiting the stage, fittingly, are simply a repetition of Antonio's, a parody of perfect translation. In response to the newly exonerated merchant's declaration, 'I am content', followed by a listing of his conditions (IV, i, 378), Shylock simply says, imitating Antonio word for word, 'I am content' (IV, i, 390). He has given up his house, his daughter, his fortunes, and now his language. His secretive and unknown interior, that which is housed beyond understanding, has disappeared, and the unknown has tipped into simple absence – empty space. The belief in soul migration occurs cryptically throughout the play, but when it actually comes up in conversation, Gratiano must, naturally, refuse belief in the action happening. The soul could not appear any more than it could in *Faustus*, since the scandals discovered in its reconciliation would become explicit. Instead, Shylock, as an avatar of the soul that cannot be visible, is purged from the stage with the efficiency of Christ's exorcism of the evil spirits. He is kept distant from the space of the stage, a place, like the celebratory parade, of signs and flesh and empty speech, a sensual, logical world from which the soul, with its mingled impossible interiority *and* overdetermined expressiveness, must be kept apart.

Jessica's fate, like Gratiano's grossly figured speech, offers a dissonant note buried in the final chords of the play. Unlike Shylock, she gains entrance into civil society, but like Shylock, she stages herself as unassimilable within her surroundings once there. Shylock's stubborn stillness of motive passes down into Jessica's physical stillness at the close. In her final exchange with Lorenzo, after their menacing flirtation ceases and as Portia's musicians approach, she utters her unsettling final line – 'I am never merry when I hear sweet music.' Lorenzo's response provides an ambivalent paean to music's power, which can stop a herd of 'unhandled colts / Fetching mad bounds' (V, i, 72–3) in their tracks. He approves her lack of merriment, though, as it indicates a reaction; it shows him that her 'spirits are attentive' (V, i, 70). The attentiveness is all in this case, not the nature of the judgement that follows: Jessica, Lorenzo implies, has the favourable trait of allowing outside forces to enter her consciousness. Sensitivity to music, concludes Lorenzo, is no less than an index of humanity: 'The man that hath no music in himself, / Nor is not moved with concord of sweet sounds, / Is fit for treasons, stratagems, and spoils; / The motions of his spirit are dull as night' (V, i, 83–6). In this manner, while Lorenzo admits to the impossibility of the soul's realisation, housed within our decaying bodies, he advocates for a different sort of harmony than Shylock's lodged enclosure. Rather, for Lorenzo the Platonist, music suggests a non-linguistic medium of external harmony, an embodiment of that which is impossible to transcribe even as it is intimately affective. But Jessica unsettles this ideal with her mere presence: after her final line, she remains onstage as all other characters reach their conclusions; she lingers, as if stopping short, like the colts, frozen after hearing music.

The ritual of Shylock's exile restores narrative coherence by erasing the possibility of selfhood necessarily existing outside of understanding, but Jessica's frustrated stillness – like Antonio's exclusion from the primary erotic pairings – prevents full resolution. Jessica and Antonio, here, act as tokens that tell us in their silence that contempt toward the usurer is not just a reflection of historical prejudice – it is a necessary manoeuvre to maintain the validity of the illusions on which their society is founded, and with it, the self-constitution of its inhabitants. And the process of sanctioned metempsychosis that ushers Shylock off the stage is not entirely complete: strands of soul remain on the scene, still gumming up the machinery. What is at stake in the play's relaxation into pastoral closure, then, is the reassertion of the fiction of the absolute humanity of the human, an imaginary sovereignty not split by an essence that claims and denies it. And what is needed to accomplish this is the branding of the unmarked soul as non-human and its subsequent conversion from animal to man, flesh to spirit.[41] Rethinking Shylock as a soul, however, reminds us that while he clearly supplies antagonistic energies that help fuel the dramatic conflict, he also serves as an uneasy reminder that Venice's humanity – the supposed quality that the romantic and comic ending recuperates – is itself stitched together by resolutely distanced, unrepresentable elements of non-humanness. The next chapter will build on this notion by examining how a city itself can lose and recreate its soul, and how the individual struggle of the soul thematised in *Merchant* can be amplified into the wider polis.

CHAPTER 3

WOUNDING THE WOUND: THE MONUMENTS OF *CORIOLANUS*

What does it mean to hide something on the stage? The theatre announces the importance of the visible in its very name, derived from *theatron* ('seeing-place'), but the consummation of its effects also depend on what is invisible and implied. Shylock's baptism, for instance, never actually occurs in *The Merchant of Venice*. Nor does the banquet that distracts him so Jessica can be ferried away from her home. But these 'scenes' are essential to the play; they tissue the dramatic action with the vitality of actual occurrences. Likewise, an implied space behind a door or window can seem as real as the actual onstage world, as with the next room in which attempts to create the philosopher's stone lead to a literally explosive climax in Ben Jonson's *Alchemist*, or the intimate familial reconciliations in *The Winter's Tale* that the gentlemen witness and then report excitedly to each other, but which we never actually see. Andrew Sofer, drawing on the language of physics, terms these immaterial but powerful aspects of the theatre 'dark matter', the 'invisible phenomena' that 'continually structure and focus an audience's theatrical experience' and 'remain incorporeal yet are crucial to the performed event'.[1] Much like the dark matter that helps construct the universe, the dark matter of theatre is both vital and, by definition, unprovable in its existence.

And yet dark matter need not even occur offstage. One way of thinking about the theatre is that it plays with the very notion of presence in its construction of what is decidedly *on*stage. Much of the discipline of performance studies has focused on a fundamental tension within the theatrical event: to perform is to stand in and represent, as if in constitution of authority, but also to become ephemeral and fleeting. To perform is, in a sense, to promise disappearance, even as performance seems to insist on its capacity to draw attention and emulate reality. In Peggy Phelan's influential account, performance thus structures itself around its 'unmarked' elements, leaving its marked appearance fragile and fluctuating. Performance, Phelan attests, can only live 'in the present. Performance cannot be saved, recorded, documented, or otherwise participate in the circulation of representations *of* representations: once it does so, it becomes something other than performance'.[2] To take this a step further: if theatre reflects – or perhaps extends – consciousness, then it reflects back to us a fundamental state not only of the elements of formally staged work, but also of the mind's play of thought that creates subjectivity. This, at least, is the view of Herbert Blau, whose prose style virtuosically emulates the very loops and slippages of thought that it describes:

> So: character actor person self. These are but declensions of the name for the unformulable act, the act of interpretation, not of character but of the play of thought, which is doubled over in performance by affinities and projections of thought, the indeterminable subject, persona mask double and double's shadow – haunted by the faulty memory of an unforgettable act.[3]

Blau connects the mysterious and inherently unstable nature of performance to the selfsame qualities that characterise memory. Performance mirrors memory's ability to congeal action into seeming permanence (the 'unforgettable act') even as it is haunted by what it has lost or suppressed. Performance, like memory, presents the illusion of bound and cohesive subjects – characters, actors, people, selves – but the raw material for these seemingly solid constructions is thought, a slippery and self-disguising medium.[4]

An astonishing scene in Thomas Middleton's *Second Maiden's Tragedy* vividly implicates memory and mourning as complicit with the quasi-presence of performance that Blau describes. The plot of

Middleton's play follows the progression of many Jacobean revenge dramas: the central antagonist, simply called the Tyrant, finds himself in the throes of delirious desire for a maiden who, rather than face his punishing passions, commits suicide. The Tyrant, bent on consummation of his love, demands that her body be exhumed so he can literally possess it. Kissing her corpse, the Tyrant attempts to fashion her death into a semblance of life. But the Tyrant is aware of, and even fetishises, her body's soullessness: 'Since the spirit has left me, / I'll clasp the body for the spirit that dwelt in't, / And love the house still for the mistress' sake.'[5] Soon after, the Lady's true love, Govianus, visits the gravesite to have a lamentation sung. However, mid-sentence, he is interrupted by a 'voice within' that proclaims 'I am not here'.[6]

The lack of the Lady speaks for her. Or does it? What is the 'I' that speaks or is spoken of? In a convex reflection of Augustine's non-self 'I' that narrates his *Confessions*, the Lady's body is elsewhere; the body is not speaking. Nor does what speaks seem to be a ghost, necessarily, but instead a remnant of the Lady that is not entirely the Lady, one that channels her tormented self. And yet the Lady herself appears, or at least the actor playing her does, with a melodramatic flourish of clattering tomb doors and howling winds, to continue her speech – which keeps insisting that she is not, in fact, present:

> I am now at court,
> In his own private chamber. There he woos me
> And plies his suit to me with as serious pains
> As if the short flame of mortality
> Were lighted up again in my cold breast;
> Folds me within his arms and often sets
> A sinful kiss upon my senseless lip;
> Weeps when he sees the paleness of my cheek,
> And will send privately for a hand of art
> That may dissemble life upon my face
> To please his lustful eye.[7]

The speech's tacit reference to the medieval liturgical trope of *Quem Quaeritis* – in which the angel informs those seeking the body of Jesus Christ that he has gone – segues into the appearance of a missing body that insists that it is still missing. The layers of mimetic and ontological confusion pile up: the Lady keeps insisting that her body doubles as her self, but her speaking self seems to have the same vitality as the corpse, if not more, by dint of being performed, presumably by the performer who played her while living.

The Tyrant's debasing acts of adoration that the Lady's non-body describes seem, at first, to be a straightforward condemnation of false belief – later, while the Tyrant adorns the Lady's corpse, one of his soldiers will call these actions 'mere idolatry!'[8] – but the appearance of a being divorced from the body, and the urgent insistence that the body be recovered, elevate the corpse's status beyond that of a hollow and heretically worshiped cadaver by investing it with an indeterminate spiritual potency. As Susan Zimmerman observes, 'the desperation with which the Lady's spirit seeks to rescue this corpse, and the intense jealousy that Govanius feels at the prospect of its violation by the Tyrant, confuse the boundaries between good and evil, living and dead, saint and strumpet'.[9] I would add to that list presence and absence, and body and soul: the exact material status of the body and soul becomes almost impossible to tease out. Here, the dead body seems to *be* a soul, or somehow have lingering traces of the soul's power. And the living body of an actor inhabits a physical realisation of the body's absence as a shred of dark matter made momentarily present. At the core of Middleton's depiction of the soul after death is a concern with how the soul can be remembered in the body – how the body can serve as a monument to what it once held. By indicating that the spiritual presence of the dead is somewhere else, within a body identical to the soul's material avatar, the (not-)Lady stages the aporia of her own death by refusing to locate her lost presence solely within any part of her remains.

This meditation on the volatility of performance and its absent presence, as it relates to the remains of the dead, finds a powerful interlocutor in Shakespeare's *Coriolanus*, the subject of this chapter. But as I aim to show, *Coriolanus* further complicates the philosophical quandary of *The Second Maiden's Tale*, which, while theatrically complex, still suggests that the restoration of the missing body would bring with it cohesion to the Lady's being.

Coriolanus locates such problems of monumentality within the living subject of Coriolanus. Specifically, Coriolanus's insistence on laying bare the dark matter between presence and absence, to live neither in worlds here nor elsewhere, models the early modern understanding of the soul's memorialisation that Middleton so memorably stages, but it situates this process in a determinedly living subject. In a crucial scene, Coriolanus refuses to show the battle-wounds that have inscribed his side with markers of his virtue.[10] The curtains of his bandages and clothes refuse to rise, and the frustrated audience within the play must settle for only what is implied, not what is extant. And what is hidden, furthermore, is itself an absence, a lack of flesh – an empty grave. As Nichole Miller elaborates,

> Coriolanus's sufferings are marked primarily by *absence*: just as he is named by removing his name, so he is defined primarily by his *missing* flesh. In the kaleidoscopic political economy of the play, names, voices, wounds, and words occupy a shifting scale of value emerging alternately as overdetermined 'superfluity' or 'surplus' (two terms that appear frequently in the opening scenes of the play, always in contested form) of meaning and as its absolute negation or dearth.[11]

Coriolanus refuses to make present a collection of absences. As Miller notes, the lack of flesh provides an echo of the missing name (the scene occurs in the hinge between the titles Caius Martius and Coriolanus). And so the scene, intended to display civic pageantry, instead showcases a series of disruptions that hobble the intended demonstration of post-victory political unity. Along with resisting this customary display of injury, Coriolanus receives a title that he will later disavow, forgets the name of someone who helped him, bristles at the possibility of receiving gifts, and proves a limited orator and altogether reluctant object of public admiration.

Counterintuitively, the series of elisions, deferrals and concealments that characterise Coriolanus's complex mode of performance in this scene and throughout – a performance that famously resists attempts at clear interpretation – present a form of monumentalisation rather than its rejection. The lost soul, in early modern England, could not be remembered as a purely reproduced entity, but instead was expressed by limning quasi-present spaces, much like those that *Coriolanus* outlines, but never makes legible: the unseen flesh under bandages, the hidden city of Corioles, the opened sky through which the Gods laugh. Memorialisation, then, depends less on the construction of an indexical stand-in for the lost soul and more on a performance that underlines the impossibility of the soul's replacement – an expressive performance that lives in the breach between theatre's capacity to represent and its unavoidable disappearance. Much has been made of *Coriolanus*'s trenchant commentary on the anti-theatrical debates in Shakespeare's day, and my aim here is not to add a new argument to that discussion. Instead, I hope to see in the difficult anti-hero at its centre a kind of performance that is resolutely theatrical but that defers representation altogether, one that twists away from even considering representative capability. Coriolanus, then, amplifies early modernity's complex memorial performances of the soul by proffering a figure who wants to escape the theatrical world – and historical record – in which he has been cast, but who, paradoxically, embodies a kind of process that calls for, perhaps even structures, memory through self-obscuring disappearance. Rather than defer the delivery of meaning, as with Shylock, or show the difficulty of conceiving the soul in performance, as with Middleton's Lady, Coriolanus continually enacts gestures of concealment, as if to carve out within the stage an unseen space that it cannot, but must, contain.

One popular understanding of the monument brings to mind a static and transcendent object that commemorates loss, such as a gravestone, or, more iconically, totemic sculptures like Christopher Wren's monument to the Great Fire, which, as Theron Schmidt describes, does not simply stand in for a piece of history but instead 'represents History itself – indeed, it *is* History'.[12] Traditional monuments like Wren's work to transcend the necessary displacement of time inherent in an act of ritualistic surrogation; they comfort through their replication of the potency of the original. Schmidt's incisive analysis of monumentality elaborates on how theatrical practice can upbraid the monument's claims to capital-H History, and many other performance and theatre theorists have similarly revitalised performance as a way to reconceptualise memory in opposition to the calcified traditions embodied in Wren's work.[13] But the kind of monumentality evoked in *Coriolanus* – and echoed in early modern cultural practice – is in opposition to static and material fixity *tout court*. Instead, it illuminates a tradition ignored in Schmidt's critique of Wren's work, one in which the monument already was, in effect, a form of performance. Closer to this kind of monument is the model offered by Alice Rayner, who explains that a knowing sense of absence – an acknowledgment of the fluid and unstable condition of performance – can act, quite literally, in service to memory. After discussing the more conventional monuments that materially placehold memory in a necessarily failed – but not forthrightly acknowledged – attempt to replicate what has been lost, Rayner turns to a more spectral understanding of memory-keeping:

> Another kind of memorial is spontaneous, ephemeral, like those appearing after sudden shocks and catastrophic disasters . . . these memorials are not meant to last. They are, rather, performative gestures of grief. They are momentarily expressive or expressive of the moment. Not assembled to combat the forgetfulness over time, they speak in the present of an otherwise unutterable sorrow . . . The placement of the flower, the candle, is the gesture of grief, not a substitute for it.[14]

These kinds of monuments articulate in the face of the unknown in a self-consciously futile way, as if an acknowledgment of their representative limits could act as homage to what is lost. By rendering grief as a gesture rather than replicating the original event, transitory memorials expose the necessary disappearance of performance, a medium that depends on its fleeting nature. The performances surrounding the displacement of the living in their death, in *Coriolanus* as in Shakespeare's day, complicate Rayner's idea further by incorporating into their execution the self-conscious effacement and rendering useless of the material monument. In other words, monuments in *Coriolanus* become effected in an acknowledgment of inevitable forgetting, and in a vivid demonstration of failure, rather than in an attempt at ephemeral or eternal remembrance.

How does Coriolanus want to be remembered? He is acutely sensitive to the possibility that he *will* be remembered, and remains attuned to how the events that surround him will become recorded and passed down. And he keeps aiming for a kind of greatness, as if hoping to afford himself a form of memory outside of the mortal and earthly world. Yet he also wants to be obscure, in both senses: he tries desperately to be difficult to determine and he hopes to be lost to memory. The scene in which Coriolanus denies the public sight of his wounds exemplifies the tension between these two impulses. After his refusal, the more traditionally-minded Cominius softly chastises his subordinate's stubbornness while maintaining his general tenor of praise:

> You shall not be
> The grave of your deserving; Rome must know
> The value of her own. 'Twere a concealment
> Worse than a theft, no less than a traducement,
> To hide your doings, and to silence that
> Which, to the spire and top of praises vouch'd,
> Would seem but modest. (I, ix, 19–25)[15]

Martius responds with a characteristically curt rejoinder: 'I have some wounds upon me, and they smart / To hear themselves remember'd' (I, ix, 28–9). The opposition of these two views plays on a doubled sense of wounding: the wounding of the flesh and the wound effected onto those wounds by displaying them.[16] Both Martius and Cominius think of the wounds in terms of memory, with Cominius worried that Martius would turn into a 'grave' of his deserving – an oblivion into which the wounds will fall, an absenting of absent spaces.

The wounds themselves are compared to graves elsewhere in the play, notably when Menenius attempts to impress the citizens with Coriolanus's prowess in war: 'The warlike service he has done, consider. Think / Upon the wounds his body bears, which show / Like graves i'th'holy churchyard' (III, iii, 47–50). The wounds are like gravestones, presumably for the enemies slain while receiving them. Menenius crucially tells the citizens to 'think' rather than see, because Coriolanus does not want them 'remembered' at all. The wounds function for Coriolanus as a private set of offstage meanings, not as publicly negotiated tokens; he craves not the abandoned selfhood in which he becomes a living monument to his own victory, but instead a kind of seamlessly bound subject separate from the exchanges and communally negotiated existence of civic life. In Stanley Cavell's formulation, he desires to lack nothing, to lack lack: 'Since to hunger is to want, to lack something, he hungers to lack nothing, to be complete, like a sword.'[17]

The scene Cavell references, in which he becomes a sword – hoisted, incredulous, into the air by soldiers he has just mocked for their cowardice – follows his victorious return to the Roman camp, where he achieves a different kind of unmarked singularity. As he approaches his compatriots, Coriolanus momentarily becomes an entire wound; Cominius asks 'Who's yonder / That doth appear as he were flayed? O Gods, / He has the stamp of Martius, and I have / Beforetime seen him thus' (I, vi, 21–4). Here, Coriolanus has momentarily fulfilled the fantasy of denying memory's inscription by becoming *all* wound, in anticipation of his desire to become all weapon. The bloody figure Cominius observes could either be a victim of Coriolanus's wrath – the recipient of his stamp – or Coriolanus himself, bereft of clear substance but maintaining his shape, another sense of 'stamp'. He is more comfortable in the flush of war, where he is all action and indeterminate, free of inscriptions. Immediately before he becomes a sword, having resolved from all wound to war-battered body, he taunts his soldiers to join him for battle if 'any be such here, / (As it were sin to doubt) that love this painting / Wherein you see me smeared' (I, vi, 67–9). He prefers the appearance of smeared paint, an indistinct blur, rather than the defined inscription that the wounds, like marks of writing on a blank page, would brand onto him. As Cynthia Marshall elaborates, in comparing Coriolanus's wounds to the medieval figure of the 'wound-man', the acknowledgment of pain would not neatly divide his body into symbols of meaning but instead render his body indeterminate. Whereas the wound-man is a passive stand-in for a human, encyclopedic and pedagogical, the visibly wounded

Coriolanus would have to possess 'the acknowledgment of pain that would establish the wound-man as a suffering person'.[18] He would be an actual porous and creased human, not a sword nor a wound entire, since when 'human identity is understood as inescapably bound up with an unruly and vulnerable body, notions of the free, whole, and coherent self are impossible to support'.[19] Coriolanus's refusal to show his wounds is thus as self-(pre)serving as it is completely sacrificial, the emblematisation of a paradox of virtue: he fears both vanity and the threat of being rendered a vulnerable, bodily human.[20]

The wounds' marks would reveal pain, but also, like the marks of archival writing, write Coriolanus into history. Suffusing many of his scenes with an uncanny sense of anxiety, Coriolanus continually seems to perceive a threat that no one else can: the terror that a mythologised version of himself will replace him during his own life. His increasingly vitriolic protests to Cominius at the failed wound-ceremony – he labels rewards as 'bribes', even though he is traditionally entitled to the spoils of war – climax with an expression of fear and disgust at the prospect of his actions turning into hagiography, as he protests that 'you shout me forth / In acclamations hyperbolical, / As if I loved my little should be dieted / In praises sauced with lies' (I, ix, 46–52). To commemorate is, for Coriolanus, to exaggerate, and to exaggerate is to lie. More offensive to him is the prospect that he would *love* to have his feats turn into lies; above all, he wants to divorce any trace of his own desire from displays of public ritual. D. J. Hopkins contrasts the public and indeterminate status of the wounds with the reward of a new name, which Coriolanus accepts: 'Though Coriolanus is attached to his new name (in both literal and figurative senses) for its power to monumentalise his own past, he will not sit by while his "nothings", acts which were performed in concealment, are retroactively made public at the discretion of others.'[21] Later, Coriolanus again fumes at the prospect of his wounds accruing specific reference; bristling at the prospect of wearing the gown of humility and appealing to the citizenry, he resents that he will have 'To brag unto them "Thus I did, and thus", / Show them th'unaching scars which I should hide, / As if I had received them for the hire / Of their breath only' (II, ii, 146–50).

His oversensitivity to public interpretation, coupled with a highly subjunctive imagination that allows him to ponder how it would appear 'as if' he felt a certain way, betray a desire of Coriolanus to conceal himself, just as he had concealed his wounds. He wants to remain away from the public eye, or even any scrutiny: he wishes to be offstage. The new name, as Hopkins suggests, offers a way for Coriolanus to carry an inarguable and undebatable reminder of his conquest, as opposed to the more semantically fungible tokens of his wounds. But he will, of course, eventually abandon his name, too, when he leaves and banishes Rome. The play almost sadistically insists on simultaneously tracking and hiding him, dilating its scenography to encompass his physical displacements while habitually leaving him outside, offstage, elsewhere. Time and again, Coriolanus suppresses the traces he might leave to history, but he does so floridly, angrily, theatrically. He makes a show of indicating the dark matter he insists remains dark.

Between Memory and Forgetting

This contradictory imperative – the need to be remembered through a wilful erasure of memory's devices – links *Coriolanus* historically and psychically to a work that has itself gained a monumental stature in early modern culture, John Foxe's *Acts and Monuments*. In witnessing the constant departure of martyrs' souls, Foxe elaborates a powerful memorial performance based on concealment and the deliberate withholding of ritual significance, one that casts Coriolanus's seemingly difficult behaviour in a markedly different light. For Foxe's section on Anne Askew, perhaps his most popular account, he reprints what claims to be her own report of her death, as earlier collected and printed by John Bale. The section is notable for Askew's wit and rhetorical resourcefulness, which force increasingly desperate measures by her Catholic torturers.[22] Her refusal is compounded in an especially mimetic moment, wherein a priest shares with her a 'similitude' – a pedagogical exemplum – of a man refusing to show his wounds and thus not being treated. Her response is that her apparent wound (apostasy) is in fact clean, and that their cure (conversion) is useless:

> Then brought he forth this unsavoury similitude: that if a man had a wound, no wise surgeon would minister help unto it before he had seen it uncovered. 'In like case', saith he, 'can I give you no good counsel, unless I know wherewith your conscience is burdened.' I answered, that my conscience was clear in all things: and for to lay a plaster unto the whole skin, it might appear folly.[23]

For Askew's torturers, the wounds of heresy must be revealed, examined, and affirmed as physical fact. The plaster, she asserts, would have to cover her smooth skin, which encompasses her entire body and, to her, is clean and healthy, whereas to the Catholics it comprises a whole wound. For Askew, it is useless as an analogy, as she is innocent and purified; for the Church, the folly of *not* showing wounds demands treatment, as with any sickness. Like Coriolanus, she rejects the revelation of her wounds, preferring instead to remain all wound or all skin, as whole as a sword, without depths to be revealed.

In her rhetoric, Askew aligns herself with a broader Reformist theme of unadorned simplicity, a mode of existence unfettered by potentially deceptive clothing. As the Homily of Good Works asks, 'what thing can be more foolish, more superstitious, or ungodly, than that men, women, and children should wear a friar's coat to deliver them from agues or pestilence, or when they die, or when they be buried, cause it to be cast upon them in hope thereby to be saved?'[24] Reformist polemics positioned such artifice in opposition to the nakedness and unadornment of the soul, as in Nicholas Breton's poem 'The Ravisht Soul', where the narrator speaks of his 'naked soul' clothed with 'the Vesture of that vertues grace', an abstract replacement for the fallen physical covering of the body.[25] Askew, it follows, would label as 'folly' the plaster that would cover her woundless body to affirm a more widespread sense of virtue. Virtue is its own clothing; the comic tension, for Askew – which she ironises with wit in her discussions with the Catholic persecutors – arises from the contrast and conflation of spiritual identity and trivially material set-dressing.

As Askew's tale makes clear, the battle over the nature of the wound imagery, and the power of its hiddenness, that characterises the tension of Coriolanus's unsuccessful hero's welcome taps into a deeper anxiety over the power of making visible a form of spiritual interiority and the strange power that can result from *denying* interiority, from remaining resolutely on the surface. Coriolanus's refusal to show his wounds marks him as a failed politician but an effective martyr – and, paradoxically, effective *because* of his political ineffectiveness. By declining to allow his body to be incorporated in the pageantry, he divests the external and material world of the possibility of connecting to his interior self. This mode of withheld and non-teleological performance is illuminated further in Bale's introduction to Askew's testimony. The iconoclastic editor, risking his own torture in shepherding Protestant texts from Germany into hostile England, situates the chronicle of Askew's death among traditions of saintly visions, and further ties this point to a larger Protestant contention with Catholics over Biblical exegesis. Evoking the visions, and subsequent death, of the first Christian martyr, Saint Stephen, Bale spitefully asks that if Catholics 'allege Steven, to maynteyne theyr purpose, that he at his deathe behelde heaven open', then 'what they were whiche see it more than his own persone?'[26] This argument centres around the phenomenology of miracles: can we, Bale asks, here in the present, pretend to know what Stephen saw as the heavens opened up? Can we claim an authority to the nature of heaven if we have not been granted access to it? He contrasts this sense of resigned unknowing to the hubristic manufacture of supposed miracles by the Catholic Church. 'The popes martyrs in dede', Bale notes, 'were moche fuller of myracles than ever were Christses.'[27] The miracles whose existence Catholics insists on were, for Bale, fantastical tricks, as opposed to the events of Stephen's death related in the Bible, which are perceived through his eyes:

> But [Stephen], being full of the Holy Ghost, looked up stedfastly into heaven, and saw the glory of God, and Jesus standing on the right hand of God, and said, Behold, I see the heavens opened, and the Son of man standing on the right hand of god. Then

> they cried out with a loud voice, and stopped their ears, and ran upon him with one accord, and cast him out of the city . . . And they stoned Stephen, calling upon God, and saying, Lord Jesus, receive my spirit. (Acts 7: 55–9)

The miracle of Stephen's vision before death is not *untrue* for Bale, but it is not visible and attainable – much less rhetorically mutable – by others. The heavens 'truly' opened up for Stephen not in a miraculous sense but instead beyond comprehension and the perception of the onlookers or those who do not believe. The spectacle is beyond spectacle, more real because unperceived: within the physical world, an unseen passageway opens for the soul to leave the body. To claim Stephen's experience as a miracle is to diminish the power of its invisibility and non-existence to any except Stephen and God. We are left only with the surface of the story and must assume that Stephen's soul has slipped away to the divine world only he can witness. The role of Bale and his audience, he implies, is more a witness *to* the act of witnessing, a twice-removed spectatorship that absorbs scenes of invisible theatre and faithfully believes in what is taking place. For Bale, the scene of heaven must remain as dark matter, vital to lived experience but not provably a part of it. By placing Askew in a genealogy whose origin is Stephen's vision and death, he implicitly suggests not only the elevation of her execution to hagiography but a belief that she embodied and underwent a miraculous, holy transformation that left no residue of spectacle or perception and encompassed unseen modes of deliverance right at the edges of sight, like Faustus seeing the saviour in his final minutes. For Bale, the unknown cements spiritual reality rather than upbraids it.

Coriolanus adapts the non-theatrical scene of Stephen's death into a more ambivalent context. Shortly before his own demise, Coriolanus, in a stunning tableau that marks his acquiescence to Volumnia's demands, faces his kneeling mother and wife in silence – only to burst out in emotion: 'O mother, mother! / What have you done? Behold, the heavens do ope, / The gods look down, and this unnatural scene / They laugh at. O my mother, mother! O!' (V, iii, 182–5). The spasmodic language describes a divine rift similar to that of Stephen's vision, but rather than witnessing the serenity of the holy father and son, Coriolanus sees the Roman deities mocking him. His usage of the word 'scene', and his rhetorical construction of a godly audience, theatricalise his vision, as does Aufidius's remark that, like a proper Aristotelian spectator, he 'was mov'd withal' (V, iii, 194). To level Bale's phenomenological inquiry on this passage, we may ask what, exactly, Coriolanus sees: does he actually observe the heavens? For Bale, it would not matter: the fact remains that we, barring an exceptionally ambitious stage director, cannot.[28] Coriolanus's evocation may be an attempt at linguistic excess, but it also suggests an acknowledgement, but not depiction, of something that escapes consideration but nonetheless does, as with Stephen's vision, 'occur', in a sense, in the play. Coriolanus here keeps something from the mimetic economy into which he is cast, just as he did with his refusal to show his wounds. Those wounds, magnified, now return to mark the scenography of the play.

The three figures of Coriolanus, Askew and Stephen are connected by the repeated gestures of not revealing something – a wound, a vision – even as they undergo specific and calculated performances that deny their audiences a representative connection to their actions. A palpable tension in these scenes arises in the unresolved dialectic of both withholding the grammar of remembrance and the insisting on being remembered, on transmitting their legacy in the future. As Jarrett Walker observes of Coriolanus's cry of 'I banish you!' in the face of his own banishment from Rome, his 'circular interpretation of banishment reveals the specific problem of identity that his view of time creates. He lives time as a single transcendent event, as though unconscious of time in a continuum'.[29] Seeking to be caught within a singular event, divorced from the quotidian march of time that marks the earthly realm he despises, Coriolanus resists any revelation of time's effects even as he desperately seeks to enter a noncontinuous and immortal mode of being. In his sole soliloquy, he belies a concern for this desire to live as constant event by pitting this desire explicitly against the day-to-day sense of time as a progression of thoroughly human events. Why, Coriolanus wonders, should he have to appeal to the citizens? He spits out that 'Custom calls me to't. / What custom wills in all things, should we do't, / The dust on antique time would lie unswept, / and mountainous error be too highly heaped / For truth to o'erpeer' (II, iii, 115–19). If we were to follow every injunction of custom, he reasons, the obscuring 'dust' and clutter of history would accrete, as would mistakes that obscure a purer sense of truth. 'Custom' seems, here, to extend radically to all human action, rather than the pure state of being that defines his desired wholeness. But the play's genius and perversion is to withhold these states of action, to keep at bay Coriolanus at his most liberated. We do not see him in Corioles, where presumably he reaches the ecstatic unity of action with being that eludes him in Rome. The first solider, witnessing this enclosure, remarks that Martius 'is himself alone / To answer all the city' (I, iv, 55–6). Only himself when he is alone and disappeared, Coriolanus can 'answer' the city of Corioles in the totality of his imagined character, divorced from the actor onto which he must be grafted when he occupies the stage. What results from this uneasy collision of disappearance and presence is a sense of memorialisation of what we cannot see, as with the opened clouds over Saint Stephen. Absence itself becomes a kind of monument, like a wound becoming a gravestone.

Between Words and Bodies

I want to trace further the contours of this mode of memorial performance by focusing on its deliberate obscuring of the two primal elements of performance itself – words and bodies. We can think of this indistinctness as kin to the tension, so palpable in *Coriolanus*, between the titular terms of *Acts and Monuments*: on the one hand, the impermanent status of an action, dependent on the ephemeral needs of the body, and on the other, the apparently static fixture of a monument, something presumably capable of resisting the erosion of history. Of course, one primary site of this conflict centres precisely on words, on the demand for an English translation of the Bible, an argument that, as evinced in Foxe's account of William Tyndale, calls for an unveiling of the truth:

> [R]ight well he perceived and considered this only, or most chiefly to be the cause of all mischief in the church, that the scriptures of God were *hidden from the people's eyes*: for so long the abominable doings and idolatries maintained by the Pharisaical clergy, could not be espied, and therefore all their labour was with might and main to keep it down, so that either it should not be read at all.[30]

If miracles must remain unseen, then the words of God, by contrast, had to be unhidden, uncovered, not 'hidden from the people's eyes'. Markers of language appropriately occupy an amorphous space throughout *Actes and Monuments*. Words are capable of delivering the message of God but also potentially acting as vessels of idolatrous corruption, as with the attempts to deceive Askew through false interpretation. The martyrs continually acknowledge this ambivalence in demanding the democratising accessibility of the scriptures, even as they deny leaving a textual residue of their own actions by refusing to sign or pledge allegiances to Mary and the Catholic Church. The scriptures, then, are not particularly more or less powerful in themselves as any other mortal concrete thing, but they access the holiness they cannot contain.

Words, on their own and without God's will behind them, are for Foxe's martyrs ineffective and artificial. As a result, the martyrs' own speeches become self-consciously useless as a mode of persuasion. After all, as the Homily makes clear, material attempts to cure spiritual sickness are bound to fail. Thus the recurring paradox in *Actes and Monuments*, made especially potent in Askew's use of wit and irony, is that it is itself a text, a collection of speeches, and yet those speeches must acknowledge their own inefficacy and embrace the inevitable end. Askew's ability to spar with her tormentors ultimately does not matter, as she herself seems to acknowledge. As Liz Koblyk explains, 'Neither forceful nor measured speech sways the papist tormentors, and the martyrs are aware of this even as they speak'; the traditional measures of success for oratory, such as persuasiveness, must be cast aside, as 'Foxe's martyrs, no matter how eloquent, deviate from common expectations of the orator's success.'[31] The words of the translated Bible depend on an unmarked connection to something beyond themselves in order to succeed.

The bodies of the martyrs, like the words they fight to protect, fulfil a tenuous role of signification; their actions are both seemingly incidental and capable of connecting to divinity. Even if they do not rely on words to express their deliverance, the martyrs express a corporeal grammar in performing the rejection of locating coherence *in* performance itself. This process is elegantly emblematised in the death of Thomas Cranmer, who relents in finally signing a declaration of heresy, yet when the fire is lit, he 'put his right hand into the flame: which he held so steadfast and immoveable (saving that once with the same hand he wiped his face) that all men might see his hand burned before his body was touched'.[32] Allowing the heretical component of his body to burn, he maintains stillness, as if to stress renunciation of action itself, so that 'he seemed to move no more than the stake to which he was bound'; as with his fellow martyrs in Foxe's book, the choreography becomes beatific as 'his eyes were lifted up to heaven, and oftentimes he repeated his unworthy right hand, so long as his voice would suffer him: and using the words of Stephen' – themselves a version of Jesus's last words on the cross – '"Lord Jesus, receive my spirit", in the greatness of the flame, he gave up the ghost'.[33] Cranmer, like Bale, deliberately evokes the proto-martyr in performing a kind of inaccessibility, marking the absence of divinity's available presence in his environs through stillness, while witnessing privately an egress for his presumably cleaned soul.[34] Foxe rehearses this inaccessibility through his narrative, reporting the quotidian reception of the event, along with the physical details of Cranmer's final moments, but without forthrightly engaging the fantastical.[35]

The text, then, gives us not a spectacle but audience after audience to a spectacle we cannot see. And the spectacle Foxe captures in these repeated scenes is the unmarked transference of his soul that cannot be detected by the reader, only assumed, through faith, to occur. The reflexive instantiation of the reader's trust into the deliberately withdrawn narrative can result in an exaggeration of the failure of what can be seen, as in one of the most gruesome passages in the collection, the death of John Hooper:

> But when he was black in the mouth, and his tongue swollen, that he could not speak, yet his lips went till they were shrunk to

> the gums: and he knocked his breast with his hands, until one of his arms fell off, and then knocked still with the other, what time the fat, water, and blood dropped out at his fingers' ends, until by renewing of the fire, his strength was gone, and his hand did cleave fast in knocking to the iron upon his breast.[36]

The torments progress inward, from the mouth – the first observed mutilation – to the chest. Hooper stresses this concentric movement with his incessant pounding upon his own breast, as if to accentuate the futility of destroying his spirit by assisting the flames in their destruction. The body might, we can only assume, transcend physicality through its terrifying disintegration, as Hooper emphasises the communication of his own interiority to Christ – his last words are, again, Stephen's: 'Lord Jesus receive my spirit.' The body is the mute and almost – but not entirely – irrelevant witness, the grotesque remainder necessary in its existence as a marker that signifies the faith that it channels but is not immanent to it.

For Cranmer and Hooper, extreme bodily death presents a structure within which faith, resistant to description, can be realised, and in which the soul, resistant to legibility, can be documented in its absence. The lack of ability to evoke piety directly through the body must be outlined through the careful orchestration of theatrics: rhetorically mapping a wound over the skin, outstretching a hand, beating the chest. A stillness that is not a *performed* stillness – like Ulysses's attempts at unmoving soulfulness in *Circe*, examined in Chapter 2 – is without the whiff of willed staging and would not, it follows, be capable of evoking a world beyond the means of the deaths' chronicle.[37] By collapsing the materiality of the body, the actions involved with death also become, in Foxe's text, immaterial remainders that serve to educate and preserve the memory of the event. The work that *Actes and Monuments* undergoes is to constellate its series of contentions of what cannot be articulated, which comprise the 'monuments' of the title, as pieces of a narrative of persecution and the passageway of the soul to heaven.

By keeping the soul at bay, and by focusing on the inadequacy of the more palpable elements of the scenes of martyrdom, Foxe creates a text that is resolutely dynamic and theatrical – a work that depends upon the interplay of reader and text to constitute its potency, and whose scenes depend upon a mutually constituted sense of spirituality rather than a straightforward, indexical depiction. Jennifer Rust compellingly argues for this communitarian dimension of Foxe's work in retracing a genealogy of the *corpus mysticum*, a concept originally conceived in the medieval Catholic Church as a communal demonstration of sacramentality rather than something realised by a single figure. The power of *Acts and Monuments*, Rust argues, is in part its ability to mingle deftly traces of these communal and theatrical dimensions within a Protestant martyrological framework. Fragments of the *corpus mysticum* give the accounts an air of interactive participation, as in the death of John Lambert, which depends upon him partaking in 'a performance of elevation at the stake' replete with an audience to bear witness: 'a community surrounds Lambert to bear amazed witness to the perseverance in these final moments, with those in the foreground most visibly affected by the performance'.[38] The sacred quality of the scene arises within the theatrical interaction of the people involved, rather than revealing itself from within a constitutive element of the execution.

Acts and Monuments, I have been arguing, gives us a strategy for reading *Coriolanus* as a meditation on how the spiritual threads through the material by way of the theatrical. The gesture of *hiding* manifests itself as an expressive manoeuvre that allows for a faithful acknowledgment of the soul without the threat of representation. Coriolanus's repeated withholdings similarly take place at the registers of word and body. The play announces with its first scene an impatience with language and bodily movement: the assembled Romans listen to the First Citizen and almost immediately become ready to *act*, chanting 'No more talking on't. Let it be done. Away, away' (I, i, 11). Soon after, the Second Citizen relates that their 'business is not unknown to the Senate; they have had inkling this fortnight what we intend to do, which now we'll show 'em in deed' (I, i, 52–4). Though Coriolanus bitterly opposes the citizens, the notion of showing 'in deed' echoes his own philosophy: to seek a purity of action that supersedes speech and temporality – to become a sword. As Coriolanus later tells the senators vetting him for election, 'When blows have made me stay I fled from words' (II, ii, 70). Words unnecessarily dress his wounds – which let him 'stay' fixed in space, with artifice, an unnecessary covering.

The desire to escape from the conventions of speech and time lends Coriolanus a deep impatience with the world around him, as if he had better things to do than be in his own play. This quality receives praise from Volumnia, who explains to Virgilia, in the chilling scene of their introduction, 'If my son were my husband, I should freelier rejoice in that absence wherein he won honour than in the embracements of his bed' (I, iii, 2–4). She would rejoice if he were absent from the interior and domestic space that the play depicts: *not* being present in Rome means he is in battle – or, more honestly, that he is offstage, or that 'Coriolanus' no longer exists. He is instead in the dark matter, the neither-here-nor-there space of theatrical absence – in his own words, a 'world elsewhere' (III, iii, 134). In fact, as Madhavi Menon points out, time and again within the play, actions that attempt to ground themselves in the physical reality of the body fail at doing so:

> However, lest we fall prey to the temptation to ground desire in these bodies and their activities, we should remember that none of these bodily activities actually leads anywhere in the play or has its desired effect. The fable of the belly fails to stamp out unrest in Rome, and indeed, ensures that even worse schemes are concocted by the plebeian Senators; Coriolanus's wounds cannot speak loudly enough to ensure his election to the Consul; and Aufidius's fist comes down on Coriolanus's head to kill all hope of a romantic future for the two of them.[39]

The body proves unstable as trope (the allegory of the body politic), ritually displayed text (the wounds), and site of desire (Coriolanus and Aufidius's physical attraction). None of these actions reach fruition. While the play, as Marshall has it, 'insists on the inescapability of the body', Coriolanus's own 'refusal to explain or reveal himself renders him an unknowable character'.[40] Simultaneously calling attention to bodies *and* dismissing them as ineffective, *Coriolanus* reveals the tension between a resolutely material world and an escape from the logic that posits the body as the stable site of political and spiritual subjectivity. It shows bodies that collapse, dissolve, and anxiously hope to slip away. As Coriolanus declares, 'I shall be loved when I am lacked', echoing his mother's desire for him to be elsewhere (IV, i, 15).

And yet Coriolanus's repeated longings to be absent, elsewhere, lacking, and concealed fail to trivialise him. Like the parade of stoically suffering and still martyrs in *Acts and Monuments*, he distrusts commemoration but hopes to be commemorated by rendering the space around him inadequate. The sense of monument that results from these actions is more verb than noun: Coriolanus *monuments* himself. Foxe affirms the ambiguity of this term in the preface to the fourth edition, where he explains his title:

> [S]o all true disposed mindes which shall resort to the reading of this present Hystory conteining the Actes of Gods holy Martyrs, and *monumentes* of his Church, may by example of theyr lyfe, fayth, & doctrine, receiue some such spirituall fruit to theyr soules through the operation of his grace, that it may be to the advauncement of his Glory, and profite of his Churche, through Christ Iesus our Lord.[41]

The term 'monument' here is both a reference to a static concrete object and a placeholder for a set of actions. Foxe plays on the word's association with mortality and use as a synonym for gravestone, a link I will explore later in the chapter. But the gravestone here is not a stone structure but a necessarily ephemeral action, the burning to death of martyrs: nothing remains. The way the monument lives on is in its rereading and rehearsing the conditions of its material disappearance. Foxe, in framing his stories, is careful to maintain constant distinction from physical commemorations, for which he reserves, confusingly, the same term as for his martrys' performances. He distinguishes carefully those 'Monuments of idolatry'[42] that signal the Catholic perversion of scripture; such blasphemous signifiers are exemplified in one of Tyndale's charged 1531 response to Thomas More that excoriates 'our false faith, in visityng the monumentes of Christ' and explains that 'therefore hath

God also destroyed them'.[43] The instability of the word 'monument' only further emphasises the term's disengagement from the logic of reference. Instead, it wilfully erases itself as a part of God's plan and resists any bond with systems of articulation, be they bodies, objects, or words.

As Tyndale's citation implies, to think of the monument as an act, rather than an idolatrous commodity, is not a radical revision of the term but a distillation of a tradition, popular in Shakespeare's time, of de-emphasising tangibility as a means of formulating memory. This process also links the soul to the performative construction of monumentality. The complicity of the soul's entanglement with memory, born in the tension that emerges between physical tomb and ephemeral performance, is palpable in both Platonic and Christian strains of thought – and, as a result, in the interplay of these ideas in the syncretic intellectual-religious landscape of early modern England. The soul, for Plato, is a fragment of eternal memory, a cosmic entity that desires to be recollected but can yield its truth only through proper maintenance of the body. As Frances Yates asserts, the 'soul's remarkable power of remembering things and words is a proof of its divinity'; caring for it could access this power and allow the bodily senses to comprehend it without resolving the soul into idolatrous matter.[44] The central doctrine of *anamnesis*, that all knowledge is remembrance, is developed in Plato's *Meno*, where Socrates characteristically rebuts the obstinate Meno's attempts to undermine his philosophy. Meno, hoping to flummox the philosopher, posits the paradoxical question of how knowledge can be acquired at all; by turning to the soul as his answer, Socrates radically subverts Meno's epistemological assumptions. There is no new knowledge, he asserts, only degrees by which we are separated from the part of us that already knows everything – the essential component that cannot find direct register on our bodies or minds. As Socrates brusquely tells his interlocutor, the soul 'is immortal and has been incarnated many times, and has therefore seen things here on earth and things in the underworld too – everything in fact – there's nothing that it hasn't learnt'.[45] The soul, here, already knows everything and imparts its knowledge to the mind by doling out wisdom in relation to its proper health and maintenance. The *Meno* only sketches out an idea that will be further realised in the *Phaedo* and *Phaedrus*, although it succinctly introduces the soul's immortality and its relation to memory.[46]

Traces of this Platonic notion resonate in the Christian rubric of *anamnesis*, which derives from the New Testament's depictions of the last supper, when Jesus asks his followers to eat and drink 'in remembrance of me' (1 Cor 11: 24). The memorial Jesus asks for is ritualistic, not static. As Bruce Morrill notes, the doctrine of *anamnesis* as it relates to the Eucharist yokes together imitation and remembrance:

> Here we find something of the mystery (mysticism) that makes the Eucharist the source and summit of the entire Christian life as a following or imitation of Christ. The invitation to imitation comes in the invitation to share at the Lord's table, to an intimate communion in the very person (body) of the crucified but risen Jesus encountered with joyous thanksgiving in the meal of the covenant (in his blood).[47]

The 'invitation to imitate' is also an invitation to remember: through imitation, spiritual fulfilment is reached. Morrill, writing from a Catholic philosophical tradition, assumes a transubstantive relationship that would, of course, be attenuated in the Anglican setting of Shakespeare's theatre. But the basic central tenet remains, whether literal or metaphoric: at the centre of Christian practice is the upkeep of memory that arises from action, not from attempts at permanence.

This concept is more profoundly realised in an alternate and textually rarer word, *mnemosunon*, translated in the King James Bible as 'memorial' as opposed to simply 'memory'. '*Mnemosunon*' occurs in two scriptural incidents. The first transpires when a woman pours over Jesus's head the contents of an 'alabaster box of very precious ointment' while he visits a leper; the disciples react in anger, to which Jesus demands of them:

> Why trouble ye the woman? for she hath wrought good work upon me. For ye have the poor always with you; but me ye have not always. For in that she hath poured this ointment on my

> body, she did it for my burial. Verily I say unto you, Whosoever this gospel shall be preached in the whole world, there shall also this, that this woman hath done, be told for a memorial [*mnemosunon*] of her. (Matthew 26: 10–13)

The word crops up again in Acts, when Cornelius receives an angelic vision; the seraph informs him that his 'prayers and thine alms are come up for a memorial before God' (10: 4). In both instances, memory is an action, whether gratuitous and spontaneous, as with the woman, or rigorous and ritualistic, as with Cornelius's prayers and donations. The monument, here, is something processual, rather than fixed; it offers a set of actions untethered to the tangible. For the woman in the leper's house, especially, the scene echoes Foxe's recurring theme of the material, consequential and economically valuable becoming denigrated in service of establishing memory. But the action in question is not the representational one of the Eucharist. The spontaneous and ultimately prophetic performance by the woman is instead radically disconnected from what it commemorates; its ambivalence to direct interpretation seems to be what, in fact, give it its power. David Gregg, in a philological study, compares the two New Testament terms for memorial – *anamnesis* and *mnemosunon* – and proposes that they can be distinguished by the form of memory they draw upon, as *mnemosunon* implies an 'element of continuity' whereas '*anamnesis*, on the other hand, characteristically designates something that is momentary and discontinuous – something that has no abiding existence of its own'.[48]

This conclusion seems counterintuitive: *anamnesis*, the term used by Jesus to ask for his name to be remembered, would more conventionally be thought of as continuous and powerful, whereas *mnemosunon*, the word used for the woman's indecorous waste of ointment, would be more of an interruption of time. But *anamnesis* is less temporally fixed, argues Julie Gittoes, and more irruptive, rather than seamless: 'the Eucharist is retrospective, and also has an anticipatory dimension. It looks backward to this Last Supper and forward to the eschaton, and is concerned with the transformation and building of the Kingdom of God in the present. Thus *anamnesis* is a word designating the connection between past and future in the present.'[49] *Anamnesis* is a form of memory-keeping that exists in typological unease within the passage of time, yet *mnemosunon*, a purer and more continuous form of memory, is used by Christ to uphold the divinity of a spontaneous act – precisely, it follows, *because* of its ephemerality and apparent waste of valued, economised matter. Continuous remembrance, for the woman in the leper's house, demands an action that lays bare its unnecessary nature, one that strips away the material and evaluated qualities of the world. It renders *anamnesis* as a non-mimetic and self-consciously useless performance, linking an external set of actions to the internal stewardship of the soul.

In a close reading of the works of the Puritan minister Stephen Denison, Peter Lake elaborates on this knowingly ineffective form of performance within the praxis of early modern Protestantism. Lake proposes that a sermon of Denison's, published as *The Monument or Tomb-Stone: A Sermon Preached at the Funeral of Mrs. Elizabeth Juxon*, serves as a model of how a certain quality of banality is needed in a properly holy life, according to the strain of Protestant faith Denison exemplifies. 'Despite the exemplary Christian virtues which Mrs. Juxon had displaced after her conversion', Lake writes, 'her fervor to hear the word preached, her scrupulous Sabbath keeping, her charitable benefactions to both poor ministers and the godly poor, the closeness of her spiritual relationship with Denison and other ministers of his ilk – she had been troubled by a certain spiritual dryness.'[50] This flatness helps Denison mould her into a model, a perfect pedagogical component of his own memorial of her, which complements her dryness with literary flourish and spiritual exhortations. Denison can construct a sermon that itself serves as a monument to her, one dependent upon the interaction between the audience and his words: 'Denison proffered his picture of Mrs. Juxon as a model for his readers, who could, he claimed, examine themselves "by these marks" of godliness set out in the sermon. "If thou dost find them in thee", he continued, it was safe with a "childlike boldness and holy confidence" to go to God and claim eternal life.'[51] Juxon does not simply die and become replaced with a material stand-in, but her memory becomes a reperformed set of actions prompted by Denison's inscription – the 'marks' to be examined – that allow for faithfulness to flourish in the reader.

Juxon's life makes for fairly insipid narrative, but that dullness is what allows for faith to occur between the lines, in the dynamic between her and her post-mortem observers: a necessary gap instantiates itself between the words and their intended effects. This gap is, for Denison, her true monument, her *mnemosunon*, and it is in this gap that *Coriolanus* occurs, forthrightly denying the efficacy of its bodies and words alone, as if outlining a 'world elsewhere' where the true wholeness of faith could be born. Remarkably, though, Coriolanus reverses Denison's formula by locating in his body the techniques that Lake explores within the textual, and by inflecting his living body with the qualities left by the dead: he embodies dryness and modulates it into performance, transforming what for Denison is between the lines into the offstage, hidden spaces of the stage. Coriolanus's words, it follows, are notably *not* lyrical and are instead spectacularly dreadful, in the truest sense of the word: as Cavell observes, his speeches are marked by absence and abjection: 'the general idea remains, indelibly, of Coriolanus's speech, when angry, as being the spitting forth of the matter of an abscess'.[52] His words furthermore mark a *lack* of good words, of what should be said: 'Accordingly, every word he speaks will mean the withholding of good words. He will, as it were, have a sword in his mouth.'[53] Coriolanus speaks, Cavell suggests, as a way of marking time, showing blatantly how the space usually reserved for beauty, consolation and other forms of public human connection are instead only invective, unhelpful and decidedly non-participatory. Kenneth Burke notes how Coriolanus effects, in the ugliness of his language, a form of Aristotelian catharsis, a demonstration of the ' "curative" function of invective', that is 'released under controlled conditions that transform the repressed into the expressed' but ultimately 'do us no damage'.[54]

What results is a play fed up with itself. Theatre is a place of bodies and words, but *Coriolanus* and especially its central character place representational value on neither: bodies fail and words act as placeholders for meanings that never arrive. The offstage spaces, anxiously neither present nor absent, constantly offer the beckoning call of fulfilment, one inaccessible through the means of the staged event. Coriolanus's hidden wounds serve as a powerful model of the larger pattern at play: *Coriolanus* keeps occluded and only gestures to what it cannot show. But as Foxe's work demonstrates, a complex theatrical grammar still attends the process of articulating this non-presence. In short, the monument to the soul is a theatrical set of actions that demonstrate its non-placement. The monument does not remember the soul in the sense of 'recall exactly'. Rather, its form of remembrance is a complex performance that fluidly resituates both the memory and the rememberer. And that form of performance is, as made clear by the wilfully useless martyrs in *Acts and Monuments*, the life commemorated by Denison's sermon, and the unseen and unknown miracles witnessed by St Stephen, an intentionally dull one – but not, crucially, an insignificant one. Obscuring himself from the public, Coriolanus's heightened distrust toward the capacity of words and bodies to mean anything places him in extreme opposition to what Rob Carson calls the 'cavalier constructivist attitude towards the truth in Rome'.[55] In a line that has been taken to signal resonance with anti-theatricalist ideals, Coriolanus indicates, moments from his demise, that 'Like a dull actor now, I have forgotten my part and I am out, / Even to a full disgrace' (V, iii, 40–2).[56] But while his death signals capitulation to the progression of mortal time that he has resisted, for much of the play he manages to become obscured from the machinations that would render him indexical and readable and instead live in abeyance of representation. By presenting himself to us as wilfully resistant, Coriolanus forces a consideration of the fact of his self without resolving into a coherent subject. He becomes and exposes the dark matter residing under the play of significance that creates his surroundings.

Acts of Monuments

Before returning more fully to *Coriolanus* to explore this peculiar performative strategy, I want to linger on the actual material artifact of the monument in early modernity to explore how it could be destabilised and rendered indistinct. Foxe's progression of departing souls gives us one side of early modern monumental performance by portraying the slipping away of the soul at the moment of death. It would follow that the concrete monuments that then stand in for lost life – both immediately, with the corpse, and later, with the gravestone – would seem to be in opposition to such action. And yet they still contain a theatrical energy that renders them *more* capable of memorialisation by deliberately defacing themselves with the same violence as Coriolanus's self-obscuring. Much has been made of the ghosts and apparitions that signal the uneasy status of the dead. But rather than focus on the supernatural, I want to see how what should be straightforwardly material and dull can still vibrate with theatrical energy.

Concerns over the properties of physical graves and monuments appear in a passage from North's translation of Plutarch's 'Life of Martius Coriolanus', the primary source for Shakespeare's play. In discussing the construction of a memorial to the three women who eventually cause Coriolanus to relent in his assault on Rome, Plutarch embarks on an extended aside on the properties of monuments to the dead. He takes up the common superstition that graves and statues can weep or bleed as phantasmagoric expressions of the life they once held. First, Plutarch allows that such phenomena can occur, but for logical reasons, since 'wood and stone do commonly receive moisture, whereof is engendered an humour, which do yield themselves, or do take of the air, many sorts and kinds of spots and colours; by which signs and tokens it is not amiss, we think, that the gods sometime do warn men of things to come'.[57] But, he continues, it is impossible for such behaviour to result from any spiritual cause, as 'a body which hath neither life nor soul should have any direct or exquisite word formed in it by express voice – that is altogether impossible. For the soul nor god himself can distinctly speak without a body, having necessary organs and instruments meet for the parts of the same to form and utter distinct words.'[58] North's Plutarch cannot allow for the belief in the soul's pure emergence; it must be mediated by the instrument of the body. And the monument that remains to stand in for the dead must remain obstinately without signs of life.

Strikingly, Shakespeare removes the construction of the memorial from his adaptation, as if reluctant to attempt as neat a distinction as Plutarch does between solid material and divine signs that linger in the wood and stone. Sidestepping the theatrical problems that Middleton realises in *The Second Maiden's Tragedy*'s staging of posthumous spiritual life, *Coriolanus* makes only a brief mention of a tribute to the women; the scene of Coriolanus's capitulation ends with him linking their silence and stillness to memory: 'Ladies, you deserve / To have a temple built you' (V, iii, 206–7). Shakespeare keeps the monument only as a possibility, ethereal as if in tribute to the lack of concrete methods employed by the women. Virgilia, Volumnia and Valeria have, in fact, already demonstrated an embodied form of memorialisation more potent than any structure could effect, one that effectively leads to Coriolanus's buckling under their will. With empirical precision, Volumnia attempts various strategies to change her son's mind. In doing so, she insinuates spiritual guilt, telling Coriolanus he 'barr'st us / Our prayers to the gods, which is a comfort / That all but we enjoy' (V, iii, 104–6); threatens to disown his filial connection, likening his siege to treading 'on thy mother's womb / That brought thee to this world' (V, iii, 124–5); and hints at the ruinous interpretation of the time that would follow his actions, channelling a possible encomium: 'The man was noble, / But with his last attempt he wip'd it out, / Destroy'd his country, and his name remains/ To th'insuing age abhorr'd' (V, iii, 145–8). We can gather from her notation of the *mise-en-scène* that he finally responds by turning away – in indifference or shame – when she prods him to say that her 'request's unjust' (V, iii, 164). After this moment, spurred by his physical reaction, she deploys her final tactic – the deliberate effacement of the stream of words and rhetorical technique she has utilised thus far. She confronts his lack with further lack, asking Virgilia and Valeria to kneel in stillness – the exact manoeuvre she first insinuated she would undertake, bitterly, at the start to her diatribe, warning that if 'we be silent and not speak, our raiment / And state of bodies would bewray what life / We have led since thy exile' (V, iii, 94–6). Her language evokes a stripping down, a 'bewraying', of her performance – a disavowal of language and recourse to a demonstration of a lack of artifice.

Much as Coriolanus attempts to take on different roles to 'frame' himself as properly humble, only to reject the very notion of performance, Volumnia strategically embodies different stock characters – seducer, confessor, matriarch – only to shake off embodiment altogether. And as much as the scene is persistently marked as theatrical, the performance that proves most fruitful is the disintegration of the rhetorical system it constructs. It is this effectiveness that leads to Coriolanus's capitulation and the Gods' parodically beatific vision of mocking laughter; it leads also, as a result, to the rending of the mechanics of the theatre that holds the play *Coriolanus* itself. Coriolanus notes that upon their return they will bear 'a better witness back than words' (V, iii, 204–5). He flees from words, and the women, better than words, act as emissaries to this aversion in their silence. Volumnia, in ceasing to speak and having the women kneel, makes any actual inclusion of a physical monument redundant – she has already embodied a disruptive elision of meaning that itself constitutes the creation of memory.

The cultural anxieties that surround the physical construction and disintegration of the monument within the body or a physical structure, as portrayed in this scene, extend to gravestones, the more quotidian markers of death. John Weever's 1631 *Ancient Funerall Monuments* explores these monuments, which feature so dominantly in *Coriolanus*'s imagistic vocabulary. Weever's full title signals kinship to Foxe's project: 'Ancient Funerall Monuments Within the United Monarchie of Great Britain, Ireland, and the Islands adjacent, with the dissolved Monasteries therein contained: their Founders, and what eminent Persons have beene in the fame interred.' The title neatly frames the work's primary conflicts in the friction between the recovery and properly directed reverence toward the monuments of the dead, and the dissolution of the idolatrous 'dissolved Monasteries' within which they are contained. Weever's nostalgic tour through these gravestones mourns for the loss of objects that are designed to mourn; he laments the disappearance of the inscription that allows for a clear remembrance of the dead. The monuments themselves are at the hinge of dissolution and coalescence that separates the spiritual and material.

And yet packaged within this sentimentality is the perverse wish for further dissolution. Weever elaborates his original mission in his opening chapter, where he begins with a seemingly straightforward declaration that, as 'generally taken', 'all religious Foundations, all sumptuous and magnificent Structures, Cities, Townes, Towers, Castles, Pillars, Pyramides, Crosses, Obeliskes, Amphitheatres, Statues, and the like, as well as Tombes and Sepulchres, are called Monuments'.[59] Weever then traverses through a variety of literary citations, from classical philosophy through the Bible and concluding with a string of glowing references to Spenser's tribute to Sidney, 'The Ruins of Time', from his *Complaints*. (I will discuss the form of the elegy more in depth in the next chapter.) The book's progression charts the very effacement of the monuments that Weever laments – and makes it its mission to remedy through chronicles of lost graves – only to conclude that, following Spenser's encomium, it is vain to 'thinke to gaine a perpetuitie after death, by erecting of pillars, and such like monuments, to keepe their names in remembrance, when it is only the Muses work which give unto men immortalitie'.[60] Weever's wandering transforms the object-based idolatry of the monument into the intangible action of admitting the folly of remembrance at all. This ending provides a test to the sentimentality that may have accrued in viewing the apparent tragedy of disappearance: while a physical structure may seem permanent and awe-inspiring, in fact, Weever argues, it is poetry (presumably his own, alongside Spenser's) that will persevere. The 'ruins of time' motif is immensely popular in Renaissance poetry, and echoes the self-willed erasure of the elegy explored in the next chapter, but what is especially noteworthy in Weever's work is its intimate connection to the defacement of the material world, which the author catalogues with zeal.[61] The graves' ruin is not antithetical to proper codes of memorialisation: it is necessary, prompting the task of cataloguing and stringing together in a poetic medium the lives of the dead and nearly forgotten. The acts of desecration fold into the poetic act, synthesising into remembrance.

John Stow's *Survey of London*, originally published in 1598, similarly enacts a form of forgetting and defacement as, paradoxically, a form of commemoration. Winding through London, the

Survey peppers its simulated *flânerie* with personal remembrances and historical digressions. And yet its power also accrues from the more banal accumulation of details to which Stow persistently attends. The work serves as a meditation on what seems to be precisely the opposite process of Foxe's martyrology: the reduction of the divine into the quotidian and tangible, rather than the deliverance of the everyday into the unknowable. The more physical 'monuments' of gravestones that Stow lists as destroyed and paved by the Broad Street church are instances of a motif to which he keeps returning.[62] In each ward, the effaced, lost and forgotten graves are listed and remembered in long lists of names, some numbering among the hundreds. Like Weever, he tasks himself with surrogating his words as replacement headstones, which have failed to promise a long cultural memory. In order to offer his encomia, however, Stow must labour to demonstrate the extent of the gravestones' destruction. In Faringdon, after relating a long history of Christ's Church, including the previous incarnation of Grey Friar's Church, Stow recites an exhaustive list of those buried, taking up the majority of the printed page. He notes at the close of this series that 'all these and five times so many more have been buried there whose monuments are wholly defaced', amplifying the effect of the sheer quantity; he then focuses on the nature of their dissolution, noting that 'there were nine tombs of alabaster and marble, environed with strikes of iron in the choir, and one tomb in the body of the church, also coped with iron, all pulled down, besides sevenscore gravestones or marble', which were in turn all 'sold for fifty pounds, or thereabouts, by Sir Martin Bowes, goldsmith and alderman of London'.[63] The monetary amount lands like a punch line, reducing the past to units of exchange. Rather than reach Weever's conclusion, which strains for the transcendental power of poetry to keep the inaccessible divine alive through lyrical embodiment, Stow lets the sudden tangibility of the monuments allow for the loss of their spiritual power – an inanimate version of Foxe's martyrs' gaining salvation through their destruction.

The deliberate facticity of the language – its strategic banality – emphasises its lack of ability to contain the past, which slips by in the background of the written record. By simply noting that which should receive more committed descriptive energies, Stow amplifies the wished-for erasure that Weever contains beneath his profession of melancholic loss. There are no celebrations of poetic remembrance, no ruins of time, only the present-tense observation in ineffective words. The lists of graves approach what Sianne Ngai calls 'stuplimity': the accretion of banalities that deny any kind of transcendence but nonetheless create a sense of beyond-ness through their obstinate repetition and duration. Stuplimity, Ngai elaborates, is

> a concatenation of boredom and astonishment – a bringing together of what 'dulls' and what 'irritates' or agitates; of sharp, sudden excitation and prolonged desensitization, exhaustion, or fatigue . . . Stuplimity reveals the limits of our ability to comprehend a vastly extended form as a totality, as does Kant's mathematical sublime, yet not through an encounter with the infinite but with infinite bits and scraps of material in repetition.[64]

Stuplimity maps out what words cannot do, marking the invisible sublime that they don't bother to attain and to which they don't even gesture. Stow's extreme detail employed in cataloguing the physical blazoning of the landscape keeps reaching a tipping point of stuplimity by marking out carefully the limits of knowledge as a tribute, of sorts, to the spiritual, which gains only minimal description. Whereas a single water pump in Lime Street Ward gains a strange power through obstinate narrative fixation – 'for the placing of which pump, having broken up the ground, they were forced to dig more than two fathom deep before they came to any main ground, where they found a hearth made of Britain, or rather Roman tile, every tile half a yard square, and about two inches thick . . .'[65] – the monuments that should provide an emotional climax are observed with a subdued voice. In Cornhill Ward, after describing an apocryphal story involving a lion attack, Stow sets to work, as always, in notating the graves. Slipped among the customary list is a sudden striking inclusion: 'Richard Garnam, 1527, buried there; Edmond Trindle and Robert Smith; William Dickson and Margaret his wife, buried in the cloister under a fair tomb now defaced; Thomas Stow, my father, 1559; John Tolus, alderman,

1548.'[66] As if a list of descendants in the Book of Numbers, the names whip past, sometimes prompting scrutiny and anecdote; the mention of Tolus, for instance, allows a digression on the sale and reparations of the church.[67] That Stow's father and grandfather are included is only incidental, allowing no hitch in the tempo of his series. What demands proper attention is the materiality of the past resolving into a present; the concrete descriptions deny synthesis to register the loss of something that cannot be reclaimed or, implicitly, even locate itself entirely into language – despite, or because of, the enormous physical detail it entails.

It seems significant, then, that the fantastical-sounding anecdote about the lion revolves around the insistent theme of engraving. The animal apparently scratched the surface of solid stone, by way of explanation of the crevices and cracks into which Stow recalls putting a 'feather or small stick' as a youth.[68] As with the tombstones, the defacement of the surface creates the structure for Stow's sentimentality as well as the imbued power of the past, which, while remaining inaccessible and whose power is barely articulated, still acts upon the present as channelled through Stow's guiding words. Stow, then, maintains his principle of preservation – but acknowledges its ironic dependence on the destruction of the perceivable world in order to texture it silently with an imagined past. The diverging voices of both Coriolanus and Cominius, arguing over the proper appropriation of physical symbolism, find their expression in the *Survey*, which understands the need for a narrative to produce memory *and* the suppression that denies its total comprehension.

The Soul Politic

The scene of Coriolanus's successful refusal, while discomforting and, as it becomes politically manipulated, infuriating to the Roman citizens, is consonant with a larger pattern in the play whereby he absents aspects of his identity that would otherwise prove more conducive to the social cohesion of the state. In this final section, I hope to recover a deeper set of questions that this observation allows us to find when coupled with the contemporary and theoretical ideas of memory and performance I have elaborated. Coriolanus, I believe, does not only provide an antagonism to the state, but also an embodiment of how *performed* absence, and its integral connection to memory production – its ability to 'act' a monument, to monument – in fact comprises the centre of political power, a theatrical strategy reserved for the dead found, here, at the centre of life.

In the opening scene, Menenius attempts to quell the possibility of plebeian rebellion by telling the hoary tale, lifted from Plutarch, of the 'body politic'.[69] His purpose is to relay the actual importance of the belly, the part that consumes nutrients yet is essential to the overall maintenance of life – an apology, naturally, for the apparent greed of the aristocracy and very real starvation of the citizenry. He frames the story in the mythical past: 'there was a time, when all the body's members / Rebell'd against the belly: thus accus'd it: / That only like a gulf it did remain / I'the'midst o'th'body, idle and unactive' (I, i, 95–8). The 'gulf' of the belly, which is defined by its lack, is in distinction to the 'other instruments' who 'see, and hear, devise, instruct, walk, feel' – in short, the bodily aspects that *act* (I, i, 100–1). The 'gulf' at the centre, the belly, is defined by its consuming, rather than any legible contribution. The scene is partially satirical: the rebellion is far more easily quelled by the granting of tribunes than the telling of allegories; however, the consumptive and absenting properties of the belly are given political analogy immediately afterwards, when Coriolanus learns of the Volscians 'in arms' (I, i, 223) and is excited by the prospect of battle. Whirling on the plebeians, he asks them spitefully to join him: 'Worshipful mutiners, / Your valour puts well forth: pray follow' (I, i, 249–50). The citizens '*steal away*' rather than fight (I, i, 250).[70] The battlefield, the site of forgetting names, erasing recognition, and obliterating all disguises save for kites and crows, is, like the belly, a gulf that feasts on identity, and the citizens, the toes of the body politic, wish to stay compartmentalised. Menenius may believe that the 'Senators of Rome are this good belly' (I, i,147), but a deeper understanding of the 'gulf' in the midst of the body is war, and most intensely,

Coriolanus, who literally – as Volumnia memorably relays – nourishes himself with blood, and who is 'devoured', in turn, by war (I, i, 257).

The power of the hollowed belly finds its re-emergence in a particularly complex, if syntactically awkward, speech by Aufidius to his lieutenant. Puzzling over Rome's rejection of Coriolanus, he lists the possible reasons for the military leader's social friction – pride, judgement, nature – and arrives at a meditative point about the very progression of history: 'So our virtues lie in th'interpretation of the time, / And power, unto itself most commendable, / Hath not a tomb so evident as a chair / T'extol what it hath done' (IV, vii, 49–53). The sentiment could be Coriolanus's in his decision to keep his blood on his body, rejection of acting, and refusal to show his wounds. The passage of time alone, Aufidius suggests, is without clear display of virtue; rather, it is the reading and interpreting of events, the granting of symbolic value, that creates positive attributes. Paradoxically, though, it is exactly this process, of extolling what is done, that inters the workings of power. The belly, invisible and devouring, cannot be articulated or aestheticised, proclaimed or denounced, in the literal marketplace where the populace rages for its display. The monologue doubles on itself by implying that, for the upcoming siege of Rome, Aufidius will be the invisible one, in the shadow of his celebrated partner – thus giving him the power to overthrow Coriolanus, whose own power would have just been forced into the centre after his military victory. When Coriolanus is 'poor'st of all', Aufidius states that 'shortly art thou mine' (IV, vii, 56–7). This pattern of power occluding itself to gain intensity, only to capitalise on its visibility and, as such, diminish, results in the rueful dialectic by which, Aufidius notes, one fire drives out another, as 'one nail, one nail' (IV, vii, 54). Coriolanus, who tents himself against commodity and refuses to gain political traction, is as such not an exilic irritant to the state, but a concentration of its own maintenance, taken to an extreme – a return of the belly as an even more obscured absence. He is capable of reflecting this phenomenon to authority without succumbing entirely to it – he is capable, in other words, of performing a monument to power without fully becoming one.

Rather than placing himself on the chair that would destroy his agency, he creates a living tomb, a self-obscuring yet persistently visible and present act.

Zvi Jagendorf has influentially connected Menenius's speech with St Paul's division of the body in I Corinthians: 'A body is not a single organ, but many. Suppose the foot were to say, "Because I am not a hand, I do not belong to the body", it belongs to the body none the less. Suppose the ear were to say, "Because I am not an eye, I do not belong to the body", it still belongs to the body . . .' (12: 14–16). What is lacking from this comparison, however, is Paul's insistence that the body is only incidental to the literally animating power of the soul, which grants the divisions life. In fact, Paul's description of bodily distinction is bracketed by bodily dissolution. Immediately preceding the breakdown of the roles of hand, ear and eye, Paul notes that 'by one Spirit are we all baptized into one body, whether we be Jews or Gentiles, whether we be bond or free; and have been all made to drink into one Spirit' (12: 12–13). The resurrected body of Jesus has the power to individuate roles but also binds its differentiated parts into one whole. The differences of body can always dissolve into the sameness of soul. But radical sameness, when recontextualised out of Paul's apostolic community-formation and into the political climate of Shakespeare's Rome, is more threatening to individuality than it is liberating. James Kuzner, drawing on the work of Leo Bersani, Judith Butler, and Giorgio Agamben, has brilliantly shown how the republicanism of *Coriolanus* renders itself vulnerable to a radical, sodomitical exteriority that valorises homogeneity, rather than the differences granted by sovereignty.[71] The externalising and queer figure that Kuzner outlines bears uncanny similarities not only to Paul's sameness but also the theatre's: Coriolanus's smeared and undone self acts as a corrosive reminder of the soul *and* stage's inherent, unsteady presence.

If Rome's political leaders are collectively the city's belly, then, Coriolanus surely attempts to be its soul.[72] Slipping out unseen at death, the soul demands remembrance. Foxe and Stow extensively document a strategy for such remembrance by cataloguing the material remains at its departure. Such demonstrations of physical fragility gains a threatening valence within the political-theatrical logic of

Rome, however, where time must be marked out and absences must be translated into ideological currency. At the edge of the tomb and life, Coriolanus is an explicit demonstration of the contradictory mechanics of memory that bind together bodies politic and corporeal.[73] As a form of concealment made explicit – without resolving into valuation through the mimetic economy – Coriolanus allows the play to absorb a mode of theatrical resistance characteristic of the scenes that bracket the soul's departure: the dry and deliberately banal body of the dying martyr and the self-obscuring and indistinct corpse and grave. He becomes the stuplime, the *mnemosunon* of strategic self-indeterminacy. By doing so, Coriolanus does not simply demonstrate a generalised anxiety over what cannot be represented, but shifts into another mode of performance altogether. He does not disappear when he 'banishes' Rome; rather, he moves into a different kind of stage. As he tells the servingman in Antium, he dwells 'under the canopy' of 'kites and crows' (IV, v, 39.43). The second servingman will later try to recall his features and fail at even basic description: 'Nay, I knew by his face that there was something in him. He had, sir, a kind of face, methought – I cannot tell how to term it' (IV, v, 156–8)'. And Aufidius does not even recognise him. The 'disguise' that he wears is not an artifice but a stripping-down of the artifice that, with feigned naturalness, attends civil life.[74] He becomes, in Cominius's phrase, 'a kind of nothing, titleless, / Til he had forged himself a name o'th'fire / Of burning Rome' (V, i, 14). Cominius relates this harrowing description after returning from an unsuccessful attempt to dissuade his attack – one of the more pedestrian attempts at straightforward persuasion that precede the women's own 'kind of nothing', the silence and stillness that lead to capitulation.

As with Shylock, Coriolanus threatens to reveal the nothingness that thrums underneath the play of life created so convincingly by theatre and state. His actions of radical concealment puncture the surface of political and even subjective construction. The soul, then, comes dangerously close to bursting into the representative schemes of the city-state, infringing on its coherence. If this makes Coriolanus like a soul – trying to escape behind the distraction of words – it also explains his perpetual ability to seem non-human. By keeping articulation at bay, he becomes wholly a body. He is made a 'sword' by the soldiers eager to follow him in war, a beast incapable of empathetic connection, a 'kind of nothing' that replicates the saint and the monster.[75] His death, appropriately, releases the suppressed urges for articulation on the smeared plane of nothingness, like Askew's self-enveloping wound, that Coriolanus embodies. 'Cut me to pieces, Volsces men and lads', he demands, as they do just that. 'Stain all your edges on me. "Boy", false hound! / If you have writ your annals true, 'tis there / That, like an eagle in a dovecote, I / Fluttered your Volscians in Corioles. / Alone I did it. "Boy"!' (V, vi, 112–17). Repeating the insulting term lobbed at him – 'boy' – Coriolanus relents to have his 'annals' written onto his body, and the Volscians release their own ecstatically brief stories with each stab: they decry 'He killed my son! My daughter! He killed my cousin Marcus! He killed my father!' (V, vi, 121–2). These micro-histories find a final, tragic pronouncement in Aufidius's last full line, delivered as he stands over Coriolanus's corpse – 'he shall have a noble memory' (V, vi, 155). Coriolanus's killers have, in a sense, now intensified his own intensification: he wounded his own wounds, which Rome had construed as not-yet-untranslated meaning; the Volscians then inscribe their own symbolic writing onto his body, making his mutilation the scratches on the wall that beg for interpretation and, with this, the restitution of a governing narrative to maintain the strength of political fictions. The play itself, in this reading, becomes in its final moments the kind of textually stable monument that it has resisted. Until that point, *Coriolanus* has accommodated a way for the soul's expressive embodiment to impinge on the theatre by replaying its essential breach between the visibly logical and the invisibly sublime. Coriolanus had staged a deep homage to memory through the counterintuitive erasure of memory's surface. But this performance must come to an end and produce, by way of Aufidius's spontaneous myth-making, a semblance of a future, at the precise moment the play's future runs out.

CHAPTER 4

MOURNING THE PRESENT: THE ELEGY OF *THE WINTER'S TALE*

The previous chapters have explored how Shylock and Coriolanus, in different ways, take on a corporeal grammar that evokes the soul – or, more precisely, a grammar that evokes the impossibility of its physical manifestation. Each of these figures subsequently becomes punished within the relentlessly mimetic worlds into which they are cast. In this chapter, I turn to *The Winter's Tale* to examine a very different outcome. While Leontes, like Shylock and Coriolanus, refuses to accept the representational logic of his surroundings, he ultimately finds himself redeemed and reincorporated into his familial and political realms. This ending is on one level an essential function of the romance genre, which allows for post-tragic revelation. But in the context of this study, such a resolution suggests the possibility of the mimetic economy to absorb the expressivity of the soul's bodily condition – an uneasy truce between two hitherto antagonistic ways of being.

One character does become sacrificed in this redemptive trajectory: Mamillius, Leontes's son. My contention in this chapter is that Mamillius's death catalyses the ending's fantastical mingling of presence and absence, expression and representation – and more specifically, as I will elaborate, breath and word. As with Shylock's deferrals and Coriolanus's concealments, the prince employs a host of bodily strategies – silence, breathing, whispering, stillness – that potentially disrupt the play of meaning-making around him. But he is not a social problem like those other characters because his expressive grammar is inherent to his status as a child. Leontes, however, becomes deeply disturbed by the connection to pre-signifying play that his son embodies, as well as the suggestion that Mamillius's sanctioned displays of incoherence are essential to the formation of signification, of meaning itself. Leontes thus absorbs Mamillius's behaviour and recontextualises it within the far more dangerous context of his adult self. The king's realisation that his conception of knowledge depends on something beyond his comprehension – particularised luridly in his charges of Hermione's infidelity – plunges Leontes into a private logic so embedded as to create a social and linguistic withdrawal that mirrors Mamillius's material exit. As Leontes admits, in a panic: 'In those foundations which I build upon, / The centre is not big enough to bear / A schoolboy's top' (II, i, 101–3).[1] In his crisis, he finds himself squarely out of joint with the world around him, the smooth operation of which depends thoroughly on the ability to read and gather prescribed references from stable foundations. He is, as Mamillius was, a soul trapped in a machinic world of representation.

To explore the play's meditation on the death of a young prince as a reflection of its meditation on the soul, this chapter first reads *The Winter's Tale* alongside the development of the Renaissance elegy, a literary form that marks the separation of soul from body. I will pay particular attention to the outpouring of mournful remembrances prompted by the passing of Prince Henry Frederick of Wales. The massive popularisation of the elegy that occurred after Henry's death gives us a rich historical context for Shakespeare's work, but the form also lets us see how *The Winter's Tale* radicalises the elegiac form by allowing for a non-textual and highly theatrical mode of remembrance – a mode that, like the monuments surveyed in the previous chapter, meditates on its own incapacity to properly represent the soul of the departed that it seeks to remember. But unlike the monument, the elegy positions itself as primarily textual, and thus is characterised by a profound theatrical and corporeal discomfort with its own status as written work.

The chapter then explores how Mamillius paradoxically embodies the soul's *lack* of representation – even when alive. I will pay particular attention to the figure of breath, an anxious trope in Renaissance culture that could signify the spiritual vitality of the soul or reject signification altogether as a form of complete absence. Leontes's panic results from his realisation, prompted by Mamillius, that the shaky foundation of meaning lie in the precarious delineation and demarcation of a form of non-meaning: the breath creates the word, the child creates the adult, the soul creates life. I will conclude as the play does, with the famous statue scene, which makes the astonishing suggestion that the very realisation that sends Leontes into terror can provide the fabric of a new form of community and understanding. The play gives us the delicate, deeply vulnerable, but ultimately hopeful prospect of balancing the soul within the stage – a way for a rough, earthy place of bodies and things to gesture towards spiritual essence without making recourse to imitation. The elegiac form becomes a practice grounded in the body, and the bodies at the close of the play become linked in a partial abandonment of their capacity to signify but united in their resolute theatricality.

We can think of the play not only alongside the elegy but as a *form* of elegy. The elegy, whose popular topos of inexpressivity allowed for repeated admissions of textual failure, invites its own embodiment: it prompts its reader to engage in a mode of theatre that acknowledges the soul's absolute absence in the realm of the living. Like an elegy, *The Winter's Tale* must admit to the impossibility of recapturing loss through mere signification; but also like an elegy, the play must also acknowledge the necessity, and powerful effects, of freely admitting that impossibility. These sequences further separate the meditations of *The Winter's Tale* from those of the preceding chapters: *The Winter's Tale* finds in its ending not an ironised representation of a world it tacitly condemns but instead a seemingly impossible concatenation of loss and presence, meaning and nonsense, soul and body. In other words, Leontes finally receives his wish for meaning and presence to merge within the confines of the theatrical, but only after he decides, with the passion of the converted, that such a wish is absurd.

Re-placing the Dead

The final moments of *The Winter's Tale*, when Leontes's apparent tragedy transforms into salvation and Hermione's apparent stone transforms into flesh, swiftly weave together multiple narrative resolutions. Within the spectacular bursts of theatrical alchemy – most prominently, the 'statue' of Hermione that descends to greet and forgive her husband – one can lose the more muted strains of the play's political concern with the throne's inheritance.[2] Leontes's last speech, delivered to Hermione, shores up this subplot and underlines its quiet importance to the play as a whole: 'This your son-in-law, / And son unto the King, whose heavens directing, / Is troth-plight to your daughter' (V, iii, 149–51). 'This' is Florizel, Polixenes's son and Perdita's fiancé. The first words Leontes devotes to his wife, thought dead for years, serve to assure her of the royal line's survival.

The final lines also hint at the staging of *The Winter's Tale* itself. After Leontes grants this comfort, he asks the company to follow Paulina 'from hence, where we may leisurely / Each one demand and answer to his part / Performed in this wide gap of time since first / We were disserved. Hastily lead away' (V, iii, 152–5). Robert Weimann, in his study of the endings of Shakespeare's plays, reads this contradiction of pace (the 'leisurely' act of storytelling and the 'hastily' led performers) as the reconciliation between 'an oral culture demanding the leisure of listeners' and 'the swiftness of actors in the economy of a Renaissance theatre'.[3] Leontes must tell his tale, which will take time, but he must also obey the rules of a carefully orchestrated theatrical event, which demands brisk movement through the finale of a dramatic arc. More broadly, the dynamic Weimann identifies, between oral culture and theatrical economy, characterises a broader pattern in the play as a whole, which flecks its dramatic narrative with traces of the folkloric. Autolycus's ballads, the dancing and singing of the Whitsun festival, the clown, and other bodily and oral traditions thread their way through the more traditionally mimetic elements of the play's construction. As Paulina remarks in the final scene, which features the apparent resurrection of Hermione, 'Were it but told you, should be hooted at / Like an old tale' (V, iii, 116–17). The tale has been translated into prescribed action – a translation hinted at when Mamillius, evoking the title of the play itself, tells his mother that 'a sad tale's best for winter' (II, i, 25).

Mamillius is conspicuously unmentioned in Leontes's final lines, though Leontes's emphatic introduction of Florizel to Hermione reminds us of the missing male heir – the void that Florizel can now fill. As such, after the triumphant return of Perdita, the revelation of her identity, the reconciliation of the 'twinned lambs' Leontes and Polixenes, and the theatrical awakening of Hermione, the concluding speech of the play asserts two linked themes that rumble underneath all of these concerns: the replacement of a missing entity with a present one, and the uneasy mixture of the mimetic action of the swift theatre and the oral storytelling of the leisurely recollection that will follow their exit. I want to explore, here, how these two elements relate by underscoring how the final scene's double gesture also provides the mission the elegy, one of the more popular early literary genres. As a medium that must gesture to its own incapacity to replace the lost soul it purports to describe, even as it attempts to flex its poetic voice to impress the reader, the elegy struck a careful balance of wilful degeneration and lyrical fabrication. G. W. Pigman places the elegy within a larger cultural preoccupation of uneasily mingling rationality with spiritual loss. The problems, as he sees it, are the lack of utility – as he asks, simply, 'why cause pain if you know it will not be effective?' – and the fact that, for the elegist, the mission of poetic tribute is oriented more towards the author's faculties than the more painful task of remembering the subject of mourning. Pigman notes that consolation 'is a defense against the breakdown of an ideal of rational self-sufficiency'.[4] *The Winter's Tale*, too, balances oral and literary traditions, and contains an untimely and tragic loss, but the medium of the elegy also suggests a strategy of reading the play as a struggle to recover order and rationality in the face of its own losses. The brief examination of the elegiac tradition that follows seeks to illuminate this strategy, which ultimately highlights the subterranean, though foundational, narrative of absence, performance, and replacement at which Leontes's last lines hint.

Mamillius's death may have reflected more real and historical struggles to its early audiences, since *The Winter's Tale*, as revived by the King's Men in 1612 or 1613, presented itself in the wake the death of an actual prince, Henry Frederick of Wales. Stephen Orgel observes that 'the play would have had an eerie topicality'.[5] The prince's death, in 1612, quickly gave rise to a competitive field of poets and dramatists vying to mourn with the most virtuosity, classical knowledge, and proper fidelity. As Dennis Kay describes:

> a major consequence of the mourning for Prince Henry was that the vernacular funeral elegy had become established almost overnight as a form (or a series of forms and strategies) which every educated person would be expected at some stage to practice. From 1613 the elegy was a canonically laureate form: but it was also established as poetry of social gesture, as a medium for self-examination, and as a form in which writers could learn to imitate, recognize, and investigate the elements of their art.[6]

Ironically, then, a genre marked by the speaker's humility and admission of inability to act in the face of providential machination also encourages formal mastery and an uneasy community of elegiac praxis. As such, specific words or rhetorical figures become borrowed, refashioned and moulded into new lamentations. The proficiency of the poet implicitly – at times palpably – jostles uneasily alongside the professed sadness at the loss of its subject. To take one particularly circuitous example, Arthur Gorges's tribute to the prince, 'The Olympian Catastrophe', borrows exact lines both from his earlier elegy for Philip Sidney and from his friend Edmund Spenser's 'Daphnaida', which Spenser had written to lyricise Gorges's own grief at the passing of his wife. The ostensible subject of the poem becomes, in these circulations, both a horizon and a red herring – the elegy's other purpose, implicit in its knowing recitation, becomes the accumulation of social capital.

Such a hall of mirrors of citation was not an uncommon quality for elegies, or early modern poetry more generally, to possess, but it seems acutely strange given the singularity of the grief that it documents. How can actual loss be registered if the poetic form that sought to communicate it prides itself on citationality, economy and mastery? The elegy, after all, seeks to capture something absolutely distinct and incapable of reproduction. What makes this loss so singular is that it is a loss of life itself – more specifically, the loss of a soul, the absolute manifestation of personhood. Souls cannot be recovered through language; in fact, they resist language altogether. They can only be analogised, pointed at, dwelled on; Edward Herbert's 'Elegy for the Prince' first rehearses a Lear-like lament in the face of the human soul's incomprehensibility by noting that 'Sense is the Soul of Beasts, because none can / Proceed so far as t'understand like Man: / And if souls be more where they love, then where / They animate, why did it not appear / In keeping him alive?'[7] If the human soul distinguishes and magnifies itself where it loves, as opposed to the brute registers of sense, then why did the beloved Henry's soul fail him? The lost soul cannot be theorised as an extension of the physical logic that attends study of the animal soul; instead of capturing through verse the singularity of the soul that eludes understanding, Herbert eulogises the absoluteness of the soul's loss by turning toward his own: 'So though we rest with him, we do appear / To live and stir a while, as if he were / Still quick'ning us? Or do (perchance) we live / And know it not?'[8] The only way to understand the prince's departed soul, for Herbert, is to imagine that we, his subjects, have actually died, and that Henry's soul provides the regenerative force of our own resurrection. Such overt messianism finds a more complex reflection in Jonathan Donne's 'Elegie on the Untimely Death of the Incomparable Prince Henry'. The title hints at the inherent paradox of analogising that which is 'incomparable'; that this notion of irreplaceability was itself a common topos of the elegy only heightens the tension in its purpose. With echoes of his own profoundly influential 'First Anniversarie', Donne asks:

> What had His growth and generation donne?
> When what wee are, his *putrefaction*
> Sustains in us, Earth, which *Griefs* animate?

> Nor hath our World now other *soule* than That.
> And could *Grief* get so high as Heav'n, that *Quire*
> Forgetting This, their new Joy, would desire
> (With grief to see him) *Hee* had staid belowe,
> To rectifie our *Errors* they foreknowe.[9]

The departure of Henry is not only the departure of *his* soul but everyone's soul, and all that is left is rotting and putrefying flesh. The world itself has become a body bereft of soul, only a place of fallen and empty grief so strong it could coax the angels to forego their joy and return Henry to the mortal sphere. The narrator writes from a typically Donnean position of searching incomprehension, struggling for coherence but finally settling for a faithful release of reason (this process is similar to his Holy Sonnet VIII, surveyed in Chapter 2). The writing must fail at describing what it pretends to know because it has lost its animating force – writing cannot help but originate from a human, and humans are now soulless. Words are resigned to absence – and as a result, we are left with the trafficking of tropes and phrases among the elegists, almost as an admission of the lack of hope to properly evoke Henry's loss.

We may, however, read the attempted mastery of language as closely connected to, rather than in opposition to, the act of mourning. As a compensatory gesture, the poet overfills the page with knowingly gratuitous demonstrations of writerly command, as if highlighting the desperate need to wrest control of language in the face of grief. Futility, after all, is baked into the very form, and demonstrations of facility only underline its failure. David Shaw identifies a 'paradox of verbal power' as characteristic of the early modern tradition:

> Though the elegist's words seem grounded in a world of imitative magic, where changing the right name, like finding the right number to dial on the phone, can channel a beneficent force or deflect a malign one, how can the efficacy of the speech act, its passage from ignorance to knowledge, be guaranteed in advance? . . . And if they are a mere audacious boast, they lack the stamp of truth. How can a word of power be empirically grounded and still bring into being the state of affairs it purports to describe?[10]

The poetry of the words *seem* to be magical, as if capable of conjuring the very thing they describe, but they must fail – and that failure, far from attenuating the power of the work, in fact provides it with a singular power. The closed course of referentiality must separate itself from the 'stamp of truth' needed to invoke properly the dead. The gap between the purported power of textuality and its obvious failure mirrors the loss of the subject and thus replicates the work of mourning.

One of the residual effects of this built-in futility is that elegies frequently gestured outside of themselves, as if straining and seeking to break from their physical forms. The physical pages of Joshua Sylvester's collection *Lachrymae Lachrymarum* vividly demonstrate this desire to escape the material confines of the work: utilising a 'white line' printing practice that would have been dated and difficult at the time, the *Lachrymae* fills its pages with huge smears of black ink upon which the words and designs are written in white, as if smudging and abnegating its own status as a static object removed from the world of the living. The medium of the elegy thus echoes its own desperately overdetermined failure, hinting instead, with its clear physical presence – its insistence on its own materiality – at the actual embodied practice of mourning. Such practice cannot be found among the textual operations of poetry, but instead among the living: the elegy seeks to displace its praxis onto the reader or speaker.

This displacement from text to ritual comprises its own elegiac topos. The poem's insufficiency produces the prompt for physical manifestations of remembrance in the actual world. In Virgil's fifth eclogue, an acknowledged classical influence on the Renaissance form, the shepherds Menalcus and Mopsus share remembrances of their lost friend Delphis.[11] But their words do not attempt to recall or describe the departed so much as delineate the rituals needed to properly commemorate him: 'Scatter the ground with flowers, all you shepherds', Mopsus asks, 'And shade with mourning trees the woodland springs – / thus Daphnis has commanded for his honor. / Then build a tomb and place on the tomb these verses: / "Daphnis" was known to these woods and known to the stars; / Lovely the flock, and lovelier still the shepherd.'[12] Menalcus's reply promises annual songs of devotion. The elegies do not make immediate compacts – they make instead promises that call for future action. They are, like Coriolanus's unfulfilled promise to build a shrine for his women, more prompts for proper and full remembrance than they are embodiments of that remembrance. Registering loss takes active work – something more than the careful arrangement of perfectly arranged words that become socially codified and canonised among peers.

The elegy's two contrary strains of textual mastery and embodied practice weave their way through *The Winter's Tale*. Mamillius is not only a lost prince when dead, though: he is a resolutely corporeal and oral one when alive, a whispering, storytelling boy whose seeming replacement by Florizel – and more crucially, as I will later elaborate, by Perdita – demonstrates not only the recovery of the kingdom but also the apparent victory of a literary logic and order over an embodied and expressive one. 'Seeming' and 'apparent' must accompany this formulation because the play beautifully complicates this appearance of victory with the statue scene, which suggests a more subtle dance between the textual and the theatrical, one reminiscent of the wobbly marriage of fixity and futility that characterises the elegy.

To draw these resonances out further, we can turn to a collection of elegies for Prince Henry – specifically, a collection by a group of dramatists: Cyril Tourneur, John Webster and Thomas Heywood. These poems seem particularly attuned to their own theatrical supplementation, to the *act* of reading that must accompany them; the capacities of the authors to write for the stage seem to inform their ability to craft themselves dialogically with their audience. As such they engage with what Bruce R. Smith, writing on Renaissance balladry, calls the 're-membering' of texts with bodily reference.[13] For Smith, instructions for singing demand physical participation from their readers in order to complete their execution by including 'somatic notation' that 'tells the reader just what to do with his or her body'.[14]

For Tourneur, Henry's passing produces a grief so great it carries the potential to physically disrupt the very act of reading: 'I cannot blame thee, if thou read'st not right, / Or understand'st not, for I know thy fight, / With weeping is imperfect, if not blind / And sorrow does (almost) distract thy mind.'[15] The language is, of course, hagiographically exaggerated, excessive, and overly compensatory. Yet the implicit braggadocio of Tourneur's words – he has the power to make you cry – also admits to an awareness of the reader through somatic notation. At one point the writing stops itself upon reflecting on the impossibility of its very subject, exclaiming 'Dead! 'Tis above my knowledge how we live / To speak it.'[16] Later, Tourneur compares Henry's ephemeral life on earth to his eternal life in art (presumably, and circuitously, in such manifestations as Tourneur's own elegy), asking 'How can *that* perish? That ever will keepe / Because th'impression of it is too deepe.'[17] As with *The Winter's Tale*, though, such considerations of art, when centred on a prince, are tied to those of succession. Henry's 'sicknesse' arrived to 'deprive Him of the fortunate / Succession of the greatnesse of the State, which he was born to'.[18] While this lament gestures to the actual 'succession' of his younger brother, Charles, we can also read the attempt to reconcile the loss of a royal subject, as a 'natural' living entity, with the written succession of the text that fills his place.

The particular element that makes this textual succession unbalanced is the soul, which Tourneur cannot contain nor even explain. Indulging in a bout of imagery still familiar today, he reports that 'I see his spirit turn'd into a starre, / Whose influence makes that His own virtues are / Succeeded justlie'. [19] The image is a slightly more tempered version of Herbert's transference of the prince's soul into the bodies of his mourners. For Tourneur, Henry's soul cannot be present on earth, but it can exert powerful influence from afar; the elegy, and the performance it prompts, must not supply a perfect substitute. Tourneur cannot replicate the power of God by reclaiming or even allowing contact with the soul, so his writing locates its power instead in breaking its own narrative by smudging its print with tears or lamenting the failure of its own vocabulary ('Dead!'). These breakages, he implies, are the symptoms of the soul's absence, and we must settle for symptoms rather than the cosmically distant self. As with Mopsus and

Menalcus, we can only make promises for the future that we will be able to properly remember: the attempt at poeticising in the present must fail and the body must be utilised to complete the proper action.

John Webster, in his contribution, likewise labours to impress the reader of his own relative frailty in recreating the true presence of the lost prince. First, he attempts to find a proper analogy, wondering why one would create such a divine being only to destroy it. Unless, he laments, 'I could imagine one so fond / To build a gorgeous pallace, but to race it: / A cunning painter that hath gone beyond / His skill, in a faire picture, to deface it / Before the world his cunning understand'.[20] But rather than follow that logic further, he turns his blame to the more lateral target of the social realm: 'What monster may we call this? / Sinne: our sinne, / When one alone (and but one) that of pride, / Cast angels from the highest *Cherubin* / All their bright gloryes in the *Abisme* to hide'.[21] The weight of our envy crushed Henry, Webster argues, before calling upon the readers to cast their eyes inward to survey their own culpability. The text operates as a prompt for its witness to confess and as a result catalyses Henry's death into a vessel of possible atonement. The call to absolution follows the reduction of the child to a mere aesthetic object, a 'palace' that is razed or 'picture' that has been defaced. With the soul gone, we are left only with the husk of Henry's body, which Webster, like Tourneur, links to the empty vessel of writing that he produces. This vessel, it follows, can pay homage to the power of the soul only by showing incapacity to engage with it – while virtuousically showing its ability to lyrically invoke its subject. The elegy de-souls Henry and renders him rational and classifiable, capable of implementation within the scheme of the work itself: the primal act of the elegy, the notation of the departure of the soul, thus allows for the virtuosity of the poet to impress itself onto the purely textual form that remains in the soul's wake and demonstrate mastery over the lifeless words, as empty as the husks of flesh that Donne observes around him. Words in a fallen world may be symbols of decay, but they also provide vehicles for lyrical showmanship. Likewise, Webster offers a call to ritual that cannot hope to change the situation but instead revels in this very hopelessness.

A twist on this manoeuvre, whereby the elegiac object is supplanted by the self-consciously empty lyricism that laments it, occurs in Ben Jonson's famous 'On My First Sonne', which refutes its sentimentality even as it suggests an incalculable and intimately felt death. The piece is worth quoting in full, so as to trace the implications of its quietly radical conclusion:

> Farewell, thou child of my right hand, and joy;
> My sinne was too much hope of thee, lov'd boy,
> Seven yeeres tho'wert lent to me, and I thee pay,
> Exacted by thy fate, on the just day.
> O, could I loose all father, now. For why
> Will man lament the state he should envie?
> To have so soone scap'd worlds, and fleshes rage,
> And, if no other miserie, yet age?
> Rest in soft peace, and, ask'd, say here doth lye
> BEN JONSON his best piece of *poetrie*.
> For whose sake, hence-forth, all his vowes be such,
> As what loves may never like too much.[22]

Tourneur and Webster attempt to cast their own poetic work as necessarily feeble substitutions of the child whose loss they catalogue. But Jonson intensifies this surrogation by inverting it. The poem is not standing in for a child. The child is in fact already a sublime form of poetry, the 'best piece' that Jonson could create. The work oddly, if logically, registers a kind of happiness at Jonson's son dying by suggesting that, since heaven surely is a greater place to be than the miserable, fleshy world of earth, lamentation is absurd. In addition, it suggests that in death, the lyrical energy of the lost son will continue to mobilise his father's creativity.[23] In death, the child, without its spiritual essence, is manageable, yoked into symbolic labour as literary muse. The vacuum of his absence allows processes of writing to rush in and fill the space of his missing body with layers of malleable textuality. Clifton Spargo has gone so far as to connect this malleability to the specifically financial language employed in the poem: 'The statement of economy in Jonson's poem is set against the form of hopeful love that dies with his son. If Jonson employs the financial conceit in the spirit of renunciation, there can be little doubt that the economics he describes come off as stingy.'[24] The child becomes a figure on the ledger, balanced out by the facility of the language.

The *locus classicus* of Renaissance elegies is surely Milton's 'Lycidas', which similarly supplants the dead with products of its own lyrical facility. While Milton writes his work long after Shakespeare's play, its brilliant playfulness with – and subversion of – the Renaissance elegy's tropes give us a powerful reflection and critique of the elements employed by Jonson, Tourneur, Webster, and others. As a more polyvocal and ambivalent work, 'Lycidas' allows tremors on its surface of textual resolution to create a troubled presentation in marked distinction to the seeming ease by which Jonson and Henry's elegists attain ethical closure. In its late movement towards regeneration, the voice of the lamenting shepherd – the uncouth swain – takes over the narrative to secure the dead Lycidas as reanimated on the ocean floor, moving quickly from the menace of the water to its reception of the sun, which sinks 'in the ocean bed / And yet anon repairs his drooping head, /And tricks his beams, and with new-spangled ore /Flames in the forehead of the morning sky'.[25] Likewise, the poem relays, Jesus allows Lycidas passage to heaven. But the story does not end there. It instead repositions this divine progression within an earthy vehicle: 'Thus sang the uncouth swain to th'oaks and rills', the final stanza asserts, noting that with 'eager thought warbling his Doric lay' the shepherd ends his day, only to rise again.[26] Divine and cosmic elements of the story locate themselves in the warbling, uneven sound of a worker calming himself before retiring: the entire poem repositions itself as the residue of a rough, aural expression lost to time. The poem answers the promise of the shepherds in Virgil's eclogue: it delivers in the present the song of mourning that Mopsus's and Menalcus's songs only assured would happen in the future.

As with Weimann's analysis of the finale of *The Winter's Tale*, the poem's closure can be thought of as somehow quasi-textual, hinting at a kinetic and oral performance that it cannot, by nature, absorb. Milton pressurises the dramatic tensions inherent to the pieces that lament Henry. And as with Tourneur's smudging of his words with tears, the reminder of orality's uneasy bind with literality allows the seeming fixity of the piece – a fixity that Jonson neatly executes – to be challenged. Milton's insistence on the theatrical qualities of the pastoral form, like the white-line blackness that punishes the pages of the *Lachrymae*, emphasises what is only implicit in its setting – that the transitory, bodily and voiced expression of grief, by echoing the breathy animations of life, provides a more fitting tribute to the dead than the neat assembly of words on the page. Such an emphasis on the 'rough' qualities of the poem chafes slightly against the popularly received notion of the pastoral as a 'utopia' or 'ideal' world, but as Eric Smith elaborates, following William Empson, 'the pastoral world may be less an ideal to be captured or recaptured than a simplification, a sample society where what are thought to be the fundamental issues of living together are brought out and discussed away from the temporal and incidental distractions of the present'.[27] And yet *Lycidas* divulges the seams of the attempt to import the complexities of mourning into the self-conscious simplification of the pastoral form. Grounding his ode in the voice, Milton resists textuality's seductive call to bring resolution and suffocate and codify the living soul as a poem, as with Jonson's son. The heteroglossic fringe between the oral and the literary realises the theatricality that Mikhail Bakhtin locates as 'an indeterminacy, a certain semantic open-endedness, a living contact with unfinished, still-evolving contemporary reality (the open-ended present)'.[28] Rather than include the carnivalesque clowns and scatological gestures that disrupt the illusion of order, however, 'Lycidas' creates indeterminacy through the constant, radical reminder that life itself, figured absolutely in the soul, belies description. Milton allows the divine its power, but can only frame it in the serene, unstable trappings of song.

The elegies surveyed here find themselves inherently and intentionally locked in crises of mourning: to narrate the loss of the soul into literary systems must admit to what cannot be translated, and at the same time the narration must attempt to retain a fragment of memory of the now-absent person. Such a fragment becomes figured as a ghost adrift in a system of meaning – a soul in search of a body, or a performance in search of a text. For Tourneur, it appears as a bodying forth of tears and metacritique of poetic faculty; for Milton, the aural songs underneath the printed tribute.

After his exit, Mamillius disappears from the stage, and beyond noting his death in cursory terms in Act III, Scene II, the play 'forgets' the child. It does not seem to attempt the elegiac, even though the cultural forces that surround it would seem to demand it. Yet *The Winter's Tale* possesses fragments of the elegiac medium even if it does not expressly orient its narrative toward the same conclusions. The play allows the rough, pastoral Whitsun festivities of Bohemia, as transitory as the swain's warble, to appear as a setting for an unsaid cry of remembering. Mamillius makes a ghostly sort of return as Perdita pines for 'flowers o'th'spring' for Florizel and begins to catalogue the different classical and heraldic associations of daffodils, violets, primroses, oxlips and the 'flower-de-luce' before exclaiming 'O, these I lack to make you garlands of, and my sweet friend, / To strew him o'er and o'er' (IV, iv, 127–9). She partakes, here, in the fecund, floral world in which Virgil's shepherds find an ample medium for remembrance – and Florizel, apparently familiar with this elegiac echo, misunderstands her and asks 'What, like a corpse?' (IV, iv, 129). As Jonathan Crewe remarks, the passage 'echoes the burial-ritual of pastoral elegy, in which flowers are strewn over the body of the dead shepherd . . . here, however, pastoral elegy is at once displaced and recontextualised by the play's movement into a world of post-tragic regeneration'.[29] The regeneration is still tinged with loss: Perdita quickly corrects Florizel, but the sudden slap of 'corpse' recalls the delicate line between celebrations of life and death – and more directly recalls the actual dead who have disappeared from the play.

While the play might overtly cite textual elements of the elegy with the ease of Gorges repurposing Sidney's lines, it also contains traces of the more unstable, bodily and theatrical practice that the elegy demands as supplement to and acknowledgement of its own failure – the tears, cries and sighs that elude semantic capture, or the smudges of black ink that show the futility of the linguistic medium at all. This unsteady kind of mourning is located in the expressions of the body itself, most vibrantly in Leontes's violent phobia in the beginning of the play. In his constant denial of the correlation of meaning with the careful play of political and social correspondences that surrounds him, Leontes represents a sinister inversion of Milton's final stanza. Rather than find comfort in discovering creaking voices that construct the textual logic of Sicilia, he becomes terrified by them. His wracks of doubt in the first act stem from irruptions of bodily, temporal and aural production into the mechanisms of his perception. Even before Mamillius dies, Leontes demonstrates an incapacity to exist in a literary logic that would assimilate death into a poem. He is *too* alive to the constant paratextual murmurings that surround him:

> Is whispering nothing?
> Is leaning cheek to cheek? Is meeting noses?
> Kissing with inside lip? Stopping the career
> Of laughter with a sigh? – A note infallible
> Of breaking honesty. (I, ii, 281–6)

This menacing fantasy of adultery escapes clear assignments of reference: bodies touching and leaning, the sounds of laughter and sighing blurring into indices of infidelity. Leontes establishes himself here as devoid of the representational virtuosity that will be necessary to comprehend the loss of his son. Such comprehension displaces itself from the central character and onto the acts of memorialising that occur in the fringes, from Autolycus's monstrous ballads to Antigonus's stories to calm the infant Perdita. Suppressing such catalyzing actions, Leontes instead attempts to deal with the enormity of messy, bodily, aural actuality.

Of course, at this point Mamillius is not yet dead. But the young prince, in his relentlessly performative qualities, embodies the exact elements of Leontes's nightmarish vision come to life. He presents an entity that exists outside of textual systems of logic and thus lacks literary articulation. Such illegibility stems inherently from Mamillius's status as a child, but is underlined in his specific actions, which expose a structural illegibility running underneath the narrative lineaments of the adult world. In other words, the play suggests the ghosts of the unassimilated not only haunt the stage, but in fact comprise the stage. And as I hope to demonstrate in the following section, the whispering resistance that the prince effects places him squarely in the realm of the spiritual as much as it does the incoherent. He is a being who, like his father, refuses the resolution of poetic assimilation, and attempts to find faith in the transitory, holy breaths of life that animate the more comprehensible and negotiable human bodies. As the soul of the play, he must, like Coriolanus, be purged from its smooth construction of imitative narrative – as must Leontes's madness, linked as it is to the prince. However, instead of returning to the production of meaning that characterises Venice and Rome at the close of *The Merchant of Venice* and *Coriolanus*, *The Winter's Tale* finds a way to register the loss of Mamillius in the bodies of its characters – it suggests a communal way that expressive and soulful performance can coexist with the economising logic of representation.

Is Whispering Everything?

An understanding of Mamillius as an expressive figure resistant to the mimetic economy of the adult world – and more abstractly, to the representative logic that a production of *The Winter's Tale* itself would demand – finds its initiation with Mamillius's behaviour in Act II, Scene I, in which the prince enters, largely oblivious to the depths of jealous rage into which his father has just descended and bantering with his attendant ladies:

> FIRST LADY. Come, my gracious lord,
> Shall I be your playfellow?
> MAMILLIUS. No, I'll none of you.
> FIRST LADY. Why, my sweet lord?
> MAMILLIUS. You'll kiss me hard, and speak to me as if I were a baby still. *(To another lady)* I love you better.
> (II, i, 1–6)

This exchange offers some possible explanations for Mamillius's troubling status. First, it positions him as liminally masculine. While he acts coy with the ladies, as if engaged in heteronormative flirtation, he also approaches re-gendering himself in the process.[30] His interest in make-up, which he learned 'out of women's faces' (II, i, 12), places him within a traditionally feminised aesthetic – and, following the popularly sexist line of thinking, as a practitioner of deceit and subterfuge. In addition, as we shortly discover from Leontes, he still had a wet nurse, a practice associated in the early modern period with domesticity and womanliness.[31] Furthermore, the dialogue positions him as, naturally, childlike: while he balks at being treated as 'a baby still', and in the prior scene has asserted to his father that, rather than 'take eggs for money' he will 'fight' (I, ii, 160), he will still sit by his mother and has not yet been breeched (I, ii, 154).

These qualities make Mamillius a creaturely variation on the full-fledged adult human.[32] While resonant with Leontes's fears, though, they are not unique to him – they are, in fact, essential to the Renaissance conception of childhood.[33] While the play may, here, softly interrogate the implications of the child's placement in schemes of political and social power (compare this behaviour, for instance, to Coriolanus's butterfly-mammocking son), Mamillius represents a different sort of problematic subject by operating as a wholly *theatrical* figure. The child's actions also make manifest a childish variation of Leontes's imagined whispering – the turning heads, hard kissing, and coy preference of a different lover, all couched in childish games, miniaturise the feverish visions of Hermione's faithlessness. Lowell Gallagher notes that Mamillius is an 'aporia, an impossible locution' who suggests 'the intervention of a temporality grounded in bodily process'.[34] Gallagher's conception situates the prince within the realm of the theatre, a medium both ephemeral and dependent on bodily manipulation. And so Mamillius signifies both a passage of time and a collection of flesh, two qualities that locate themselves outside of the semantic cohesion that characterises rhetorical and literary narrative. As a confluence of forms of narrative resistance, Mamillius marks the text with his theatrical presence and interferes in more textual and representational communicative channels. This quality is present in his first mention, in the first scene, in which he is associated with inscrutable sound: 'You have an *unspeakable* comfort of your young prince Mamillius', observes Archidamus, addressing Camillo (I, i, 32–3, emphasis mine).

Mamillius demonstrates a similar strategy of theatrical irritation by lodging his body as a silent presence in his father's attempts to speak with him. Again, such silence is implicated in Mamillius's age by recalling the etymological link of *infant* to *infans*, or speechlessness. The supposedly quiet nature of children was enough of an established trope that Ben Jonson could satirically deploy its expectations in *Epicene*, where a young boy successfully poses as a quiet, seductive woman.[35] Mamillius's silence, however, worries itself into Leontes's consciousness in a more fundamental fashion than mere childish reflection.[36] In the play's proper opening, as the king laments his state with self-doubt and loathing, his attempt to narrate his emotional trajectory stutters as it encounters reminders of the lingering Mamillius's presence:

> Inch-thick, knee-deep; o'er head and ears a fork'd one.
> Go, play, boy, play: thy mother plays, and I
> Play too: but so disgraced a part, whose issue
> Will hiss me to my grave: contempt and clamour
> Will be my knell. Go, play, boy, play. (I, ii, 184–8)[37]

He ends, later, with the question 'How now, boy?' (I, ii, 207). Mamillius's body refracts the speech's intended progress: Leontes's rhetorical facility falters over discursive stopgaps, marked by the repeated phrase 'Go, play, boy, play' as it proceeds to its conclusion, and finally he questions, rather than demands, his son's exit. Although Mamillius remains textually silent, he remains theatrically present, persistent in his mere form. As readers, we can infer his lack of movement as he prompts the desperate refrain from his father. Yet the desperately prolix Leontes also finds himself seeking identification in the silent and bodily child he compulsively attempts to banish. As T. G. Bishop explains, the tension of the speech derives from this betrayed desire for familial sameness:

> Leontes' search for connection to his son thus gives him both less and more than he desires: less in that it does not seem satisfactorily to still the doubts and intimations that prompted it in the first place, more in that it revives in him thoughts and modes of thought long thought overcome or put aside – thoughts that re-emerge from the strange amalgam of childhood, friendship, rivalry, and courtship that the scene anneals.[38]

The conflation of desire's surplus and lack results in a failed scene of identification but a successful scene of association. Without saying anything, Mamillius reminds his father of the imagined 'playing' of Hermione. This evocation of bodily betrayal is occasioned by the son's role as evidence of sexual encounter – and, it follows, a reminder of the selfsame erotic action that prompted Hermione's present pregnancy – but also in his strategy of being merely a body, silent and obstinate. Mamillius insinuates his body into the increasingly failed narrative of his father, and his presence becomes measured by the ripples of the language he stirs.

The foundational instance of Mamillius evoking spiritual vocal disturbances in the field of writing, however, is his whispering to Hermione. His mother asks Mamillius to 'sit by us, / And tell's a tale' (II, ii, 22–3) but the prince ignores the 'us' and, upon joining Hermione, insists on telling it 'softly' so that 'yon crickets', the ladies, 'shall not hear it' (II, ii, 30–1). The audience cannot hear it either, yet it occurs before our eyes. The story he tells his mother is 'a sad tale' that's 'best for winter' about 'a man' who 'Dwelt by a churchyard' (II, ii, 29–30). This is the tableau that Leontes witnesses amidst his dialogue with Antigonus that prompts him to stop his speech and demand that Hermione 'Give me the boy' (II, ii, 56). The terror of this moment originates not only from the tale possessing a strikingly similar label as the play itself (a resonance that has led to many Mamillius-centred staging decisions by theatre directors). By whispering his tale, unheard, Mamillius implies his silent and invisible role as author of the governing narratives of his adult counterparts – and of the storytelling and physical production of voice needed to construct the appearance of a staged reality. He offers a brief revelation of the resolutely theatrical elements that covertly create ordinarily seamless mimetic coherence.[39] This situation particularly implicates Leontes, given his professed fear of whispering and aversion to associating himself with the performative qualities of his son. And yet, as Mamillius states simply: 'I am like you, they say' (I, ii, 207). His actions reflect Leontes's panic back to him, both in details of the brief snippet of the story we hear – the man in the churchyard echoing Leontes's belief that he will be hissed into the grave – and, again, in the fact that the story is whispered. The hushed, secret, withheld story, far from being 'nothing', in fact threatens to be the very construction of his logical world.

The non-verbal might prompt Leontes's terror, but the infantile practice of Mamillius's insistent presence also links the whispering and murmuring childish prince with the soul that remains both distanced from and conjoined with the body. Specifically, the non-linguistic instance of *breath*, as a non-material yet palpable event, recalls the strategies of conceiving of the soul without compromising its form into something overly tangible and worldly. Breath is precisely what the elegies beg for as complement to their self-consciously airless construction. Breath also figures Mamillius as a soul-figure – the elegies' missing yet monstrous pulse of life. More broadly, the narrative of recovery and resolution that follows his death makes a radical proposal as to breath's relation to liveliness, performance and meaning.

The foundation of breath's associations occurs, naturally, in Genesis, where, having made the world, God 'formed man of the dust of the ground, and breathed into his nostrils the breath of life; and man became a living soul' (Gen. 2: 7).[40] The breath is what separates Donne's putrefying bodies from cosmic communion, dust from creature. In the early modern era, finding ways to reconcile life's essential breathiness with humankind's legal, political and humanistic modes of self-definition created significant dramatic and poetic *frisson*. Later in the seventeenth century, Milton, in rewriting the story of the Fall, gives Eve one of the more profound meditations on the matter. Contemplating her sin, she professes that

> one doubt
> Pursues me still, least all I cannot die,
> Least that pure breath of Life, the Spirit of Man

Which God inspir'd, cannot together perish
With this corporeal Clod; then in the Grave,
Or in some other dismal place who knows
But I shall die a living Death? O thought
Horrid, if true! Yet why? It was but breath
Of Life that sinn'd; what dies but what had life
And sin? the Bodie properly hath neither.
All of me then shall die . . .[41]

When Eve sinned, was her breath or dusty vesture responsible? Breath, after all, is the only component of her subjectivity that could sin, since it is life itself, and yet the soul cannot die, so how could proper punishment be doled out? She ends with a desire for the unity of soul and body, but this unity is the result of the soul chaining itself, as penance, to the innocent but dreadfully inanimate human form. Gertrude, in *Hamlet* – notably framed as a version of Eve after her expulsion[42] – wrestles with a similar scandal when confronted with her son's demand that she not tell anyone of his secret disclosures: 'Be thou assur'd, if words be made of breath, / And breath of life, I have no life to breathe / What thou hast said to me' (III, iv, 197–9). Words and logic are crafted from the physical manipulation of breath, which carries life. The soulful whispers of God that animate the body must always be the foundations of the logic that proceeds from their manipulation, much as a non-speaking child is the originator of the adult whose language creates systems of order. Eve is able to hold both breath and word together, exposing their inherently frictional coexistence, just as Gertrude ties together her own livelihood – which has just been explicitly threatened by her son – to her silence, retaining an inward breath that keeps her body from being merely body.

Breath could be figured as alternately non-linguistic spiritual component or empty nothingness; this ambivalence threads through several potent religious meditations on its relation to word and Word, holiness and absence. By eluding clear meaning, breath could avoid the deceptive potential of language that for Catholic and Protestant alike provided a path to sinfulness. In Genesis, direct infiltration of God's breath links Adam to divinity more than the animals, also formed of the earth, who lack this animating force and whose identities arise instead through the names inscribed by Adam himself (2: 19).[43] Eve, born of Adam's own flesh, contains the trace of the breath, but the beasts do not. As such, humanity contains the insubstantial mark of separation from the animal, though all share the same material foundation. Augustine, in *City of God*, meditates on the origin and nature of breath in this passage to explain that the breath of God is 'a soul which he had already made, or rather by willing that the actual breath which he produced when he breathed on him should be the soul of man', because, he concludes, 'to breathe is to produce a breath'.[44] After considering how the breath of God could be or transform into a soul, Augustine ends in strategic redundancy: breathing produces breath. The paucity of description marks the necessary lack of linguistic means available to describe the soul's foundations, which necessarily exist beyond comprehensibility.

Attempting to position the soul's status as a breath of life, among its several competing metaphors, manifestations, incarnations and rhetorical usages, proves difficult work. Yet this positioning also proved essential for Reformist iconoclasts who sought a reassessment of the entire terrain of humankind's relationship with the divine. Heinrich Bullinger, the successor to the Swiss Church after the arch-Reformer Huldrych Zwingli, continued his predecessor's theoretical provocations, questioning the ontological assumptions of Catholic and less fervent Reformation theology. His relative extremism presents a limit case that emphasises the shared concern with breath's spiritual properties: both Augustinian–Catholic and more hard-line Puritanical traditions allowed for its simultaneous kinship to the soul and the potential danger of it being undetectable. In his sermon 'Of the reasonable Soule of man', Bullinger takes up the musing on Milton's Eve on the soul in terms of its rhetorical, and perhaps physical, proximity to breath, spirit, body and God. The words used to stand in for the soul are, according to Bullinger, empty and useless vessels given solely metaphorical import – an echo of the Zwinglian rejection of transubstantiation – and harmless as such. It follows, however, that the implication of understanding the soul, and of having the very seat of reason *be* a soul, must simply be incorrect. Summing up the necessary incomprehensibility of the soul, Bullinger arrives where Eve begins. The soul's ineffability, he concludes, is why we conceive of it as a breath, an insubstantial and physically unclaimable, though palpable, movement of air. He proposes

> that the nature or disposition of the same might after a sort be shadowed out, and that by the workes or actions thereof, & by such qualities as the scripture doth attribute. There are some therfore which haue said that the soule is the spirite of life, created after the image of god, & breathed into ye bodie of man.[45]

The soul, then, does not inject itself directly into the faculties of reason, yet neither is it wholly absent or utterly incapable of producing phenomena within the world. Instead, Bullinger argues, with poetic delicacy, it 'might after a sort be shadowed out', cloaked yet perceptible – hence, the sense of the spirit as inspiration, an invisible but palpable breath. These shadowings-out of reality are precisely what terrify Leontes. They form the evidence that he feels must be real, despite – or, in fact, *because* – of its lack of tangibility. The swain's warble and Tourneur's smudges all perform this shadowing-out, and so too does Mamillius, who exposes the breathy foundations of an epistemic logic that falters as it covers its tracks.

Determining the difference between a whisper and a breath – an empty expression of air and a life-giving divine trace – is a critical activity for Catholics and puritans alike, and for *The Winter's Tale*. Bullinger's semantic problem, which rapidly coheres into a spiritual and ontological one, is that the soul must be accounted for even though it cannot attach itself to the actions and words that evoke it. His approval of breath imagery, as a rhetorical strategy that navigates the soul's paradox, thus found itself at the crossroads of disappearance and faith. Breath emerges, appropriately, in one of the more contested scriptures in early modern debates, the Book of James.[46] A principal body of evidence for Counter-Reformists hoping to undermine the Pauline dictum of 'faith alone', the book attempts to differentiate between the shadows of souls in the world and the whispers of heretics. In a passage widely cited by Catholic opponents to the Reformation, the narrator asks: 'What doth it profit, my brethren, though a man say he hath faith, and have not works? Can faith save him? If a brother or sister be naked, and destitute of daily food, and one of you say unto them, Depart in peace, be ye warmed and filled; notwithstanding ye give them not those things which are needful to the body; what doth it profit?' (2: 14–17). This point is emphasised soon after by relating faith and action to body and soul, respectively: 'For as the body without the spirit is dead, so faith without works is dead also' (2: 26). The slipperiness of breath is such that it can be marshalled to prove the exact opposite of the point Bullinger makes: breath, as the animating spirit of the body, is an action, not an imprint of faith – faith is, in fact, like flesh alone, inanimate. Breath is action, but action is inherently without morality.

Proper knowledge of the distinction between the breath of faith becoming animated into action, on the one hand, and devilish speech, on the other, proves critical to proper spiritual practice. If the borders between them shift, one could fall into an extreme state of doubt, recoil from the ability of words to correlate to deeper meaning, and place too much faith in the imperceptible. The line between inward faith and sinful licentiousness is delicate enough that Thomas More can label them as one and the same in his defence of Catholic doctrine. Responding to attacks on the belief in purgatory, he attacks the notion of *sola fide*, implying – in an echo of the narrator of the Book of James – that mere faith means 'you may do what you want, and that if you obey any law or ruler, that is all of your own courtesy and not because of any duty at all, faith having set you in such a licentious liberty'; he concludes that this 'and many a mad, mad delusion will be the gospel that then will be preached'.[47] Delusions are exactly what initiate the dramatic mechanisms of *The Winter's Tale*, with Leontes bracingly addressing his own 'affection' in a peculiar inward dialogue:

> May't be
> Affection? – Thy intention stabs the centre,
> Thou does make possible things not so held,

Communicat'st with dreams – how can this be?
With what's unreal thou coactive art,
And fellow'st nothing. Then 'tis very credent
Thou mayst co-join with something and thou dost,
And that beyond commission, and I find it,
And that to the infection of my brains
And hard'ning of my brows (I, ii, 137–46)

The speech begins addressed to his son, then plunges inward to speak to his own affection, which stabs at his 'centre' and speaks to him through his dreams. David Ward has carefully excavated the peculiar rhythms of this speech through a historical understanding of the term 'affection'; as Ward explains, drawing from Richard Hooker's discussion in *Of the Laws of Ecclesiastical Polity*, the word links this speech to the Aristotelian soul:

> In the contemporary psychology, affections were held to be aspects or manifestations of the appetite. They were thus a product of the operations of the sensitive soul rather than of the rational or intellective soul, and were therefore to some extent independent of the Will and of the Reason . . . Since they are appetitive rather than voluntary, according to Hooker, they are incapable of discriminating between what is possible and what is impossible. It is only the Reason which can distinguish, and the Reason operates through the Will, not through Appetite.[48]

If affections become unruly, the reasonable soul cannot keep them in check – it can only inquire, examine, and guess at their condition and effects on the overall human soul and body. Leontes's monologue gives voice to this inquiry and locates the symptoms of his affections' 'stabbing' at his centre – his soul – and leaking out into his rational perceptions, shuttled out in dreams and infections. If we accept this definition of affection, Ward persuasively argues, other seemingly puzzling aspects of the speech click into place. The 'intention' that Leontes mentions would refer a particular valence of the term as 'an intensification and multiplication of symptomatic disorders which arise from the affections in such a way that the soul is swamped, wounded, and cannot cope'.[49] The threshold between possible and impossible becomes inscrutable and the rational soul becomes overwhelmed with a preponderance of possibly false images and thoughts. In a tragically lucid moment, Leontes gives voice to his rational acceptance of his inevitable irrationality. The 'centre' of his soul returns soon thereafter in the image of the centre in those 'foundations' he builds upon not big enough to bear a 'schoolboy's top'. If we take the centre to be his rational soul, we are given a glimpse at its rapid miniaturisation as it is overcome by the affections that obscure Leontes's capacity to gauge the possible.

But as this book has maintained, this instability is something coiled within the construction of the soul as much as it is a form of spiritual disease. The uneasy threshold of the breath of life and the whisper of madness finds a reflection in the unsteady borders of the soul's maintenance of sanity. Leontes is both sick with delusion and hyper-aware of an essential condition of spiritual life.

Interpretation should Abuse

The conflicts elaborated in Leontes's speech to his affection hover over *The Winter's Tale* as a whole. The play is filled with whispers, breaths, and the anxieties of determining which is which. Repeatedly, and with increasing urgency, its characters attempt to narrate the potentially damaging immediacy of the expressive present, which finds ephemeral 'meaning' only in its own gestures and behaviour, into a fixed and possibly mastered mimetic narrative – to not have the breath alone exist in its unruly, illegible (and possibly spiritual) presence, but to recategorise it as essentially linked to meaning, economisable and accountable. In elegiac terms, the play positions itself as torn between the unknowability of the soul, which it positions as *already present* in the living body, and the capacity to narrate meaning out of the belief, however illusory, in the absolute power of word and gesture to correlate to essence. The dramatic action progresses at the hinge of non-sense transforming into either an affirmation of faith or an irruption of disorder. Polixenes introduces the dangers of unheard murmuring when he initially declines Leontes's offer to have him stay longer: 'I am questioned by my fears of what may chance / Or breed upon our absence, that may blow / No sneaping winds at home' (I, ii, 11–13). The illegibility of rumour and insult in Bohemia gives him pause and prompts fears of political unrest. Polixenes, here, is a more subdued and socially adept version of his twinned lamb, who will shortly fear sneaping winds everywhere.

Polixenes, however, still covets the pure, and notably presexual, spirituality of childhood, even if it can resemble an engine for dangerously whispering winds. In recounting his fraternal bond with Leontes to Hermione, the Bohemian king stresses their essential innocence as boys, despite encroaching aspects of adulthood. Had the two 'pursued that life' and retained the innocence of childhood, their 'weak spirits' would 'ne'er been higher reared / With stronger blood', and they would 'have answered heaven / Boldly, "not guilty", the imposition cleared / Hereditary ours' (I, ii, 71–5). This hypothetical trial, a prefiguration of the actual trial of Hermione to follow, expresses the fantasy of having no sinful action, only the natural, hereditary 'spirit' of childhood to allow passage to heaven – a parodic recasting of Protestantism's pure 'faith alone' in the soul as Edenic nostalgia. Polixenes, here, wishes to remain in the spiritual innocence and soulful totality of childhood without participating in actions inherent to the child exemplified in Mamillius's behaviour.[50] The irony, not lost to Hermione, is that what corrupted their spirits with blood is the sexual awakening her gender presumably brought about – the monarchs' respective queens flooded childhood's spirit with bodily blood. During her actual trial, as Leontes spits forth the unfounded reasons for his rage, Hermione responds that he uses 'a language that I understand not' (III, ii, 78). A maddening, illegible figure, Leontes, uncannily like his son, withholds his meanings – even as he attacks a form of illegibility that terrifies him. He attempts instead to return forcibly to the logic of youth that Polixenes wistfully mourns from a distance.

Later in the play, in the festal scene of celebration in Bohemia so reminiscent of the pastoral elegy, Polixenes further demonstrates the importance of maintaining fixed meanings, rather than the rough immediacy of bodily theatricality, in his exchange with Perdita. Masked as an old peasant, Polixenes's mode of speech is notably pedagogical. He inquires why the apparently lower-class, though strikingly fair, Perdita would not deign to plant the 'carnations, and streaked gillyvors' that, according to her, 'some call nature's bastards'; she responds that the plants' hubris offends her sensibility: 'I have heard it said / There is an art which in their piedness shares / With great creating nature' (IV, iv, 82–3, 86–7). Polixenes presses on, rhapsodising on the tenuous and sublime relationship of artifice to nature and offering again that she should 'make your garden rich in gillyvors'; still Perdita insists on exiling the 'bastard' plants (IV, iv, 98–9). The irony of the exchange for the audience is, naturally, the knowledge of the complex doublespeak at work. Polixenes, as we soon find out, is furious at his son's mingling with an untamed flower of the 'wildest stock', but he pretends to favour botanical and class miscegenation when speaking in disguise. He tests her by demanding a facile rhetorical ability in demonstrating knowledge of a natural order and maintenance of phylogenetic and sociocultural boundaries. The further irony is that, in a classic instance of Romantic plotting, her 'natural' knowledge of this order belies her actual situation as higher than her apparent class. She thus demonstrates her nobility by demurely refusing the possibility of its entrance into her life.

She will later, with more obviousness, betray her royal stature by showing an ability to cite Ovid in talking with Florizel. She compares herself to Proserpina, violets to Juno and Cytherea, and primroses to Phoebus as she proceeds through a bouquet of emotional indexes (IV, iv, 116, 121–2). How she has learned these stories is not explained; certainly it is not by her adoptive father, an uneducated shepherd. A fantasy of nature and knowledge commingling as the *sui generis* production of narrativity, Perdita coolly counters Polixenes's Socratic needlings and buffers her arguments with appropriate quotations from classical texts, proving the impossible paradox that Polixenes finds in nature, the 'art / Which does mend nature – change it rather' that also 'itself is nature' (IV, iv, 95–7).[51] She becomes the pure poem of Jonson's dead son, except among the living. She becomes, in other words, a digestible, wholly literary version of the soul without sacrificing her very tangibility. This transformation both makes her a perfect replica of the soul and, by its very nature as a replica, the soul's antithesis. Appropriately, Florizel, in proposing to her, shrugs off his father's wish that he purchase her a wealth of artificially beautiful goods from Autolycus – a 'pedlar's silken treasury' (IV, iv, 355) – despite the fact that, Polixenes warns, if 'your lass / Interpretation should abuse and call this / Your lack of love or bounty, you were traited / For a reply' (IV, iv, 357–60). The prince instead insists, with treacly romanticism, that the 'gifts she looks from me are packed and locked / Up in my heart, which I have given already, / But not delivered'; he proceeds to 'deliver' these gifts by pledging to Perdita: 'O, hear me breathe my life / Before this ancient sir' (IV, iv, 362–6). The sentiment that tokens of emotion cannot suffice in expressing love is well-worn, but it relies on the asignifying, total soul of breath as its ambassador. The gentle satire of young lovers and stern fathers in Bohemia scaffolds itself, then, with a variation of the theologically complex dictum that led to tragedy in Sicilia: that the unsayable breath of life could, if interpretation is abused, be surmised as a lack of love.

Much as the prince and seeming peasant efface the materiality of courtship, they also frame themselves as independent of their bodies. Perdita's art-as-nature literary fabrication, capable of citing knowledge while wiping away the traces of labour needed to attain it, replaces, in the immediate context of the pastoral celebrations of Act IV, another figure of markedly different characteristics – the Shepherd's dead wife. When she was alive, the Shepherd tells us, she would 'sing her song and dance her turn, now here / At upper end o'th'table, now I'th'middle; / On his shoulder and his, her face o'fire / With labour' (IV, iv, 58–61). Singing, dancing, and giving men sips from her jug of alcohol, his late wife was both bawdy and bodily, whereas Perdita, as her paternal stand-in notes, is 'retired / As if you were a feasted one / And not hostess of the meeting' (IV, iv, 62–3). The implied staging emphasises this failed substitution, placing Perdita downstage of the whirling, dancing satyrs (IV, iv, 347).

The replacement of the bodily wife by the literary Perdita might be explicitly articulated, but it suggests the more profound and unsaid act of surrogating Mamillius. Rather than Mamillius's whispered nothings and silent body, Perdita demonstrates here why she, perhaps even more than Florizel, will attempt to serve as the replacement for the dead prince at the close of the play. She has clarified voice into writing while retaining the holy innocence of the spirit, all without marking herself with the theatre necessary to do so.[52] She is, in other words, a mimetic replica of the singular and expressive holy breath of life and not a presence of dangerous air. The possibility of double-casting the same performer in both siblings' roles, perhaps originally executed by the same boy actor, highlights this surrogation in performance.[53] Carol Rutter's review of Edward Hall's doubling of Mamillius and Perdita unearths such a discrepancy, as the actor, 'in a dress, made no attempt to conceal his masculinity. His Perdita never erased Mamillius; rather, harrowingly, [he] showed the brother underneath, the lost in the found, refused permission for the dead child to be restored in the living sister – or forgotten.'[54] The theatre makes vivid the fissures between loss and recovery. The body, as performative residue, persists while the text seemingly forgets. Perdita's fantasy of nature and art cohering becomes exposed as a fiction of words produced by muscled breaths.

Other scenes in the play similarly meditate on the ambivalence of its own medium by attempting to assert the capacity of performance to evoke holiness yet also admit the pure eventness of bodies and voices that disrupt the social order. An elegant summation of this process occurs in the speech of the First Gentleman, who recalls with wonder the moment of Leontes recognising his daughter when the shepherd confirms her royal lineage: 'There was speech in their dumbness, language in their very gesture; they looked as they had heard of a world ransomed, or one destroyed' (V, ii, 13–15). The gentleman must translate the theatrical and non-verbal qualities of the interaction, the event that is denied his, and our, witness, and is communicated instead in 'speech' and 'language' that he himself supplements in describing the scene in his own words to Autolycus. The revelations of the opened fardel, which carry the evidence needed to unravel the mysteries of Perdita's origin, can only be related. We receive the elegy, not the body. The sixteen-year gap in the centre of the play, a temporal manifestation of the vast waters that separate the two kingdoms, is similarly withheld from us, narrated instead by the character of Time. 'Impute it not a crime / To me or my swift passage that I slide / O'er sixteen years', relays Time (IV, i, 4–6). The 'crime' here is presumably both in Shakespeare's writing, as the chorus admits to the liberal use of theatrical licence and the inherently tragic aspect of widening gulfs of separation. Time the character relates what actual time performs – a passage of an event that is recorded and calcified as a false, but necessary, story.

Policing the border between breath and air, *The Winter's Tale* concludes with an unsteady merging of the two. The statue scene offers Leontes a chance to accept the signifying ability of an object – and noise – to narrate him into existence and coherence. He, too, is showered with the 'graces' that Hermione asks the gods to pour upon Perdita's head (V, iii, 122). Before this, however, he is gripped by a grotesque vision of Hermione's return that demonstrates the delicacy of his eventual redemption. In conversation with Paulina, Leontes becomes trapped in a ritualistic, self-lacerating dialogue on his guilt and the singularity of the seemingly dead queen. He suggests that remarriage to a 'worse' woman would make Hermione's 'sainted spirit / Again possess her corpse, and on this stage, / Were we offenders now, appear soul-vexed, / And begin, "Why to me?"' (V, i, 56–60). Recasting his plight into the popular, macabre archetype of a widow's revenge story, Leontes imagines a hideous corpse stalking the twin theatres of his observed life and Shakespeare's play itself.[55] Paulina picks up the narration and further makes the details horrific, imagining that if she were 'the ghost that walked, I'd bid you mark / Her eye, and tell me for what dull part in't / You chose her', and then she would 'shriek that even your ears / Should rift to hear me, and the words that followed / Should be, "Remember mine"' (V, i, 63–7). Spewing noise and shrieking curses, this monstrous Hermione, who presumably stalks Leontes's consciousness – his affection is impinging upon his dreams, exactly as he feared – is nakedly a creature of all noise and animated actorly body, nonsensical and accusatory. Hermione's spectre has risen before, for the sceptical Antigonus, as a 'creature' in 'pure white robes' who weeps violently and imparts a curse on the presumed murderer of her daughter (III, iii, 18–35). These visions seem to erase the possibility of Hermione's earthly recuperation by establishing the potential horror at her soul reinvigorating her body.

Her actual return does not so much eliminate the qualities of her prefigured terror as repurpose them as spiritual revelation. Rather than formed from a theatre of bodies and noise, Hermione's statue is crafted from the purity of breath; in discussing its creation, the Steward and Gentleman recount the artist, Giulio Romano, as a 'master' who, 'had he himself eternity and could put breath into his work, would beguile Nature of her custom' (V, ii, 95–7).[56] A creator – or more appropriately resurrector – capable of nearly approaching Nature, an imperceptible breath short of actually creating life, Romano is, by reputation, almost able to achieve the paradoxical synthesis of craft and total originality that Perdita embodies. When the 'statue' is revealed and is utterly still, rather than the shrieking, weeping, porous body of his nightmares, Leontes greets its silence with silence. Paulina approvingly notes this reciprocation: 'I like your silence; it the more shows off / Your wonder' (V, iii, 21–2). The final movement of awakened faith and redemption is Leontes's ability to detect her soul – and correctly attribute this noise as a force of life. In fact, he labels precisely the insubstantial marker of the soul that haunts both the elegiac form and the Christian life force – the very sign that tragically eludes Lear in his desperate wish for Cordelia's revival, repurposed here not as mocking impossibility but as vehicle of faith. Leontes is convinced that an 'air comes from her' and wonders what 'fine chisel' could 'ever yet cut breath?' (V, iii, 78–9). Somewhere between life and death, Hermione is, for Leontes, neither ghost nor body, theatre nor spirit. She is a shadowing-in of the soul. Leontes, like Hermione, has also attempted to cut himself off from words and gesture, yoking his abusive interpretations to the dangerously silent and still Mamillius. But his enclosure in childhood's presignifying grip was not the spiritual bliss that Polixenes imagined, and instead a concentration of the blood that rushed in to corrupt it – in other words, Leontes was on the wrong side of the divide between breath and nothingness, and in seeing Hermione he awakens his 'faith' as purity, rather than in its other guise of madness.[57]

Of course, this awakening is itself an illusion. There is no statue, even within the play's scheme, but rather a body straining for stillness. And *this* 'illusion', the illusion of non-theatre, of cutting breath to resemble a soul without revealing the sick affections it must entail, only underlines what, echoing Hermione, might be called the 'grace' necessary for Leontes to submerge himself finally into his literary environment and remedy his self-diagnosed earlier state of playing so 'disgraced a part' (I, ii, 186) in his own play. Grace allows the body to express the soul without breaking the boundaries of aestheticised reality; it carves out a space in which the soul's unknowability can be registered without being expelled and laminated over by the illusion of its presence. It is expressed, not represented. This term, 'grace', rings throughout the play. Hermione has declared, for instance, 'Grace to boot!' (I, ii, 79), 'O, would her name were Grace!' (I, ii, 98), and ''Tis Grace indeed' (I, ii, 104). The term also recalls, today, a term of aesthetic philosophy utilised by Michael Fried, in his engagement with sculpture, the very medium which Hermione and the actor playing her seek to emulate.[58] Fried locates 'presentness' as the grace that imbues the non-art object with artistic aura. Presentness keeps at bay the dangerous quality of theatricality so dreaded by Fried, as theatre bears a 'profound hostility to the arts' by troubling the material borders of the artistic piece.[59]

But grace on stage takes sweat, regardless of what it otherwise professes. Hermione's presentness merges bodily labour with artistic mimicry. Objecthood becomes so concentrated that it is spirit. Stone gives birth to breath. The grace of presentness that Leontes must attain, however, must fundamentally offer itself through the illusion of theatre, which effaces its disruptive potential in order to imagine itself as a totality of presence – a performed soul that tries to deny its bodily means of performance. When still, the statue's grace, its cut breath, performs its own presence and presentness and eliminates the harrowing echo of the theatrical, unheard whisper that undergirds the breath of life but remains incapable of textual articulation within that narrative. But this presentness is itself an illusion – and a theatrical one at that: Hermione is pretending to be a statute and an actor is pretending to be Hermione. The statue presents less a celebration of theatre than an exposure of its mechanics.

Before attending to this scene further, I want to note its particularly powerful historical subtext. Any examination of theatricality in the statue scene invites a broader discussion of how it negotiates potentially idolatrous demonstrations of faith. Rich critical debate has found it alternately supportive of what we may broadly call a 'Catholic' ontological mode: the faith that awakens Hermione, it follows, shows the possibility of residual mystical capacities in a post-Reformation theological landscape. Or perhaps the scene portrays precisely the opposite – the seeming revival of the worshipped object contains and empties out the potential of materiality to become invested with divine energy. The scene, in this latter reading, suggests the dominance of Pauline interiorised spirituality (it is Paul-ina, after all, who asks for an awakening of faith) over more sacrally charged demonstrations.[60] Interpretations of the scene quickly become symbolically fraught analyses of a much wider historical debate between how theatre in Shakespeare's day navigated the religious implications of its craft. The tradition of reading the statue theologically is a vital one, and my reading cannot sidestep it, though I believe a more nuanced view opens up as an alternative to labelling the scene as supportive or critical of certain spiritual dispositions. In fact, it seems to be both, for precisely the reasons thus far articulated: it is both theatrical and anti-theatrical – we might apply the ungainly but accurate term *semi*-theatrical, which I elaborate upon in the book's conclusion – in its ambivalence. As I have shown, we witness the smoothing-out of the theatre's origins as breath and flesh and subsequent assertion of a symbolic and mimetic economy. But we also must see the statue move and breathe as a result of the actor playing it labouring to stand still. And we see and hear Leontes's sobs and register his silence: the scene asserts a kind of non-mimetic theatrical presence, a return of Mamillius's soulfulness and a reminder of the fragility it engenders.

To further texture this as a reflection of a historical condition, I turn to the powerful suggestion by Ethan Shagan that the Reformation did not necessarily prompt a directly antagonistic relationship between reformer and traditionalist, stripper of altars and newly stripped. Instead, what occurred was a tenuous but potent collaboration to dialogically craft ideological structures that were localised, varied and amorphous: 'The amphibiousness and ambidexterity of new religious ideas is exactly what allowed them to penetrate English culture, seeping into the myriad crevices in the dominant belief system where ideas and practices were not fully aligned.'[61] Shagan encourages narratives of integration rather than direct conversion. Change emerged, he argues, not from bottom-up nor top-down processes but within the mediation of different interests. And so supposed idolatry was not only violently destroyed – it was tacitly done so in a complex exchange between those practicing supposedly 'Reformist' attitudes and those clinging to supposedly more 'traditional' or Catholic beliefs. He elaborates this idea in a wide survey of sales of possibly idolatrous objects by local parishes, who then gained publicity and funding in the exchange:

> By ostentatiously using the proceeds of embezzlements to support the government's religious programme, these communities made it hard for the regime to complain. In collaborating so visibly in evangelical pursuits, these parishes publicly established themselves as complicit with the Reformation, and doing so they won themselves considerable immunity from government interference. We have no evidence that anyone in these parishes had converted to Protestantism, but they certainly understood the priorities of a Protestant regime, and if it allowed them to keep ecclesiastical wealth within the community, at least some parishioners were happy to cooperate.[62]

It may seem inappropriate to think of Leontes's transcendental moment of recognition in terms of ruthless, pragmatic self-sufficiency; indeed, Shagan co-opts the term *collaboration* from historical studies of negotiation between dictatorships and the oppressed. But we do gain a way of seeing the scene outside of the potentially reductive binary of idolatrous or sacred and instead have a structure of interpretation that allows for a knowing trade-off by the participants that shepherds in cohabitation among different understandings. It is as if Leontes were acknowledging that he could give in to the sacredness and power of the image without consciously conscripting himself to a specifically articulated cause. Allegiance to specific ideological and epistemological positions becomes less important here than the desire simply to muddle through the necessary exchanges of the moment. Leontes willingly gives up his desire to know – the provenance of the rational soul – and allows for the stabbing affections to remain, for the limit of the possible to stay blurred. In exchange he gains a moment of grace, something that resists strict economisation but still gives itself over as a gift. We can recall Stanley Cavell's distinction, evoked in the introduction, between knowledge and acknowledgment: Leontes gains no knowledge, in fact gives up on the very criterion of knowledge as constituency of liveliness, but he does gain the capacity to recognise, to see and allow. 'The slack of acknowledgement', writes Cavell in *The Claim of Reason*, 'can never be taken up by knowledge.'[63] Elsewhere, in 'The Avoidance of Love', an essay on *King Lear*, he notes that 'acknowledging in a theatre shows what acknowledgment really is'.[64] Acknowledging in a theatre *really is* acknowledgment as it is in 'real' life. The 'grace' that seems apparent in Hermione's return is authorised by a kind of theatricality, one that proffers her body as a spectacle, replete with curtain and music.

The Hermione-as-statue figure aestheticises Wittgenstein's 'picture of the soul' not as an embodiment or representation, but instead as a diagram of the struggle with the impossibility of the soul's capacity to be represented at all. What the statue emblematises is the folly of trying to 'have' a soul as a tethered epistemological construct: the still statue is actually a bodily, gestural, breathing person. As Garrett Hallett shows, the soul, for Wittgenstein, provides the myth of descriptive correspondence: Wittgenstein notes that 'We say that a *spiritual* activity corresponds to these words';[65] Hallett explains that we say this 'Because we cannot specify any one action or event to which we might attach the desired term.'[66] This sense of 'soul' is the stand-in used by Portia in her relentless spiritual analogising – a process that leads to her embarrassment when she confronts the impossibility of her imagery resolving into reality. But this form of soul is not simply an empty or false idea. Nor is it precisely mystical – or, more accurately, its mysticism is not found in any kind of ether but instead in the rough and ordinary grammars of bodily action. The soul also encompasses the very *desire* for an explanation at all – the need to ask for meaning when none is needed, to look past the immediacy of expression and beg for hidden reference. Perdita emerges from the play as the fantasy of fulfilling this kind of desire, but her effortlessness ultimately proves ironised by both Hermione's return and the faith it instantiates. One of this book's guiding inquires has been to see how an expressive framework – or perhaps de-framing – of the soul engages with early modern conceptions of the soul as a holy fragment of selfhood. Thinking of the soul as the fundamental impulse to *explain* meaning as something other than what is exemplified and performed – the futility of standing still and willing oneself into transcendence – we can view the statue scene as the staging of that desire without making any effort to satiate it.

Leontes, as a result, becomes aware of the futility of his own need for knowledge. His reaction to Hermione's descent from her stage is not terror but an admission of this not-knowing. His brush with affection, which hinted at whispering and breathing forces complicit in the logic of language, has vaccinated him against the potential terror of such a moment. Unlike Coriolanus's outburst and terrifying fantasia of divine mockery, Leontes signals this return with the acceptance of a reciprocal stillness that similarly risks conflation with non-being. As Sarah Beckwith describes, the scene's layers of theatre-disguising-theatre create an acknowledgment of artifice rather than blind conscription into a new aesthetic regime. And from this acknowledgment arrives a deeper and more vital form of grace than the image of fulfilment borne from self-concealment. Beckwith describes the delicate structure of faith that accommodates this situation:

> The condition of wonder that the scene seeks to cultivate is not at all attendant upon belief but rather of immediate attunements

> and attitudes. The statue scene . . . rests on commitments, not opinions. We do not need to rely on notions of make-believe. The primacy of belief-based modes of analysis then only obscures the working of this scene and its modes of recovery precisely from the epistemic modes of understanding. So it is also vital that Leontes' faith is as foundationless as his doubt has been. This is what makes it, and the new community founded on it, so fragile and so central.[67]

Leontes has not gained a form of belief, but instead given himself over to the lack of proof that characterises faith.[68] The implication is that this community-formation doubles Leontes's earlier community-destruction. The new abandonment of knowledge allows for an attunement to the others in and missing from the room. Still, weeping, and listening, the king has become Mamillius as surely as Florizel and Perdita have tried to supplant the lost and unmentioned prince. We might say that he gives himself over to the nonsensical theatre that sutures all illusions of pure meaning. And in this way he embraces the kinds of non-mimetic theatricality that have proven so poisonous in the earlier case studies of this book. Shylock's deferrals and Coriolanus's concealments provided corporeal strategies of expressing soulfulness by resisting mimetic incorporation. But these strategies lead to their death. Leontes finds here a way to absorb soulful performance without losing his self-definition.

For the once-jealous king, it is ultimately a sensitivity, a *lack* of blindness, towards the constant unruliness of life that jettisons him from the civilised world and into a seizure of doubt. As with the First Gentleman, interpreters of language in *The Winter's Tale* must always discover it founded and unfounded within gesture and silence, encoded in bodies and action. The play, then, sponsors a philosophy that accounts for the non-verbal as complicit in all seemingly literary and mimetic consideration – that is, a world that registers the threatening, unruly, and distinctly non-representative valences of the soul. Leontes finds himself as audience to the flickering parade of events calcifying into shadowings-in of narrative and then breaking anew into events, an act of constant unfolding that offers a glimpse at the interminglings of soul and body. By both admitting to the creation of theatre's totalising illusion while abandoning himself to the instability and insufficiency of the world around him, Leontes finally allows for a world to emerge not just as a seamless play of representations awaiting mastery, like lines of an elegy to be swapped among poets, but as an acknowledgment of the loss of meaning that must inherently accompany spiritual perception. In crafting an elegy for the present, he allows himself to live in it.

CONCLUSION

THE SEMI-THEATRICAL PREJUDICE

I began with a desire to speak with the dead.

Stephen Greenblatt

Why seek ye the living among the dead?

Luke 24: 5

In this pastiche dialogue, Greenblatt's famous confessional opening to his *Shakespearean Negotiations* finds a bewildered answer from the angels that attend Jesus's empty tomb.[1] The angels' words reappear in the *Quem Quaeritis* liturgical trope, which, according to a popular genealogy, theatricalised the medieval church: a dramaturgical climax that hinges on a revelation of absence, which in turn confirms an awakened presence elsewhere.[2] The mildly necromantic impulses of the present-day early modern scholar, then, mimic the motivating mystery of the theatre: Why do we try to find signs of life in a medium that, as Herbert Blau memorably has put it, consists of watching people 'dying in front of your eyes?'[3] What do we desire when we see a reflection of our consciousness, embodied and oftentimes bloodied, but not altogether alive, in the traffic of the stage?

This book has found in Shakespeare's drama the suggestion that these questions mirror the means by which early modern

England explored the precarious limits of death and life through the figure of the soul. But for Shakespeare, these limits, culturally parsed out carefully in rituals of death – reciting the mythology of metempsychosis, effacing the material monuments, marking the limits of sense-making and mastery in poetic elegies – are also the limits of the human *within* the human. Each ritual, furthermore, carries with it a self-collapsing knowingness. Metempsychosis is acknowledged as false, the monuments must be dissolved to be realised, and the elegy admits its own incapacity as the source of its potency. The ritual, like the *mnemosunon* of wasted ointment that Jesus valorises, consists of conscripting its own seeming failure as a form of affirmation. So too does the soul bury within the living the potential of life's undoing, a fragment of death that threatens to cancel out confirmations of full-bodied existence. Shylock, Coriolanus and Leontes each encompass the contact point that comprises the soul, and they do so in relentlessly mimetic worlds that insist, desperately at times, on clearer partitions of livelihood.

But this conflict is not simply one of rejecting theatricality or representation. These three figures are not noble harbingers of truth, fighting against the falsities of their social environments. In fact, by way of a conclusion, I want to pursue a line of thought that has emerged as a consequence of the readings I have staged, which I now wish to make explicit. Throughout this study the seeming binary of 'theatrical' and 'antitheatrical', terms that still retain purchase in literary and cultural studies of Shakespeare's time, has become complicated, to say the least. My aim here is to look headlong at this complication by examining how Shylock's deferrals, Coriolanus's concealments, and Leontes's denials and whispers all, in fact, demonstrate an embrace of theatre's totality, an examination of the self-devouring centre of the theatre's ontology rather than a place beyond its borders. This embrace arises from accepting the nothingness that doggedly attends the theatre not as a symptom of early modern theatricality but as its essential fabric. Breath, noise, bodies, gestures elsewhere, concealed absences: these are the building blocks of mimesis, a process that paradoxically thrives on the illusion of presence and that covers its tracks so expertly. The 'anti-theatrical prejudice' popularised by Jonas Barish's foundational book of the same name helps categorise a strain of criticism but refuses to look under the hood: if you scratch theatricality you find thriving anti-theatricality; if you interrogate the assumptions of anti-theatricality you find a profound investment in theatre's fundamentals, disguised as its antagonists.

I began this book with a prompt from Wittgenstein, whose famous dictum that the human body is the best picture of the soul helps unmoor the assumptions of the theatre that pin it strictly to representation and instead allow for an exploration of expression as performance. I want to bracket that observation with a related directive from the same philosopher, one that provides a refrain throughout *Philosophical Investigations*: the equally idiomatic notion that language is a 'life-form'. This definition appears numerous times within a discussion of what 'definition' consists of at all. In one exchange, a discussant suggests that 'the *speaking* of language is part of an activity, or of a life-form'.[4] For Stanley Cavell, in *The Claim of Reason*, this aphorism carries with it a pedagogical imperative to avoid a strictly atomist model of learning. In imagining that teaching language consists only of learning the *names* of things – rather than the form of life that comprises the learning itself – Cavell declares that we 'imagine that we have explained the nature of language when we have only avoided a recognition of its nature'.[5] Instead of framing a scene of education as indoctrination, we should instead frame it as one of invitation, in which we do not simply learn words but 'are initiate of the forms of life which give those words the point and shape they have in our lives'.[6] To take on a language is to enter the game that comprises its scene of absorption. We enter a life-form and adopt the norms of that game, as a result slipping free from obligations to screen meaning from the experience of life.

It follows that Shakespeare's plays, as read in the previous chapters, stage dilations, not ruptures, of theatre's capacity. The strict meaning-making regimes enforced in Shakespeare's Venice, Rome and Sicilia all favour the atomist and narrowly mimetic position, while Shylock, Coriolanus and Leontes give us – despite or because of their characterological carapace of 'unlikeability' and social rejection – an incitement to consider performance as the totality of its scene. The theatre thus models learning in a Wittgensteinian fashion, with the audience taking the playing of plays as an ephemeral passage of time and bodies. To position this witnessing of theatre as a witnessing of the soul is to get at the early modern soul's fundamental and irresolvable condition as a (perhaps *the*) life-form, a sum total of its embodiment – but an embodiment that rejects any framework that positions it as indexical or capable of apprehension. The revelation of an embrace that accepts, or perhaps even dissolves into, the tranches of experience that constitute meaning, all within an environment that believes in meaning as economised and representable, cannot help but wear the disguise of a catastrophe. And the refusal to cathect to the mimetic apparatuses of juridical and social systems carries with it the cathartic labelling of transgressor, enemy, or exile. But at its heart this refusal is also an acknowledgment of a wider structure, one filled with the play of bodies and sounds and timely occurrences, all interacting but not insisting on shared foundations.

Spencer Golub has also noted the affinity between Wittgenstein's ordinary language philosophy and theories of performance: 'It is not too much of a stretch to see that Wittgenstein was, at least at one time in his thinking, describing "liveness" and that his claim for liveness constituted as a limited whole provides a model for life. And with this proposition, Wittgenstein entered the realm of theatre, of performance.'[7] Yet no sooner is this kinship proposed, Golub explains, than an immediate 'stumbling block' arises when the world revealed in liveness is conflated with the world itself, because in 'struggling to ascertain the meaning of understanding's agreement with itself, we are misled by external signs that inherently cite other signs, leading not so much to looking as to overlooking not only what a sign or object means but meaning itself'.[8] When grammar widens to encompass life, life cannot help but tempt consciousness with definitions and apparently concrete understandings of the world – which is to say, with a picture of the totality of the world at all. What results is a push and pull between therapeutic acknowledgments of limitation and furtive pursuits of meaning. Shakespeare tracks a third possible form of performance to arise from the absorption into language-games: the enactment of meaning's ruse, be it through absorbing into performance the knowingly empty words of the elegy, the erasure of the monument's inscriptions, or the citation of the soul's myth as flying entity. The plays percolate with moments that usher in this possibility through invitations to fall into the wide grammar of life-forms rather than the narrow grammar of language-as-representation.

Hamlet is exemplary here because of its frantic and compulsive attempts to demonstrate the friction between grammars of mimesis and life-forms. Shakespeare's iconic play also leads us back to *Second Death*'s title by invigorating a sense of virtuality. That is, it engages with a model of the soul that is both fleshy and material *and* sublime and effervescent; it describes a spiritual form that occupies the contact point between knowing and not-knowing, and as such occupies a grey zone between senses of what is staged and unstaged, here and there. *Hamlet* continually, pathologically proffers the body as a site of indexical meaning, only to whisk the body away, both physically as a human corpse and conceptually as a field of knowledge. The repeated demand for bodies – in the face of puzzlement as to what Hamlet's father's ghost is, or as a need for ritualistic closure, or as a posthumous enactment of longing, or as a judicial apparatus to attend Horatio's proposed play in the closing lines – confronts, over and over, the impossibility of them yielding precise meaning, and as a result the play repeatedly confronts the impossibility of the theatre's bodily assemblage yielding precise cohesion. In its explicit and more subterranean strains of metatheatricality, *Hamlet* famously grapples with its own dramatic construction through repeatedly stymied attempts at theatrical presentation, most saliently in the play-within-a-play but also in the many performances that crowd its *mise-en-scene*, from the ghost's evening appearances to Hamlet's self-conscious character construction to the puppet-skulls in the graveyard to Horatio's proposed undead staging. These struggles are, in one sense, failures. They never quite take off. But as soulful enactments, they are successful – or, more accurately, they slip out of teleological intention altogether – and as such act as calls to accept a wider frame, to abandon hope of strict atomist rule-making and instead, in Hamlet's own Calvinist-tinged announcement, 'Let be' (V, ii, 220)[9]. It is ultimately this quality of invitation, of a salutary injunction to dissolve into an expressive grammar, that supplies the coda to this study.

As we have seen, on stage, the figure of the soul in Shakespeare contains both life and death, presentness and absence – it is both, as Hamlet quizzically declaims, when confronted with his father's return, '*Hic et ubique?*' (I, v, 64). The 'ghost' of Hamlet's father provides a telling reflection of a Shakespearean soul, though not for obvious reasons. It is not merely that he is quite clearly an entity from beyond death; it is rather his formal and even aesthetic construction, and the physical array of bodies that attend to his appearances, that link him to the expressive manifestations of the soul. He is resolutely solid, still victim to the 'most instant tetter' that resulted from his brother's poison, his skin now 'lazar-like, with vile and loathsome crust / All my smooth body' (I, v, 71–3). Of course, this speech rehearses already-hoary elements of the revenge tragedy, but its return to the body as the site that reflects indeterminate justice troubles the supposedly ethereal nature of the ghost. Puzzled by the intoned demand to 'swear' that emanates from below, Hamlet scrambles to find an appropriate locale from which to vow silence. His difficulty in coming to rest demonstrates physically the more abstract challenge of locating an appropriate relation to his dead father's ghost, or, for that matter, what this ghost even *is*. Solid and ethereal, silent then talkative, here and everywhere, the elder Hamlet is dead, but also the spirit of life that allows Hamlet to attempt purpose as revenger, an injection of *elan* that gives his son an odd sense of buoyancy when he deals with the incredulous Horatio and Marcellus. Running across the stage, laughing and exclaiming, he calls his father, who was very recently a source of terror, a 'boy' (I, v, 58) and a 'mole' (I, v, 170) – a child and an animal, a pair of not-quite-humans standing in for the life that has departed.[10] Locking in to a purpose deeper than the outward show of his mournful trappings, Hamlet binds himself, momentarily, to a powerful semi-fiction of the soul made briefly incarnate – he feels the thrill of connecting action to spirit, the expressly forbidden and theatrically impossible point of contact – only when it is gone. The rest of the play, naturally, challenges and dissipates the apparent rigor of this contact, but in the moment of the pact, soulfulness and theatricality seem to have reached a brief accord by negotiating disappearance, not – as with Hermione's resurrection – an interplay of liveliness.

As I stated in my introduction, this is not a book about the dead, nor of ghosts, but rather the maintenance of the soul in the living. But Hamlet's father's ghost is not necessarily dead, and seems somewhat alive. In fact, like the soul, he turns the tables by implicating the practice of living as being somewhat deathly. Hamlet's self-directive that follows the ghost's exit promises an erasure of the sediments of identity that render him in part alive: 'from the table of my memory / I'll wipe away all trivial fond records, / All saws of books, all forms, all pressures past / That youth and observation copied there' (I, v, 98–101). Hamlet's life also takes on a deathly quality in its resemblance to an actor's role, a habitual recurrence where lines are recited, exits and entrances are prescribed, and characters are remembered when they leave the stage and effectively stop existing, even while their presence lingers in repeated intonations. As the rest of *Hamlet* unfolds itself, this is precisely the crisis that keeps surfacing for the young prince: to what degree, as conglomerates of bodies and performances, are we already ghosts, and thus already dead? The two manifestations of the ghost in the first act, first as a pock-marked hideous body, second as an unseen voice, mark the twin components between which living identity floats.

The scenes of Hamlet's father find their bookend in the proposed play that ends *Hamlet*, which Horatio exhorts Fortinbras to begin rehearsing: 'Give order that these bodies / High on a stage be placed to the view, / And let me speak to th'yet unknowing world / How these things came about' (V, ii, 382–5). Corpses, here, are actors, theatrical manifestations of Horatio's tale made rotting flesh; unseen and recounted history meets present-moment bodies. We have had a preview of this mode of performance in the graveyard scene, in which Hamlet imagines a parade of material human remains – of a possible politician, courtier, lawyer, and finally Yorick – reconstituting themselves as inanimate; recalling Aristotle's definition of the soul as 'whatness', the prince asks

'Where be his quiddities now, his quillities, his cases, his tenures, and his tricks?' (V, I, 97–8). The skulls, like the ghost, force a reckoning with the soul's essential lifelessness and its tacit cooperation with theatre to appear lively. Corpses cast as characters: an anti-theatricalist's fantasia, but also a demonstration of the soul's invisible but necessary kinetic force.

And yet as much as *Hamlet* focuses on the materiality of the body, it also stresses the distance inherent to conceiving selfhood. I want to develop further this duality of distance and proximity, a lurid embodiment of the in-between-ness that flags Shylock, Coriolanus and Leontes as disturbances in their mimetic economies. *Hamlet*'s propulsive acts of distancing are noted in one of its paradigmatic critiques, Jacques Derrida's *Specters of Marx*. In his introduction to *Spiritual Shakespeares*, Ewan Fernie links Derrida's reading, which explicitly examines Hamlet's encounter with his father, to Shakespearean literary analysis to uncover new interpretive possibilities that stem from alienation, among them that the 'fantasies of the afterlife' entertained by Hamlet act 'as intense experiences of the foreignness of the self: of its simultaneously thrilling and frightening non-coincidence with itself'.[11] Such self-alienation and disassembly might seem to engender insanity, arising from severed responsibility; however, Derrida, in *Specters*, argues just the opposite case. A traumatic dis-joinment of the present – 'the time is out of joint' – is in fact, says Derrida, where responsibility begins, in an essential breakage of the present moment. This is a point to which he returns again and again:

> To be 'out of joint', whether it be present Being or present time, can do harm and do evil, it is no doubt the very possibility of evil. But without the opening of this possibility, there remains, perhaps, beyond good and evil, only the necessity of the worst. A necessity that would not (even) be a fated one.[12]

We find ourselves in a world of extreme possibility arising from violent injections of distance. Linking this breakage to Hamlet's vow, and with it, speech act theory more broadly, Derrida begins folding in a familiar post-structuralist critique – locating the constantly at-play acts of dissolution and dissemination of meaning – by labelling the promise of Marxism the 'originary *performativity* that does not conform to pre-existing conventions' but instead 'whose force of *rupture* produces the institution or the constitution, the law itself, which is to say also the meaning that appears to, that ought to, or that appears to have to guarantee it in return'.[13] The disjointure of meaning is for Derrida, with echoes of Saint Paul, the very condition of the present, giving way to the birth of law from violence.[14] Hamlet exemplifies this rupture with clear lucidity when he demands a shared vow of silence to justify bloody action.

Yet I want to pressurise Derrida's usage of 'performativity' by insisting that, like all theatrical events, the act of producing rupture – the performance of the vow that inaugurates the law – may indeed rend the self from spatiotemporal engagement, but so too does it create a proximity, a becoming, a seduction. Originary performativity might try to deny pre-existing convention in its disjointure, but it also demands a re-joining with the bodily and nontextual, or, as Hamlet promises to Marcellus and Horatio, at the very moment of his self-alienation, that 'with all my love I do commend me to you' (I, v, 190). As much as the characters surveyed in this study are shocked and distanced by soulful interjections into their mimetic economies, they too perform gestures of mournful intimacy that attempt, albeit fruitlessly, to close the distance: Lorenzo and Jessica languish in melancholic, romantic remembrance; Aufidius, perhaps tacitly in erotic conjoinment with Coriolanus, stands over his body and orders the production of nobility; Leontes promises communal renewal, but Hermione remains strangely silent, never entirely convincing as a newly awakened and lively self.[15] Mourning permeates the scene of the soul's exit, and that mourning arrives in the form of calls for closeness, as if to counteract the essential distancing of the soul. But the soul is also never solely distanced: it also comprises the essential centre; it produces an encounter with the body *and* the decorporealising sublime, both ethereally offstage ('Swear!') and in the stinking, lazar'd-over body of the present.

What opens the way to this twinned affinity and distance is, I propose, a sense of the soul's virtuality. In the present moment of writing this conclusion, the technological changes of late capitalism have ironically produced a possible answer to the question of distanced empathy by proposing a form of spiritual kinship eerily similar to the dynamic of the soul in Shakespeare: the virtual avatar. Introducing the soul into contemporary cybernetic theory, with its discussions of computerised hybridisations of personhood, is not as far-fetched a proposal as it might seem on the surface; scholarship on technology finds itself habitually grappling with its spiritual inheritance. Erik Davis, in *Techgnosis*, claims the term 'soul' as an explanatory tool in delineating the ritualistic implications of the hyper-mediated world: soul, for Davis, refers to 'the creative imagination, that aspect of our psyches that perceives the world as an animated field of powers and images'; the soul 'finds and loses itself in enchantment; it speaks the tongue of dream and phantasm, which should never be confused with mere fantasy'.[16] Curiously, Davis's soul is also rendered material and earthy, as it 'remains in the mesmerizing vale of tears and desires, a fecund and polytheistic world of things and creatures, and the images and stories that things and creatures breed'.[17] In surveying the chaotic, knotted lines of connectivity in contemporary popular culture, Davis finds in the soul a useful explanatory device – one he uses in opposition to 'spirit', which he reserves for loftier, more divine, sensations. This 'soul' might seem to occupy a position thoroughly at odds with the notion of the soul insisted upon by early modern theorists: instead of resisting the body, it embraces it, making manifest the phantasm that arises from a charmed concentration, not rejection, of tangible desires.

Despite apparent semantic conflict, however, Davis's notion of the soul opens up the somehow-both-tangible-and-absent contradiction of the soul and performance – the sublime *and* organic qualities that position it between life and death. I do not intend, in noting its lexical return, to evoke cyber-theory simply to chart how the meaning of the word 'soul' has altered itself historically, but rather try and view Davis's notion as a legitimate practice that prompts backward-looking questions on the soul's figure in early modernity. Was a soul, for citizens of Elizabethan England, similar to an avatar for us? The comparison has an unshakeable and anachronistic awkwardness to it, but the friction it produces is illuminating to both sides of the equation. N. Katherine Hayles, in a foundational text on the merging terrains of cybernetics and posthumanism, *How We Became Posthuman: Virtual Bodies in Cybernetics, Literature, and Informatics*, defines her subject as

> an amalgam, a collection of heterogeneous components, a material-informational entity whose boundaries undergo continuous construction and reconstruction [. . .] the presumption that there is an agency, desire, or will belonging to the self and clearly distinguished from the 'will of others' is undercut for the posthuman, for the posthuman's collective heterogeneous quality implies a distributed cognition located in disparate parts that may only be in tenuous communication from one another.[18]

Hayles sounds the death of the liberal humanist subject (whose funeral has been marked by enough various critical discourses at this point to birth its own army of vengeance-seeking ghosts) only to attempt and recuperate it as cybernetics by another name. She calls for a middle ground between embodiment and information; the signature qualities of the posthuman cyber-being – its reflexivity, multiple possessions, and hesitancy in identifying with the body – are not so different than the traditional 'enlightened' human. Hayles's notion of recovering a natural hybridity focuses on the particulars of technological interface; a natural extension of her inquiry is committed to diving into virtual worlds, such as Second Life, whose very name suggests the elision of a material-information divide.

Second Life, once synonymous with a futuristic use of cyber-technology, has now become a quaint remnant of its past. Like the ruins surveyed by Weever and Stow in Chapter 3, entire virtual and depopulated worlds still exist in the 'cloud', which houses receptacles of lingering algorithms and glitches.[19] They have become literal ghost towns, not simply locales populated by ghosts but ghostly constructions unto themselves, virtual worlds rendered more indistinct by the removal of human attention. But Second Life continues to be synonymous with a world that is neither concretely here nor utterly offstage, a dynamic realised succinctly in its former slogan: 'Ready to create a new digital you?'[20]

The question bluntly posits the infinite tension between those two words, 'new' and 'you'. How can it be new if you're already you? The question is a familiar one in Shakespeare; your new avatar, I am suggesting, is as much you as Portia's lead casket is she, or as much as Coriolanus's hidden scars are he, or as much as Mamillius is Leontes, or as much a character is an actor – which is to say, radically *somewhat*, in a constant performance of difference and sameness.[21] Ann Weinstone, in *Avatar Bodies*, draws from Tantric teachings to arrive at an understanding of the avatar that vibrates within the paradox that Second Life suggests; the 'state of nonstatic relationship which "I" *am*, this thoroughfare, this nexus of relationality is the avatar body', an entity that 'signals a shift away from the concept of avatar as a representational envoy of a relation between that which is essentially separated and toward a concept of avatar as expressive of a general *condition* of entanglement'.[22] An acknowledgment of entanglement is exactly the proposition that horrifies early modern culture when facing the soul within the living, just as it horrifies the characters who smoothly operate within the mimetic schema of Shakespeare's plays when facing those who demand to account for the truly spiritual under the skin of its supposed assimilation. Weinstone returns to the avatar's spiritual roots, but her terminology could easily apply in considering the segments of the self that flake off of consciousness and embed themselves in our computerised realms. An 'avatar' performs a type of hybridity between heavenly separation and proximal becoming, an embrace of difference *as* a component of subjectivity, not a step towards critiquing or transcending it. She maintains the divide that Hayles's critique seeks to eliminate but repurposes it as a containment of ensnarled flows, a set of separations that produce a fluctuating condition without assimilating its internal differences.

Weinstone's notion encapsulates several of the soul's properties; I hope to mobilise her claims further by thinking of her embrace, like Derrida's distancing, as a form of theatre – a performance *of* an embrace, an action that is constituted temporally. After all, what clasps the contradiction of self-and-other *as* self with more robust acuity than the theatre? A forum where the play between selves becomes the realisation and effacement of a new, emerging subject – where in the present, the audience reacts to the action on stage *as if* it were 'real' and *as if* the characters were 'actual' yet reminding itself that neither are, that the whole ritual is repeated and the characters are 'people' like them – the theatre claws at the walls of its own imprisonment, insisting that it replicates our own modalities of living while flaunting its artifice. Theatre gives us the chance to embrace contradictions; it is, like the soul, an avatar that embodies the very condition of embodiment's struggle. It outlines the space in which we can acknowledge our expressiveness – an expressiveness that, Stanley Cavell reminds us, is our tragic fate: we are condemned to it.[23] At its tragic origins, the theatre is a place of fate effected. And certainly in *Hamlet*, the desperate wish that theatre replicate life perfectly, despite the level of virtuosity, mirrors the struggles to represent totally the soul – and mirrors too the mechanics of tragedy. Hamlet panics at the exact techniques of acting that prevent exposure of its status as craft, as with his celebrated advice to the players, which he will spend the rest of the play failing to follow himself. But by allowing for an escape from expression's potential for tragedy, the theatre too can give us a place of acknowledgment, of falling into our virtual fates as necessary condition, of letting be. Viewing the soul as an entanglement, as Weinstone does, approaches viewing it as a theatre rife with contradictions, and as the play, in all senses of the word, among aspects that appear far from human when viewed alone, pocked corpses and ethereal spirits that need performance to keep them both separate and linked.

To be virtual is not merely to be split between selves on the screen and in the world – it is not a synonym for the online, or technological, but instead an energy that pushes beyond these cybernetic notions into a more complex ontology.[24] Well before the advent of the technological avatar, Antonin Artaud, in his essay 'The Alchemical Theater', outlines how, like alchemy, theatre engages with a deeper and more archetypal level of reality. In its aesthetic languages, it always hints towards the chaos underneath perception – existing, as such, in a 'virtual reality' between pure fiction and unseen truth. The latter, more deeply hidden, world exists as utterly beyond all logic, containing 'an infinite perspective of conflicts' that elude our totalising grasp; only 'poetically and by seizing upon what is communicative and magnetic in the principles of all the arts' can we evoke it, plunging into 'states of an acuteness so intense and so absolute that we sense, beyond the tremors of all music and form, the underlying menace of a chaos as decisive as it is dangerous'.[25]

Artaud's description of virtuality sounds almost like an imperative – you must locate the terrifying depths of art! – and, as such, like a possible way to 'solve' the theatre's condition. But I hesitate to follow suit by framing this conclusion as a way to furrow out an accurate critical model for the soul. Part of this reluctance arises from the belief that the soul's riddle needs no answer: I am not employing theory as a solution, nor ready-made lexicon, but instead as another conversation partner, a prism through which certain strains of light can become visible. In fact, as I have hopefully been demonstrating, the soul has – as it long has insisted – much to offer philosophy, as much as vice versa. The soul and philosophy are traditionally linked at the roots of any genealogy of knowledge, but they remain strange bedfellows, as each is charged with the ability to reconstitute the structure of the other. Furthermore, the soul's simultaneous super-saturation into the time and flesh of earthly beings and self-extrication into the wings suggests a distinct *lack* of potential, a switching-off of possibility rather than a tempting telos that glitters at the end of dialectical progression. Put differently, if with more deliberate contradiction: the soul is the embrace of what cannot be possible for the subject as an essential component of the subject.[26] It stages the very impossibility of a coherent self; it performs performance's failure. And it does this to unlock the potential of something 'beyond' performance, even while its formation is complicit with performance's execution.

Viewing the soul as an avatar, as a constant performance of performance's limits, disengages altogether with the production of meaning. My wager, again, is that we can recast this process as an openness, perhaps even as excess, rather than the sentencing of a limitation. Performing performance's limits is what Hamlet spends much of his time doing; much as his own performance is dislodged by the ghost, he seeks to disrupt the theatre he helps orchestrate – the staging of *The Murder of Gonzago* rebranded as 'The Mousetrap' – by injecting himself into its narrative and fashioning himself as a living ghost that disjoints the temporality of the players. Giddily interrupting the action with his own glosses, as if insecure of the embedded juridical device he has previously confidently trumpeted, his ruptures make him 'as good as a chorus', according to Ophelia (III, ii, 240); he responds that he 'could interpret between you and your love if I could see the puppets dallying' (III, ii, 241–2). The players are, like Ophelia and her imaginary lover, insufficient alone – Hamlet must supplement them with abusive interpretations by trying to remove himself from their theatrical logic and deploying excesses of meaning that render them dangerously semi-human. The further he distances himself from the stage, and attempts to place himself as an interpreter, rather than actor, the more his surroundings become, themselves, excessively theatrical – lifeless puppets needing animation, like the corpses in Horatio's morbid history play. Like Shylock, Coriolanus and Leontes, Hamlet seems to realise, with mounting dread, that he is inescapably on stage – a rogue and peasant slave – trapped within its constantly attempted exchanges of meaning. The performative of the ghost's promise, seductively literal though it seemed, reveals itself to be exactly that: a performance, but a performance only, fluidly shifting its connotations over time, denying its apparent seamless and literary ability to remain steady in its signification.[27] Similarly, the play he has planned immediately seems incapable of effecting the result he craves. Despite the assurance of the ghost, both in his words and more forthrightly in his puzzling manifestations, Hamlet cannot use theatre to do what he wants. He can no more transcend his surroundings than Shylock's soul could actually fly from his body, Coriolanus build a faithful monument to his wife and mother, or Leontes see evidence of his wife's infidelity.

In its revelation of theatre's limits *and* dependence on performance, the double bind that captures *Hamlet* in a mousetrap of its own, the soul invites a reappraisal of the very notion of 'antitheatricality'. The term has gained currency largely due to the influence of Jonas Barish's imposing *The Antitheatrical Prejudice*, which maps historical currents of cultural unease across a wide variety of periods and locales. Laying out his sweeping philosophical and historical claims, Barish writes that the antitheatrical prejudice is, in fact, 'more than a prejudice'; it is 'a kind of ontological malaise, a condition inseparable from our beings, which we can no more discard than we can shed our skins'; furthermore, this malaise 'would seem to reflect something permanent about the way we think of ourselves and our lives'.[28] 'Antitheatricality' is still used regularly in scholarly descriptions of attitudes towards the stage, although it elides, I am arguing, the constant, immanent formations of the theatrical that the soul prompts within the subject.[29] Historically, there might very well be a firm anti-representational or anti-imitative prejudice, but the theatre itself is not ever coherent enough to present itself as something to be against at all; it is always inescapable and endlessly shaded. We can stay within Barish's framework – thinking of antitheatricality as a practiced bias – but still, I hope, recover some nuance when considering the ambivalence that the soul instigates. Recalling the ambiguity of theatricality – its processual, hollowing-out spacing – put forth in the first chapter, I want to suggest that the soul's theatre is one that is constantly in play as the subject seeks definition. Regardless of costumes, properties, or pretences, early modern personhood already staged itself *within* as well as without itself, instantiating and crossing distances as it both reifies and defies the terms of its spiritual essence.

The second death and second life of the soul, its avatar of livelihood and terrifying threat to being, help form what I am calling the 'semi-theatrical' nature of the early modern subject. A virtual presence invested between the dutiful critical dyads of audience and actor, text and performance, and non-human and human, the soul renders us all semi-theatrical, expressive but not always indexical, retaining the limitations of its ineffability and the capacity to transcend the material components of its environments. We can recall from the Book of Revelation's scene of spiritual torture, cited in the first chapter, that the soul must somehow be tangible enough to be threatened by its second death amidst the pains of hellfire, yet insubstantial enough that it can never be fully grasped in this world. This is surely a terrifying proposition: the soul must be understood and yet it must not resolve itself into a pedagogy of meanings and things. But it is a proposition Shakespeare's drama grapples with exquisitely, even ecstatically, as an essential, paradoxical condition that defines the virtual and expressive theatre of the everyday, one located neither in the living nor the dead but instead in the curious impulse to divide one from the other in the first place.

NOTES

Introduction

1. Stephen Greenblatt, *Hamlet in Purgatory* (Princeton: Princeton University Press, 2001), p. 199.
2. See, for instance, *Political Theology and Early Modernity*, ed. Graham Hammill and Julia Reinhard Lupton (Chicago: University of Chicago Press, 2012); and *Spiritual Shakespeares*, ed. Ewan Fernie (New York: Routledge, 2005). An interest in religion, more broadly, also characterises more canonical works, such as G. Wilson Knight's *The Wheel of Fire: Interpretations of Shakespeare Tragedy* (New York: Routledge, 2001 [1930]).
3. See also Marjorie Garber, *Shakespeare's Ghost Writers: Literature as Uncanny Causality* (New York: Routledge, 1997) and, further back to modernist criticism, Edward Gordon Craig, 'On the Ghosts in the Tragedies of Shakespeare', *On the Art of the Theatre* (New York: Routledge, 2008), pp. 128–36. For the 'ghost' of Shakespeare as canonical icon, see David Schalkwyck, 'Shakespeare's Ghosts', *Shakespeare* 1.2 (2005), pp. 219–40.
4. Gail Kern Paster, *The Body Embarrassed: Drama and the Disciplines of Shame in Early Modern England* (Ithaca: Cornell University Press, 1993), p. 5.
5. John Davies, *Nosce Teipsum* (London, 1599), p. 10.
6. Davies, *Nosce Teipsum*, p. 11.
7. Ibid., p. 21.
8. Ibid., p. 22.
9. Ibid., p. 47.
10. Ibid., p. 13.

11. Ibid., p. 40. For more on the soul's femininity, see Sarah E. Johnson, *Staging Women and the Soul-Body Dynamic in Early Modern England* (Burlington, VT: Ashgate, 2014).
12. Ptolmey, *Tetrabiblos*, trans. Frank Egleston Robbins (Cambridge, MA: Harvard University Press, 1940), pp. 333–5.
13. Katharine Eisaman Maus, *Inwardness and Theater in the English Renaissance* (Chicago: The University of Chicago Press, 1995), p. 32.
14. All Biblical citations in this book are from the King James Version.

Chapter 1

1. All citations from *King Lear* are from the Arden 3 edn, ed. R. A. Foakes (Walton-on-Thames: Thomson, 1997).
2. The *OED's* first definition is: 'Of close tenacious substance or texture; strongly cohesive, so as to be pliable or ductile; not easily broken, divided, or disintegrated; not fragile, brittle, or tender' (tough, adj. (and adv.) and n'., *OED Online* (accessed 29 September 2015).
3. Jonas Barish, *The Antitheatrical Prejudice* (Berkeley: University of California Press, 1981), pp. 92–3.
4. Huston Diehl, *Staging Reform, Reforming the Stage: Protestantism and Popular Theater in Early Modern England* (Ithaca: Cornell University Press, 1997), p. 22.
5. William Hazlitt, 'Character of Shakespeare's Plays', *The Complete Works of William Hazlitt,* vol. 5, ed. P. P. Howe (London; Toronto: J. M. Dent and Sons, Ltd., 1930–4), p. 247.
6. For more Romantic idealism, see *Coleridge on Shakespeare: The Text of Lectures of 1811–12*, ed. R. A. Foakes (New York: Routledge, 2008). Margareta de Grazia offers a potent critique of this Romantic endeavour and its palpable afterlife in Shakespeare studies today in *Hamlet Without Hamlet* (Cambridge: Cambridge University Press, 2007).
7. See Stephen Greenblatt, *Shakespearean Negotiations: The Circulation of Social Energy in Renaissance England* (Berkeley and Los Angeles: University of California Press, 1988), pp. 94–128.
8. Thomas Betteridge, *Shakespearean Fantasy and Politics* (Hatfield: University of Hertfordshire Press, 2005), p. 20.
9. Ellen MacKay, *Persecution, Plague, and Fire: Fugitive Histories of the Stage in Early Modern England* (Chicago: University of Chicago Press, 2011), p. 132.

10. Laurie Shannon, 'Poor, Bare, Forked: Animal Sovereignty, Human Negative Exceptionalism, and the Natural History of *King Lear*', *Shakespeare Quarterly* 60.2 (Summer 2009), p. 196.
11. Ludwig Wittgenstein, *Philosophical Investigations*, trans. G. E. M. Anscombe (Malden, MA: Blackwell, 2001 [1953]), p. 152.
12. Ibid.
13. Stanley Cavell, *The Claim of Reason: Wittgenstein, Skepticism, Morality, and Tragedy* (Oxford: Oxford University Press, 1979), p. 357.
14. Marie McGinn, *Wittgenstein and the* Philosophical Investigations (New York: Routledge, 1997), p. 155, emphasis mine.
15. Wittgenstein, *Philosophical Investigations*, §297.
16. Cavell, *The Claim of Reason*, p. 334.
17. Francis Palmer, 'Master *John Fletcher* his dramaticall Workes now at last printed', *Comedies and Tragedies* (London, 1647), no pagination.
18. Citations from *Cymbeline* are from the Arden edn, ed. J. M. Nosworthy (Walton-on-Thames: Thomson, 1955).
19. See especially the finale to *Epicene* (*The Alchemist and Other Plays*, ed. Gordon Campbell (Oxford: Oxford University Press, 1995), pp. 119–208). His plays can also be obsessively self-aware of their own theatrical capacities throughout, as with *Bartholomew Faire* (*The Alchemist and Other Plays*, pp. 327–433), which features countless modes of performance that end up hoodwinking, distracting, or otherwise deceiving their audiences.
20. Margaret Ferguson, 'Saint Augustine's Region of Unlikeness: The Crossing of Exile and Language', *The Georgia Review* 29.4 (1975), p. 853.
21. Samuel Weber, *Theatricality as Medium* (New York: Fordham University Press, 2004), p. 3.
22. Ibid., p. 27.
23. Toril Moi, *Henrik Ibsen and the Birth of Modernism: Art, Theater, Philosophy* (Oxford: Oxford University Press, 2006), p. 234.
24. Plato, *Phaedrus*, trans. Robin Waterfield (Oxford: Oxford University Press, 2002), p. 38. See also Jacques Derrida, 'Plato's Pharmacy', *Disseminations*, trans. Barbara Johnson (Chicago: University of Chicago Press, 1981), pp. 61–171.
25. Ibid., p. 39.
26. Robert Watson, 'Horsemanship in Shakespeare's Second Tetralogy', *English Literary Renaissance* 13.3 (September 1983), p. 275.
27. Plato, *Republic*, trans. Robin Waterfield (Oxford: Oxford University Press, 2002), pp. 128–9.
28. Ibid., p. 134.

29. Plato, *Republic*, p. 129. Of course, Homer and his poetic ilk would be banned from the city-state theorised in the *Republic* due to their ability to imitate virtue (see *Republic* pp. 297–326).
30. Paul Kottman, *A Politics of the Scene* (Stanford: Stanford University Press, 2008), p. 35.
31. Ibid., p. 134.
32. Aristotle, *De Anima* (*On the Soul*), trans. Hugh Lawson-Tangred (New York: Penguin Books, 1986), p. 213.
33. Ibid., p. 127.
34. Michael Frede, 'On Aristotle's Conception of the Soul', *Essays on Aristotle's* De Anima, ed. Martha Nussbaum and Amelie Oksenberg Rorty (Oxford: Oxford University Press, 1992), pp. 105–6.
35. David Charles, 'Aristotle on Desire and Action', *Body and Soul in Ancient Philosophy*, ed. Dorothea Frede and Burkhard Reis (New York: Walter de Gruyter, 2009), p. 306.
36. Aristotle, *Aristotle's Nicomachean Ethics*, trans. Robert C. Bartlett and Susan D. Collins (Chicago: University of Chicago Press, 2011), p. 13.
37. For a dialogue on the role of Aristotle's *Nicomachean Ethics* in Shakespeare's day, see David Beauregard, *Virtue's Own Feature: Shakespeare and the Virtue Ethics Tradition* (Wilmington: University of Delaware Press, 1995) and a critical response by Sarah Coodin in 'What's Virtue Ethics Got to Do With It?: Shakespearean Character as Moral Character', *Shakespeare and Moral Agency*, ed. Michael Bristol (New York: Continuum, 2010), pp. 184–99.
38. Jean-Luc Nancy, 'On the Soul', *Corpus*, trans. Richard A. Rand (New York: Fordham University Press, 2008), p. 126.
39. Augustine of Hippo (Saint Augustine), *Confessions*, trans. Henry Chadwick (Oxford: Oxford University Press, 2008), p. 184.
40. Peter Lake and Michael Questier, *The Antichrist's Lewd Hat: Protestants, Papists, and Players in Post-Reformation England* (New Haven: Yale University Press, 2002), p. 318.
41. Nandra Perry, *Imitatio Christi: The Poetics of Piety in Early Modern England* (Notre Dame: Notre Dame University Press, 2014), p. 5.
42. mimesis, n'., *OED Online*, Oxford University Press, 26 September 2015.
43. Nandra Perry, *Imitatio Christi*, p. 52.
44. Martin Luther, 'Preface to Latin Writings', *Martin Luther: Selections from His Writings*, ed. John Dillenberger (New York: Random House, 1962), p. 11, emphasis mine.

45. Martin Luther, 'Preface to Romans', *Martin Luther: Selections from His Writings*, p. 23.
46. Martin Luther, 'Secular Authority', *Martin Luther: Selections from His Writings*, p. 383.
47. Michael O'Connell, *The Idolatrous Eye: Iconoclasm and Theater in Early-Modern England* (Oxford: Oxford University Press, 2000), p. 144.
48. Thomas Betteridge, *Literature and Politics in the English Reformation* (Manchester: University of Manchester Press, 2004), p. 3.
49. John Calvin, *Institutes of the Christian Religion*, trans. Henry Beveridge (Peabody: Hendrickson, 2008), p. 108.
50. Diarmid MacCulloch, *The Reformation: A History* (New York: Penguin, 2003), p. 581.
51. See Ludwig Lavater, *Of Ghostes and Spirits Walking* (London, 1572).
52. 'Homily of Faith', *Voices of the English Reformation: A Sourcebook*, ed. John N. King (Philadelphia: University of Pennsylvania Press, 2004), p. 62.
53. Henry Greenwood, *A Treatise on the Great and Generall Daye of Judgement* (London, 1606), pp. 68–9.
54. John Webster, *The Duchess of Malfi* (Manchester: Manchester University Press, 2009 [1963]), IV, ii, 124–32.
55. Michael Frede, 'On Aristotle's Conception of the Soul', p. 102, emphasis mine.

Chapter 2

1. Simon Critchley and Tom McCarthy, 'Universal Shylockery: Money and Morality in *The Merchant of Venice*', *Diacritics* 34.1 (Spring 2004), p. 5.
2. All citations from the play are from the Arden 3 edn, ed. John Drakakis (New York: Bloomsbury, 2011).
3. Quoted in Kevin Corrigan, *Reading Plotinus: A Practical Introduction to Neoplatonism* (West Lafayette: Purdue University Press, 2005), p. 8.
4. David Schalkwyk, *Speech and Performance in Shakespeare's Sonnets and Plays* (Cambridge: Cambridge University Press, 2002), p. 60.
5. Ibid., p. 67.
6. Harry Berger, Jr., *A Fury in the Words: Love and Embarrassment in Shakespeare's Venice* (New York: Fordham University Press, 2013), p. 36.

7. Ludwig Wittgenstein, *Philosophical Investigations*, §36.
8. Ludwig Wittgenstein, 'The Blue Book', *Major Works* (New York: HarperCollins, 2009 [1958]), p. 143.
9. Ovid, 'The Epistle', *Ovid's Metamorphoses*, trans. Arthur Golding, ed. John Nims (Philadelphia: Paul Dry Books, 2000), ll. 12–14.
10. Ibid., ll. 24–5
11. Ibid., ll. 26–32
12. Ibid., l. 40.
13. Ovid, *Ovid's Metamorphoses*, XV, 184–7.
14. Ibid., ll. 188–92.
15. Michel de Montaigne, *Essays Written in the French by Michel Lord of Montaigne*, trans. John Florio (London, 1613), pp. 239–40.
16. Montaigne, *Essays*, p. 240.
17. Ibid., p. 312.
18. John Donne, 'Holy Sonnet VIII', *The Complete Poetry and Selected Prose of John Donne*, ed. Charles M. Coffin (New York: Modern Library, 2001), ll. 5–8.
19. Ibid., ll. 12–14.
20. Christopher Marlowe, 'The Tragical History of Dr. Faustus', *Doctor Faustus and Other Plays*, ed. David Bevington and Eric Rasmussen (Oxford: Oxford University Press, 1995), V, ii, 99–104. My citations are from the A-Text. The B-Text, with its coda of Faustus's peers discovering and carrying off his severed limbs, offers a comically macabre and determinedly physical type of metempsychosis. His soul may not dissolve in elements, but his body, the scholars remind us, surely will.
21. Andrew Sofer, *Dark Matter: Invisibility in Drama, Theater, and Performance* (Ann Arbor: University of Michigan Press, 2013), p. 17.
22. For the role of speech in early modern animals, see two works of Erica Fudge: *Perceiving Animals: Humans and Beasts in Early Modern English Culture* (New York: St Martin's Press, 2000) and *Renaissance Beasts: Of Animals, Humans, and Other Wonderful Creatures* (Urbana: University of Illinois Press, 2004). Fudge takes up the concerns of this chapter, the interface of the animal and the soul, in *Perceiving Animals*, pp. 34–63; her final conclusion ultimately resides in the notion of animal difference not predicating itself on conscience, or the soul, but rather 'eloquence'.
23. Giovanni Batista Gelli, *Circes*, trans. Henry Iden (London, 1558), p. 143.

24. Ulysses's soul makes an appearance in the last book of Plato's *Republic* as the representative of a proper life: the souls assembled at the Spindle of Necessity choose their next lives; the last in line is Ulysses. After remembering its 'former sufferings', his soul finally decides upon 'the life of a private individual who did his own work', and it declares 'it would have done so even if it had drawn the first-place lot, and chose it gladly' (p. 325).
25. Gelli, *Circes*, p. 163 (emphasis in original).
26. Edward Topsell, *The Historie of Four-Footed Beastes* (London, 1607), p. 676. See also Laurie Shannon, 'Eight Animals in Shakespeare; or, Before the Human', *PMLA* 124.2 (March 2009), pp. 472–9.
27. Plutarch, *Morals*, trans. Philemon Holland (London, 1603), p. 562. See also Edmund Spenser, *The Faerie Queene*, ed. Thomas Roche (New York: Penguin Books, 1978) for another appearance of this pig, who Plutarch named Gryllus: 'That had an hog beene late, hight *Grille* by name, / Repined greatly, and did him miscall, / That had from hoggish forme him brought to natural' (II, xii, 92–4). For a history of literary incarnations of Circe and her animal cohabitants, see Judith Yarnall, *Transformations of Circe: The History of an Enchantress* (Champaign-Urbana: University of Illinois Press, 1994).
28. John Rawlinson, *Mercy to a Beast: A Sermon* (Oxford, 1612), pp. 51–2.
29. Thomas Watson, *Holsome and Catholyke Doctryne concerninge the seven Sacraments* (London, 1558), p. 149.
30. Jacques Derrida, 'What Is a 'Relevant' Translation?', trans. Lawrence Venuti, *Critical Inquiry* 27.2 (2001), p. 185.
31. Ibid., pp. 174, 184.
32. Ibid., p. 190.
33. Ronald Sharp, 'Gift Exchange and the Economies of Spirit in *The Merchant of Venice*', *Modern Philology* 83.3 (February 1986), p. 256. For more on Portia and the play's economics, see Natasha Korda, 'Dame Usury: Gender, Credit, and (Ac)counting in the Sonnets and *The Merchant of Venice*', *Shakespeare Quarterly* 60.2 (Summer 2009), pp. 129–53; and Karen Newman, 'Portia's Ring: Unruly Women and Structures of Exchange in *The Merchant of Venice*', *Shakespeare Quarterly* 38.1 (Spring 1987), pp. 19–33.
34. *The Merchant of Venice* actually supplies the *OED* with the first case of 'estimable' meaning 'Valuable, worth a great price; of worth' ('estimable, adj. and n., *OED Online*, Oxford University Press, 26 September 2015).

35. Drew Daniel, *The Melancholy Assemblage: Affect and Epistemology in the English Renaissance* (New York: Fordham University Press, 2013), p. 101.
36. The pound of flesh has also been read as a lurid appropriation of circumcision as castration, as it existed in the anti-Semitic imaginary. See, most recently, Amy Greenstadt, 'The Kindest Cut: Circumcision and Queer Kinship in *The Merchant of Venice*', *ELH* 80.4 (Winter 2013), pp. 945–80. As its title suggests, the essay, like Daniel's, links the violence of the pound of flesh to the queer relation of Shylock and Antonio.
37. The historical role of blood in the determination of Judaism as a 'race' is a contentious field of research, within which *Merchant* has proven a powerful touchstone. For blood in relation to market economics, see Aaron Kitch, 'Shylock's Sacred Nation', *Shakespeare Quarterly* 59.2 (2008), pp. 131–55; for the medieval inheritance of blood laws, see M. Lindsay Kaplan, 'Jessica's Mother: Medieval Constructions of Jewish Race and Gender in *The Merchant of Venice*', *Shakespeare Quarterly* 58.1 (2007), pp. 1–30. Kaplan engages with and critiques Janet Adelman's provocative arguments in 'Her Father's Blood: Race, Conversion, and Nation in *The Merchant of Venice*', *Representations*, 81.1 (Winter 2003), pp. 4–30. Adelman expands her inquiry in her book *Blood Relations: Christian and Jew in 'The Merchant of Venice'* (Chicago: University of Chicago Press, 2008).
38. For a reading of Shylock as an overly literal figure, see Anne Barton's introduction to *The Merchant of Venice* in *The Riverside Shakespeare* (New York: Houghton Mifflin, 1997), pp. 284–7. For a critique of Barton's introduction, see Alice Benston, 'Portia, the Law, and the Tripartite Structure of *The Merchant of Venice*', *Shakespeare Quarterly* 30.3 (Summer 1979), pp. 367–85.
39. Kenneth Gross, *Shylock is Shakespeare* (Chicago: University of Chicago Press, 2006), p. 24.
40. Julia Reinhard Lupton, *Citizen-Saints: Shakespeare and Political Theology* (Chicago: University of Chicago Press, 2005), p. 87.
41. The notion of policing the borders of the human by subjugating animals sounds a popular theme among animal studies in eighteenth-century scholarship. See Felicity Nussbaum, *The Limits of the Human: Fictions of Anomaly, Race, and Gender in the Long Eighteenth Century* (Cambridge: Cambridge University Press, 2003); Michael Newton, *Savage Girls and Wild Boys: A History of Feral Children* (London: Faber and Faber, 2002); and Richard Nash, *Wild*

Enlightenment: The Borders of Human Identity in the Eighteenth Century (Charlottesville: University of Virginia Press, 2003). For a review of Nussbaum, Newton and Nash, see James Steintrager, 'Humanity Gone Wild', *Eighteenth-Century Studies* 38.4 (Summer 2005), pp. 681–9.

Chapter 3

1. Andrew Sofer, *Dark Matter*, p. 4.
2. Peggy Phelan, *Unmarked: The Politics of Performance* (New York: Routledge, 1993), p. 146.
3. Herbert Blau, *To All Appearances: Ideology and Performance* (New York: Routledge, 1992), pp. 168–9.
4. Another popular conception of the theatre's negotiation of presence and absence is put forward by Marvin Carlson in *The Haunted Stage: The Theatre as Memory Machine* (Ann Arbor: University of Michigan Press, 2003). For Carlson, the theatre and its inhabitants cannot help but evoke past lives: productions and previous roles that 'haunt' the stage and performing body, respectively.
5. Thomas Middleton, 'The Lady's Tragedy' ('The Second Maiden's Tragedy'), ed. Julia Briggs, *Thomas Middleton: The Collected Works*, ed. Gary Taylor and John Lavagnino (Oxford: Oxford University Press, 2007), IV, iii, 112–14. This edition of the play features side-by-side comparisons of two versions of the play. My references are to the 'A' text.
6. Ibid., IV, iv, 40.
7. Ibid., IV, iv, 67–76.
8. Ibid., V, ii, 20.
9. Susan Zimmerman, 'Animating Matter: The Corpse as Idol in *The Second Maiden's Tragedy*', *Renaissance Drama* 31 (2002), p. 227.
10. For clarity I will use the name 'Coriolanus' to refer to this character throughout this chapter, even though he is named 'Martius' in the beginning of the play.
11. Nichole E. Miller, 'Sacred Life and Sacrificial Economy: *Coriolanus* in No-Man's-Land', *Criticism* 51.2 (Spring 2009), p. 275.
12. Theron Schmidt, 'Unsettling Representation: Monuments, Theatre, Relational Space', *Contemporary Theatre Review* 20.3 (2010), p. 293.
13. Perhaps the most salient theoretical model proffered to dismantle the authority of materiality as memory-maker is the titular duality

of Diana Taylor's *The Archive and the Repertoire: Performing Cultural Memory in the Americas* (Durham, NC: Duke University Press, 1997). Taylor argues persuasively against the colonialist and chauvinist assumptions of archiving memory, a process that grants the illusion of stability, and for the cultural memories passed down through repertoires of performances.

14. Alice Rayner, *Ghosts: Death's Double and the Phenomenon of Theatre* (Minneapolis: University of Minnesota Press, 2006), p. 67.
15. All citations of *Coriolanus* are from the Arden 3 edn, ed. Peter Holland (New York: Bloomsbury, 2003).
16. For a consideration of wounds in early modern England, see Sarah Covington, *Wounds, Flesh, and Metaphor in Seventeenth-Century England* (New York: Palgrave, 2009). For a discussion of the wounds in relation to early modern corporeal understandings of acting, see Eve Rachele Sanders, 'The Body of the Actor in *Coriolanus*', *Shakespeare Quarterly* 57.4 (Winter 2006), pp. 387–412.
17. Stanley Cavell, '*Coriolanus* and the Interpretations of Politics', *Disowning Knowledge in Seven Plays of Shakespeare* (Cambridge: Cambridge University Press, 2003 [1987]), p. 149.
18. Cynthia Marshall, 'Wound-Man: *Coriolanus*, Gender, and the Theatrical Construction of Interiority', *Feminist Readings of Early Modern Culture: Emerging Subjects*, ed. Valerie Traub, M. Lindsay Kaplan and Dympna Callaghan (Cambridge: Cambridge University Press, 1996), p. 103.
19. Ibid., p. 114.
20. While Plutarch is the obvious urtext for determining the historical inheritance of Roman *virtus* in relation to wounds, A. D. Nuttall suggests that Shakespeare may have also been influenced by Seneca. See his *Shakespeare the Thinker* (New Haven: Yale University Press, 2008), p. 294. For the influence of Livy, see Anne Barton, 'Livy, Machiavelli, and Shakespeare's "Coriolanus"', *Shakespeare Survey* 38 (1985), pp. 115–29. For more on Roman virtue in the play, see Phyllis Rackin, '"Coriolanus": Shakespeare's Anatomy of Virtus', *Modern Language Studies* 13.2 (Spring 1983), pp. 68–79; for a more genre-based treatment of this issue, see Norman Rabkin, 'Coriolanus: The Tragedy of Politics', *Shakespeare Quarterly* 17.3 (Summer 1966), pp. 195–212. See also Jeffrey Blits, *Spirit, Soul and City: Shakespeare's* Coriolanus (Lanham, MD: Lexington Books, 2006). For a broad consideration of Shakespeare and Rome, see Paul Cantor, *Shakespeare's Rome: Republic and Empire* (Ithaca: Cornell University Press, 1976).

21. D. J. Hopkins, *City/Stage/Globe: Performance of Space in Shakespeare's London* (New York: Routledge, 2008), p. 176.
22. For more on Askew's verbal facility, gendered self-awareness, and rhetorical strategies, see Megan Hickerson, 'Gospelling Sisters "Going Up and Downe": John Foxe and Disorderly Women', *The Sixteenth Century Journal* 35.4 (Winter 2004), pp. 1035–51; Frances Dolan, '"Gentlemen, I Have One More Thing to Say": Women on Scaffolds in England, 1563–1680', *Modern Philology* 92.2 (November 1994), pp. 157–78; and Christina Luckyj, *'A Moving Rhetoricke': Gender and Silence in Early Modern England* (New York: Palgrave, 2002), pp. 123–7. For a reading of the homoeroticism of Askew's death, see James C. W. Truman, 'John Foxe and the Desires of Reformation Martyrology', *ELH* (Spring 2003), pp. 35–66.
23. John Foxe, *Foxe's Book of Martyrs: Select Narratives*, ed. John King (Oxford: Oxford University Press, 2009), p. 27.
24. 'Homily of Good Works', *Voices of the English Reformation*, p. 63.
25. Nicholas Breton, *A Divine Poem, Divided Into Two Parts: The Ravish't Soule, and the Blessed Weeper* (London: John Brown, 1601), E2.
26. John Bale, 'John Bale to the Christian Readers', *The First Examinacion of Anne Askew Lately Martyred in Smithfield* (Marburg, 1546), p. 5.
27. Ibid.
28. While my reference is somewhat ironic, the staging of the play clearly affects its reception as artistic and political text. Robert Ormsby links stage audiences to the audiences depicted within the play in 'Coriolanus, Antitheatricalism, and Audience Response', *Shakespeare Bulletin* 26.1 (Spring 2008), pp. 43–62. See also Jean Howard, 'Figures and Grounds: Shakespeare's Control of Audience Perception and Response', *SEL Studies in English Literature 1500–1900* 20.2 (Spring 1980), pp. 185–99.
29. Jarrett Walker, 'Bodies and Bodiless Voices: The Drama of Human Perception in *Coriolanus*', *Shakespeare Quarterly* 43.2 (Summer 1992), p. 179.
30. John Foxe, *Foxe's Book of Martyrs: Select Narratives*, p. 17, emphasis mine.
31. Liz Koblyk, 'The Reader's Object in John Foxe's *Actes and Monuments*', *Acts of Reading: Interpretation, Reading Practices, and the Idea of the Book*, ed. Thomas P. Anderson and Ryan Netzley (Newark, DE: University of Delaware Press, 2010), p. 238.

32. John Foxe, *Foxe's Book of Martyrs: Select Narratives,* p. 196.
33. Ibid. In the Gospel According to St Luke, Jesus's final words are reported as: 'and when Jesus had cried with a loud voice, he said, Father, into thy hands I commend my spirit: and having said thus, he gave up the ghost' (23: 46).
34. In *Martyrdom and Literature in Early Modern England* (Cambridge: Cambridge University Press, 2005), Susannah Monta carefully disproves the idea that Foxe simply abolished miracles. Instead, scenes of the martyrs' death maintain certain 'subtle' miracles in the final moments of death that a Catholic reader would recognise as a more saturated part of religious life as a whole.
35. This lack of the supernatural coincides with A. C. Bradley's observation of the lack of the fantastical in *Coriolanus*; see *A. C. Bradley on Shakespeare's Tragedies: A Concise Edition and Reassessment*, ed. John Russell Brown (New York: Palgrave, 2007).
36. John Foxe, *Foxe's Book of Martyrs: Select Narratives*, p. 70.
37. Tracy C. Davis calls this unseen marking of theatricality a 'hiss' that enables fictionalisation; see '"Do You Believe in Fairies?": The Hiss of Dramatic License', *Theatre Journal* 57.1 (2005), pp. 57–81.
38. Jennifer Rust, 'Reforming the Mystical Body: From Mass to Martyr in John Foxe's *Acts and Monuments*', *ELH* 80 (2013), pp. 652–3.
39. Madhavi Menon, '*Coriolanus* and I', *Shakespeare* 7.2 (June 2011), p. 164.
40. Cynthia Marshall, 'Wound-Man . . .', p. 95.
41. John Foxe, *Acts and Monuments* (London, 1583), p. 16.
42. Ibid., p. 104.
43. William Tyndale, *An Answer to Sir Thomas More's Dialogue* (Cambridge: Cambridge University Press, 1850), p. 86.
44. Frances Yates, *The Art of Memory* (Chicago: The University of Chicago Press, 1966), p. 45.
45. Plato, *Meno and Other Dialogues*, ed. and trans. Robin Waterfield (Oxford: Oxford University Press, 2005), p. 114.
46. William Engel, in *Death and Drama in Renaissance England: Shades of Memory* (Oxford: Oxford University Press, 2002), elaborates on Renaissance appropriation of Platonic *anamnesis* in a close reading of *The Spanish Tragedy*.
47. Bruce Morrill, *Anamnesis as Dangerous Memory: Political and Liturgical Thought in Dialogue* (Collegeville: The Liturgical Press, 2000), p. 183.
48. David Gregg, *Anamnesis in the Eucharist* (New York: Grove Books, 1976), p. 23.

49. Julie Gittoes, *Anamnesis and the Eucharist: Contemporary Anglican Approaches* (Burlington, VT: Ashgate, 2008), p. 3.
50. Peter Lake, *The Boxmaker's Revenge: 'Orthodoxy', 'Heterodoxy', and the Politics of the Parish in Early Stuart London* (Stanford: Stanford University Press, 2001), p. 25.
51. Ibid., p. 26.
52. Stanley Cavell, '*Coriolanus* and the Interpretations of Politics', p. 159.
53. Ibid., p. 163.
54. Kenneth Burke, '*Coriolanus* – and the Delights of Faction', *The Hudson Review* 19.2 (Summer 1966), p. 201.
55. Rob Carson, 'Hearing Voices in *Coriolanus* and Early Modern Skepticism', *The Shakespearean International Yearbook* 6.1 (2006), p. 155.
56. The towering texts of early modern antitheatricalist writing are Philip Stubbes, *The Anatomie of Abuses* (London, 1595) and William Prynne, *Histriomastix, The Players Scourge, or Actors Tragedy* (London, 1633). For a more ambivalent take, see Thomas Heywood, *An Apologie for Actors* (London, 1612), and for a close reading *of* the complexities of Heywood's ambivalence, see Ellen MacKay, *Persecution, Plague, and Fire*, pp. 23–45.
57. Plutarch, 'The Life of Martius Coriolanus', *Shakespeare's Plutarch*, ed. T. J. B. Spencer (New York: Penguin, 1964), pp. 359–60.
58. Ibid., p. 360.
59. John Weever, *Ancient Funerall Monuments* (London, 1631), p. 1.
60. Ibid., p. 6.
61. This motif is found throughout Spenser and more widely in the Renaissance's appropriation of classical mythology; critics concerned with genre have noted its usage and historical elaboration across poetry and drama of the era. Northrop Frye connects the 'ruins of time' trope to Roman culture in his *Notebooks on Renaissance Literature*, ed. Michael Dolzani (Toronto: University of Toronto Press, 2006), p. 75. As Dolzani notes in the introduction, the ruins of time are customarily built into 'mansions of eternity' (xxxviii).
62. For further historical-cultural criticism on Stow, see Ian Archer, 'The Arts and Acts of Memorialization in Early Modern London', *Imagining Early Modern London: Perceptions and Portrayals of the City from Stow to Strype*, ed. J. F. Merritt (Cambridge: Cambridge University Press, 2001), pp. 89–116, which considers Stow's descriptions of the defaced gravestones and theorises in relation to memory and theatre more generally.

63. John Stow, *Survey of London, Written in the Year 1598*, ed. William J. Thomas (London: Whittaker, 1842), p. 120.
64. Sianne Ngai, *Ugly Feelings* (Cambridge, MA: Harvard University Press, 2005), p. 271.
65. John Stow, *Survey of London*, pp. 60–1.
66. Ibid., p. 75.
67. To take an exemplary passage from Numbers: 'And these are the names of the men that shall stand with you: of the tribe of Reuben; Elizur the son of Shedeur. Of Simeon; Shelumiel the son of Zurishaddai. Of Judah; Nashon the son of Amminadab. Of Isaachar; Netheneel the son of Zuar' (1: 5–8); and so on.
68. Ibid., p. 64.
69. For an analysis of this famous speech that connects, provocatively, the 'belly' of the city to Volumnia's womb, see Arthur Riss, 'The Body Politic: Coriolanus and the Revolt of Language', *ELH* 59.1 (Spring 1992), pp. 52–75. See also Tetsuya Motohashi, 'Body Politic and Political Body in *Coriolanus*', *Forum for Early Modern Language Studies* 30.2 (April 1994), pp. 97–112. For a more political reading, see James Holstun, 'Tragic Superfluity in *Coriolanus*', *ELH* 50.3 (Autumn 1983), pp. 485–507, which frames the monologue as an example of the classical notion of political embodiment, connecting it with Ernst Kantorowicz's magisterial *The King's Two Bodies: A Study in Mediaeval Political Theology* (Princeton: Princeton University Press, 1957).
70. Bryan Reynolds, in ' "What is the City but the People?": Transversal Performance and Radical Politics in Shakespeare's *Coriolanus* and Brecht's Coriolan', *Performing Transversally: Reimagining Shakespeare and the Critical Future* (New York: Palgrave, 2003), pp. 88–110, assesses this infamous stage direction and its importance to political readings of the play that believe Shakespeare scorns the insurgent populism.
71. James Kuzner, *Open Subjects: English Renaissance Republicans, Modern Selfhoods, and the Virtue of Vulnerability* (Edinburgh: Edinburgh University Press, 2011), pp. 84–124.
72. As an example of a reading that seeks to over-corporealise Coriolanus, see Sean Benson, ' "Even to the Gates of Rome": Grotesque Bodies and Fragmented Stories in *Coriolanus*', *Comitatus: A Journal of Medieval and Renaissance Studies* 30.1 (1999), pp. 95–112.
73. The 'body politic' and 'body natural' division elucidated so influentially by Ernst Kantorowicz in *The King's Two Bodies* has spawned a

wealth of critical responses. See, for instance, Eric Santner, *The Royal Remains: The People's Two Bodies and the Endgames of Sovereignty* (Chicago: University of Chicago Press, 2011) and a special issue of *Representations* 106.1 (2009), dedicated to Kantorowicz's work.

74. This stripping-down echoes the revelation of what Giorgio Agamben calls 'bare life' throughout *Homo Sacer: Sovereign Power and Bare Life,* trans. Daniel Heller-Roazen (Stanford: Stanford University Press, 1998). Bare life is both outside of juridical law and at its centre, as the figure of the exception from which the law is born.
75. The term 'nothing' could, due to its potential proximity to the transcendental, carry with it deep spiritual associations, especially in the mystical Christian tradition; the theologian Jacob Boehme, in *Forty Questions of the Soul*, trans. John Sparrow (London, 1663), equates the moment of deliverance with the transference of the body into a holistic soul without presence.

Chapter 4

1. All citations of *The Winter's Tale* are from the Arden 3 edn, ed. John Pitcher (London: Methuen, 2010).
2. For a powerful and problematic reading of primogeniture and sovereignty as it relates to Shakespeare, see Carl Schmitt, *Hamlet or Hecuba: The Intrusion of the Time into the Play*, trans. David Pan and Jennifer R. Rust (Candor, NY: Telos Press, 2003).
3. Robert Weimann, *Author's Pen and Actor's Voice: Playing and Writing in Shakespeare's Theatre* (Cambridge: Cambridge University Press, 2000), p. 230. Weimann's considerations here fall into the larger rubric of his critical model which distinguishes between the terms *locus* and *platea*. Weimann culls these terms from spatial distinctions of late medieval theatre: the *locus* is a more symbolically focused area, such as a scaffold or throne, while the *platea* is an undifferentiated downstage area closer to the audience. We can see his idea of the ending of *The Winter's Tale* as a permeation of these two spaces, and their attendant dramatic *gests*. For Weimann's initial elucidation of the terms, see *Shakespeare and the Popular Tradition in the Theater: Studies in the Social Dimension of Dramatic Form and Function* (Baltimore: Johns Hopkins University Press, 1987), esp. 73–84.

4. G. W. Pigman, III, *Grief and the Renaissance Elegy* (Cambridge: Cambridge University Press, 1985), p. 6.
5. Stephen Orgel, 'Introduction', *The Winter's Tale* (Oxford: Oxford University Press, 1996), p. 16.
6. Dennis Kay, *Melodious Tears: The English Funeral Elegy from Spenser to Milton* (Oxford: Oxford University Press, 1990), p. 203.
7. Edward Herbert, 'Elegy for the Prince', *Occasional Verses of Edward Lord Herbert, Baron of Cherbery and Castle-Island Deceased in August,* 1648 (London, 1665), p. 22.
8. Ibid.
9. John Donne, 'Elegie on the Untimely Death of the Incomparable Prince Henry', *The Complete Poetry and Selected Prose of John Donne*, ll. 55–62.
10. David W. Shaw, *Elegy and Paradox: Testing the Conventions* (Baltimore: Johns Hopkins University Press, 1994), p. 4.
11. As Peter M. Sacks elaborates, the adaptation of a pastoral elegy, a classical influence on the elegy, served as a kind of testing-ground for early modern poets. See *The English Elegy* (Baltimore: Johns Hopkins University Press, 1985). Sacks identifies a powerful parallel between the recovery from unspeakable loss of life that marks the content of the elegy and the poet's own rehabilitation into a rarified idiom.
12. Virgil, 'Eclogue V', *The Eclogues of Virgil*, trans. David Ferry (New York: Farrar, Straus and Giroux, 1999), p. 39.
13. Bruce R. Smith, *The Acoustic World of Early Modern England: Attending to the O-Factor* (Chicago: University of Chicago Press), p. 121.
14. Ibid., p. 112
15. Cyril Tourneur, 'A Griefe on the Death of Prince Henrie', *Three Elegies on the Most Lamented Death of Prince Henrie* (London, 1613), i.
16. Ibid., B1.
17. Ibid., C.
18. Ibid., B2.
19. Ibid., C2.
20. John Webster, 'A Monumental Columne, Erected to the Living Memory of the Every-Glorious Henry, late Prince of Wales', *Three Elegies on the Most Lamented Death of Prince Henrie,* p. B2.
21. Ibid., B3.
22. Ben Jonson, 'On My First Sonne', *The Workes of Benjamin Jonson* (London, 1616), pp. 781–2.

23. The obvious discomfort of admitting that the dead will be happier if they are in heaven is exploited for comic effect in *Twelfth Night* (Arden edn, ed. J. M. Lothian and T. W. Craik (London: Thomson, 1975)), where Feste gently mocks Olivia's prolonged mourning for her brother: 'The more fool, Madonna, to mourn for your brother's soul, being in heaven' (I, v, 68–9).
24. R. Clifton Spargo, *The Ethics of Mourning: Grief and Responsibility in Elegiac Literature* (Baltimore: Johns Hopkins University Press, 2004), p. 100.
25. John Milton, 'Lycidas', *The Complete Poetry and Selected Prose of John Milton*, ed. William Kerrigan, John Rumrich, and Stephen M. Fallon (New York: Random House, 2007), ll. 168–71.
26. Ibid., ll. 186–93.
27. Eric Smith, *By Mourning Tongues* (Ipswich: The Boydell Press, 1977), p. 1.
28. M. M. Bakhtin, *The Dialogical Imagination: Four Essays*, ed. Michael Holquist, trans. Caryl Emerson and Michael Holquist (Austin: University of Texas Press, 1981), p. 7.
29. Jonathan Crewe, 'Elegy in English Drama, 1590–1640', *The Oxford Handbook of the Elegy*, ed. Karen Weisman (Oxford: Oxford University Press, 2010), pp. 522–3.
30. Many contributions have been made to situate Mamillius as a site of gender and sexuality construction; see Gail Kern Paster, *The Body Embarrassed*, p.269; Janet Adelman, *Suffocating Mothers: Fantasies of Maternal Origin in Shakespeare's Plays,* Hamlet *to* The Tempest (New York: Routledge, 1992), pp. 225–7; and Susan Snyder, 'Mamillius and Gender Polarization in *The Winter's Tale*', *Shakespeare Quarterly* 50.1 (Spring 1999), pp. 1–8.
31. Wet nurses were common in the formation of male child subjectivity, but this fact this does not diminish the discourses of woman's milk and female company that dogged such practices with associations of femininity. For more on this problem of early modern domesticity, see Wendy Wall, *Staging Domesticity: Household Work and English Identity in Early Modern Drama* (Cambridge: Cambridge University Press, 2002), especially pp. 137–8; and Valerie Fildes, *Breasts, Bottles, and Babies: A History of Infant Feeding* (Edinburgh: Edinburgh University Press, 1986). Mamillius is linked specifically to the femininity of nursing through the etymology of his name, which recalls *mamilla*, or breast.
32. The term 'creature' is especially appropriate in defining childhood, since the term shares a semantic connection with 'future', implying an

unformed subjectivity; the complexity of creaturehood is developed in a reading of *The Tempest* by Julia Reinhard Lupton in 'Creature Caliban', *Shakespeare Quarterly* 51.1 (Spring 2000), pp. 1–23.

33. For recent work in Renaissance studies that reassesses the figure of the child and its historical formation, see *Shakespeare and Childhood*, ed. Kate Chedgzoy, Susanne Greenhalgh and Robert Shaughnessy (Cambridge: Cambridge, 2007), especially A. J. Piesse, 'Character Building: Shakespeare's Children in Context', pp. 64–79. In addition, Michael Witmore's *Pretty Creatures: Children and Fiction in the English Renaissance* (Ithaca: Cornell University Press, 2007) details the connection of children to the fabrication of fiction.
34. Lowell Gallagher, ' "This seal'd-up Oracle": Ambivalent Nostalgia in *The Winter's Tale*', *Exemplaria* 7.2 (1995), p. 474.
35. For Jonson, the boy-posing-as-woman deception opens up onto to an even wider sense of confusion, as it cleverly points out what is hidden before the audience's eyes – that the actor playing Epicene is himself a boy; the audience is treated to a revelation of what it already knew.
36. Silence, in early modern England, was not only problematically positioned along the axis of sacred and profane; it was complexly implicated in formations of gender. See Lynn Enterline, ' "You speak a language that I understand not:" The Rhetoric of Animation in *The Winter's Tale*', *Shakespeare Quarterly* 48.1 (Spring 1997), pp. 17–44, and Margaret Ferguson, 'Running On with Almost Public Voice: The Case of "E.C." ', *Tradition and the Talents of Women*, ed. Florence Howe (Chicago: University of Illinois Press, 1991), pp. 37–67.
37. For more on the notion of a text 'stuttering', see Thomas Anderson, *Performing Early Modern Trauma from Shakespeare to Milton* (Burlington: Ashgate, 2006), where he notes that the stage directions in *Titus Andronicus* reflect a wider historical anxiety.
38. T. G. Bishop, *Shakespeare and the Theatre of Wonder* (Cambridge: Cambridge University Press, 1996), p. 140.
39. For more on the performative and philosophical conditions of *The Winter's Tale*, see Joseph Roach, ' "Unpath'd waters, undream'd shores": Herbert Blau, Performing Doubles, and the Makeup of Memory in *The Winter's Tale*', *Modern Language Quarterly* 70.1 (March 2009), pp. 117–31. Teasing out the doublings of performance and haunting of memory through the play, Roach thus evokes his longstanding interest in the idea of surrogation – ways by which performance replaces and erases memory.

40. For one of many examples of this precise imagery winding its way through religious and humanist texts, see William Hunnis, *A Hyve Full of Hunnye* (London, 1578).
41. John Milton, *Paradise Lost*, ed. David Scott Kastan (Indianapolis: Hackett Publishing, 2005), X, 782–92.
42. Citations from *Hamlet* are from the Arden edn, ed. Harold Jenkins (Walton-on-Thames: Thomson, 1997 [1982]). Extending the connections between *Hamlet* and Genesis, the ghost of Hamlet's father describes his poisoning in decidedly Edenic terms: ''Tis given out that, sleeping in my orchard, / A serpent stung me – so the whole ear of Denmark / Is by a forged process of my death / Rankly abus'd – but know, thou noble youth, / the serpent that did sting thy father's life / Now wears his crown' (I, v, 35–40).
43. For more on Adam naming the animals, see what might be the foundational text in animal studies: Jacques Derrida, 'The Animal That Therefore I Am (More to Follow)' in *The Animal That Therefore I Am*, ed. Marie-Louise Mallet, trans. David Wills (New York: Fordham University Press, 2008), pp. 15–18.
44. Augustine of Hippo (Saint Augustine), *City of God*, trans. Henry Bettenson (New York: Penguin, 1972), p. 504.
45. Heinrich Bullinger, 'Of the reasonable soule of man', *Fiftie Godlie and Learned Sermons* (London, 1587), p. 757.
46. The Book of James's exclusion from the canon was famously argued by Luther, who called it 'an epistle full of straw'; see 'Preface to New Testament', trans. Bertram Lee, ed. John Dillenberger, *Martin Luther: Selections from his Writings*, p. 19.
47. Thomas More, 'The Supplication of Souls', *The Four Last Things, The Supplication of Souls, A Dialogue on Conscience* (New York: Scepter Publishers, 2002), p. 121.
48. David Ward, 'Affection, Intention, and Dreams in *The Winter's Tale*', *Modern Language Review* 82 (1987), p. 546.
49. Ibid., p. 549.
50. For a reading of the play's strategies – oftentimes at cross purposes – of recovering youth across generations, see Robert Reeder, 'Siring the Grandchild in *The Winter's Tale* and *The Fawn*', *SEL Studies in English Literature 1500–1900* 48.2 (Spring 2008), pp. 349–71. Reeder responds, in part, to David Lee Miller's reading of the play in *Dreams of the Burning Child: Sacrificial Sons and the Father's Witness* (Ithaca: Cornell University Press, 2003). Both authors unlock the scandal at work in Leontes's facing an inaccurate 'copy' of him that implicates his role in reproduction, yet also distances paternal filiation; as Miller's

title implies, he draws from Freud's account of the burning child to question the ethical role of fatherhood reckoning with itself.

51. Andrew Gurr identifies this conversation about nature and art as the fulcrum between two counterbalancing figures in the play, the bear and the statue – art and nature, respectively. See his brief article 'The Bear, the Statue, and Hysteria in *The Winter's Tale*', *Shakespeare Quarterly* 34.4 (Winter 1983), pp. 420–5.
52. In this sense, Perdita aligns more with Walter J. Ong's regimented teleologies of language, in which orality must historically be subsumed by writing. See *Orality and Literacy: The Technologizing of the Word* (New York: Routledge, 2012 [1982]).
53. In *The Cambridge Guide to Shakespeare on Stage*, ed. Stanley Wells and Sarah Stanton (Cambridge: Cambridge University Press, 2002), Gary Taylor speculates as to this original doubling by the King's Men (p. 7).
54. Carol Chillington Rutter, *Shakespeare and Child's Play: Performing Lost Boys on Stage and Screen* (New York: Routledge, 2007), p. 147.
55. For an engaging close reading of *The Gast of Gy*, one such 'widow's revenge' text, see Stephen Greenblatt, *Hamlet in Purgatory*, pp. 107–33. For Greenblatt, the questions behind the text similarly invigorate the questions of purgatory, and eventually feed into a reading of *Hamlet*'s ghost as a singular manifestation of this contentious conceptual terrain. Mary Ellen Lamb engages with a broader analysis of childish and oral folk traditions informing Shakespeare's drama, with a focus on *Macbeth*, in 'Engendering the Narrative Act: Old Wives' Tales in *The Winter's Tale, Macbeth,* and *The Tempest*', *Criticism* 40.4 (Fall 1998), pp. 529–54.
56. For a more thorough consideration of Romano's role in the play, including his odd inclusion as a sculptor, rather than painter (which, historically, he was), see Richard Meek, 'Ekphrasis in *The Rape of Lucrece* and *The Winter's Tale*', *SEL Studies in English Literature 1500–1900* 46.2 (Spring 2006), pp. 389–414.
57. The imperceptible line between madness and wonder is examined in lieu of ethical choices by James A. Knapp in 'Visual and Ethical Truth in *The Winter's Tale*', *Shakespeare Quarterly* 55.3 (Autumn 2004), pp. 253–78.
58. For a treatment of Fried in relation to performance theory, see Marvin Carlson, *Performance: A Critical Introduction* (New York: Routledge, 2003), pp. 123–44.
59. Michael Fried, 'Art and Objecthood', *Art and Objecthood: Essays and Reviews* (Chicago: University of Chicago Press, 1998), p. 160.

60. A good starting point for exploring this debate would be Huston Diehl, '"Strike all that Look upon with Marvel": Theatrical and Theological Wonder in *The Winter's Tale*', *Rematerializing Shakespeare: Authority and Representation on the Early Modern English Stage* (New York: Palgrave, 2005), pp. 19–33. Diehl disagrees with critics such as Michael O'Connell, Julia Reinhard Lupton and T. G. Bishop, who find remnants of Catholic structures of wonder in the statue scene. The statue scene, she avers, is self-consciously referential of Catholic modes of worship as a way to draw attention to how they can translate into Protestant piety.
61. Ethan Shagan, *Popular Politics and the English Reformation* (Cambridge: Cambridge University Press, 2003), p. 7.
62. Ibid., p. 298.
63. Stanley Cavell, *The Claim of Reason*, p. 338.
64. Stanley Cavell, 'The Avoidance of Love', *Disowning Knowledge in Seven Plays of Shakespeare*, p. 103.
65. Ludwig Wittgenstein, *Philosophical Investigations*, §36.
66. Garrett Hallett, *A Companion to Wittgenstein's Philosophical Investigations* (Ithaca: Cornell University Press, 1977), p. 32.
67. Sarah Beckwith, *Shakespeare and the Grammar of Forgiveness* (Ithaca: Cornell University Press, 2011), p. 145.
68. James Kuzner, drawing from the distinction mapped by Saint Paul, characterises Leontes's letting-go as the embrace of a 'law of faith' over a 'law of works'; see '*The Winter's Tale:* Faith in Law and the Law of Faith', *Exemplaria* 24.3 (Fall 2012), p. 261.

Conclusion

1. Stephen Greenblatt, *Shakespearean Negotiations*, p. 1.
2. Carol Symes has bracingly critiqued this dominant narrative by pointing out how the texts that remain to document the *Quem Quaeritis* served originally to police, not delineate, the liturgical performance. The actual performance was surely more dynamic and less codified than we have been led to believe. See 'The Medieval Archive and the History of Theatre: Assessing the Written and Unwritten Evidence for Premodern Performance', *Theatre Survey* 52 (2011), pp. 1–30.
3. Herbert Blau, *Blooded Thought: Occasions of Theatre* (New York: Performing Arts Journal Publications, 1991), p. 134.

4. Ludwig Wittgenstein, *Philosophical Investigations*, §23.
5. Stanley Cavell, *The Claim of Reason*, p. 177.
6. Ibid., p. 184.
7. Spencer Golub, *Incapacity: Wittgenstein, Anxiety, and Performance Behavior* (Evanston: Northwestern University Press, 2014), p. 5.
8. Ibid., p. 6.
9. All citations for *Hamlet* are from the Arden edition, ed. Harold Jenkins (Walton-on-Thames: Thomson, 1997 [1982]).
10. Peter Stallybrass uses the 'mole' image to link *Hamlet* to 'The Eighteenth Brumaire of Louis Bonaparte', wherein Marx frames revolution as the ghostly return of Hamlet's father. Hamlet's strange, giddy attitude toward his father is, for Stallybrass, a parodic stripping of authority to assume a subversive claim of legitimacy – like the paternal, revolutionary workings of France and the possible revolution of Europe. See '"Well Grubbed, Old Mole": Marx, Hamlet, and the (Un)Fixing of Representation', *Marxist Shakespeares* (New York: Routledge, 2001), pp. 16–30.
11. Jacques Derrida, *Specters of Marx: The State of the Debt, the Work of Mourning and the New International*, trans. Peggy Kamuf (New York: Routledge, 2010 [1993]), p. 15.
12. Ibid., p. 34.
13. Ibid., p. 37, emphasis mine. For a critique of Derrida's own criticism of speech act theory – levelled most forcefully in *Limited Inc*, ed. Gerald Graff (Evanston: Northwestern University Press, 1977) – see Toril Moi, '"They Practice Their Trades in Different Worlds": Concepts in Poststructuralism and Ordinary Language Philosophy', *New Literary History* 40.4 (2009), pp. 801–24.
14. For more on the Pauline notion of temporal rupture, and with it political and even ontological reconstitution, see Giorgio Agamben, *The Time That Remains: A Commentary on the Letter to the Romans*, trans. Patricia Dailey (Stanford: Stanford University Press, 2005); Alain Badiou, *Saint Paul: The Foundation of Universalism*, trans. Ray Brassier (Stanford: Stanford University Press, 2003); and Slavoj Žižek, *The Puppet and the Dwarf: The Perverse Core of Christianity* (Cambridge, MA: The MIT Press, 2003). The dialogue among these texts has provided a potent interlocutor in Shakespeare studies; see, as a foundational such work, Julia Lupton, *Citizen-Saints*, pp. 19–48.
15. Linking ghosts to mourning is not a move lost to Derrida, who names mourning in the full subtitle of *Specters of Marx*: 'The State

of the Debt, the Work of Mourning and the New International'. Ultimately, for Derrida, the 'work' of mourning is opposed to the 'specters' of Communism that can be endlessly disavowed because they cannot truly ever be present. Derrida twists the Freudian notion of mourning. For Freud, both mourning and melancholy involve the subsuming of the ego within a larger 'work', whereupon the ego is objectified due to the internalisation of murderous thoughts; this can lead to suicide, a ghostly end that itself haunts Derrida's critique of the post-Marxist scramble for identification. See Sigmund Freud, 'Mourning and Melancholia', *The Standard Edition of the Complete Psychological Works of Sigmund Freud*, trans. and ed. James Strachey (London: The Hogarth Press, 1971), pp. 243–58.

16. Erik Davis, *Techgnosis: Myth, Magic, and Mysticism in the Age of Information* (New York: Three Rivers Press, 1998), p. 6.
17. Ibid.
18. N. Katherine Hayles, *How We Became Posthuman: Virtual Bodies in Cybernetics, Literature, and Informatics* (Chicago: University of Chicago Press, 2004), pp. 3–4.
19. For an overview of abandoned Second Life worlds, see Patrick Hogan, 'We Took a Tour of the Abandoned College Campuses of Second Life', *Fusion*, 13 August (last accessed 26 September 2015).
20. 'What is Second Life?', *Second Life*, accessed 15 June 2009.
21. As with any dominant cultural force, Shakespeare has his parallel in Second Life. For a tour of three now defunct virtual Shakespearean theatres (Renaissance Island, the SLiterary Globe Theatre and 'Foul Whisperings') see Katherine Rowe, 'Crowd-Sourcing Shakespeare: Screen Work and Screen Play in Second Life', *Shakespeare Studies* 38 (2010), pp. 58–67. For a reading of heritage and archaeology in Second Life, see Rodney Harrison, 'Excavating Second Life: Cyber-Archaeologies, Heritage and Virtual Communities', *Journal of Material Culture* 14.1 (2009), pp. 75–106. For a performance studies exploration of virtual communities as anti-patriarchal demonstrations of feminine technologies, see Sue-Ellen Case, 'Dracula's Daughters: In-Corporating Avatars in Cyberspace', *Critical Theory and Performance*, ed. Janelle G. Reinelt and Joseph Roach (Ann Arbor: University of Michigan Press, 2007), pp. 547–62.
22. Anne Weinstone, *Avatar Bodies: A Tantra for Posthumanism* (Minneapolis: University of Minnesota Press, 2004), p. 124. For more on the overlap of the spiritual and cybernetic, see the 'Mediatization of

Religion' special issue of *Northern Lights* 6.1 (June 2008), particularly Ryan G. Hornbeck and Justin L. Barrett, 'Virtual Reality as a "Spiritual" Experience: A Perspective from the Cognitive Science of Religion' (pp. 75–90). See also Heidi Campbell, *When Religion Meets New Media* (New York: Routledge, 2010).

23. Stanley Cavell, *The Claim of Reason*, p. 357.
24. Virtuality is also a major concept for the related field of affect theory. See Brian Massumi, *Parables for the Virtual: Movement, Affect, Sensation* (Durham: Duke University Press, 2002), which places emphasis on process over positionality, movement over codification, and paradox over determinism. Affect, the intensity that is unclaimed, undifferentiated, but resoundingly present, can for Massumi produce actuality in its emergence; for an account of how this can be mobilised politically, see Lawrence Grossberg, *We Gotta Get Out of This Place: Popular Conservatism and Postmodern Culture* (New York: Routledge, 1992); for an affect-based theory of film reception, see Marco Abel, *Violent Affect: Literature, Cinema, and Critique after Representation* (Lincoln: University of Nebraska Press, 2007). Rei Terada locates the roots of affect in deconstruction's primary gestures, rather than (as traditionally conceived) any friction between post-structuralism and feeling, in *Feeling in Theory: Emotion After the 'Death of the Subject'* (Cambridge, MA: Harvard University Press, 2003).
25. Antonin Artaud, *The Theater and Its Double*, trans. Mary Caroline Richards (New York: Grove Press, 1958), pp. 50–1.
26. The deliberate contradiction here finds symmetry with the ethical claims of Jacques Rancière; see 'Who is the Subject of the Rights of Man?', *South Atlantic Quarterly* 103.2–3 (Spring/Summer 2004), pp. 297–310. Rancière surveys a brief genealogy of human and humanitarian rights, primarily those of Hannah Arendt and Giorgio Agamben, as a way to critique a pervasive tradition of assuming the political and private spheres are rigidly separate. For a more in-depth exploration of the fundamental question at play here – namely, how the borders of the legal and human are secretly codified under the auspice of their disappearance – see Rancière's *The Philosopher and His Poor*, ed. Andrew Parker, trans. John Drury, Corinne Oster, and Andrew Parker (Durham: Duke University Press, 2003).
27. A recent production of *Hamlet* by the experimental theatre company The Wooster Group stages the exact tension between the theatrical

and literary that so flummoxes Hamlet himself. With a decaying, skipping film of Richard Burton's 1964 production playing in the background, the actors recreate the action – and the mechanics of the film itself, such as zooms and pans. What is staged is the exact impossibility of total fidelity to a pre-existing script, even one supposedly as encoded as a film. Like Hamlet's belief that the promise of the ghost is non-performative – a promise that is broken as it is revealed to be fluid and theatrical – the promise of the play is that it will be an exact recreation. It never is.

28. Jonas Barish, *The Antitheatrical Prejudice*, p. 2.
29. A sampling of the formidable literature on antitheatricality across disciplines includes: Martin Puchner, *Stage Fright: Modernism, Anti-Theatricality, and Drama* (Baltimore: Johns Hopkins University Press, 2002); Laura Levine, *Men in Women's Clothing: Anti-Theatricality and Effeminization 1579–1642* (Cambridge: Cambridge University Press, 1994); Paul Whitfield White, *Theatre and Reformation: Protestantism, Patronage, and Playing in Tudor England* (Cambridge: Cambridge University Press, 1993); Michael Quinn, 'Anti-theatricality and American Ideology: Mamet's Performative Realism', *Realism and the American Dramatic Tradition*, ed. William W. Demastes (Tuscaloosa: University of Alabama Press, 1996), pp. 235–54; and David Hawkes, 'Idolatry and Commodity Fetishism in the Antitheatrical Controversy', *SEL Studies in English Literature 1500–1900* 39.2 (1999), pp. 255–73.

INDEX

Notes: Titles are plays by Shakespeare unless stated otherwise; 'n' indicates notes.